COGNITIVE THERAPY

Treatment Approaches in the Human Services

Francis J. Turner, Editor

COGNITIVE THERAPY

A Humanistic Approach

Harold D. Werner

Fp

THE FREE PRESS
A Division of Macmillan Publishing Co., Inc.
NEW YORK

Collier Macmillan Publishers
LONDON

Copyright © 1982 by The Free Press
A Division of Macmillan Publishing Co., Inc.

The Free Press
A Division of Macmillan Publishing Co., Inc.
866 Third Avenue, New York, N.Y. 10022

Collier Macmillan Canada, Ltd.

Library of Congress Catalog Card Number: 81-68217

Printed in the United States of America

printing number

1 2 3 4 5 6 7 8 9 10

Library of Congress Cataloging in Publication Data

Werner, Harold D.
    Cognitive therapy.

    (Treatment approaches in the human services)
    Includes bibliographical references and index.
    1. Cognitive therapy.   I. Title.   II. Series.
RC489.C63W47   616.89′14   81-68217
ISBN 0-02-934640-1   AACR2

To
Hilda

and to the memory of
Robert Penn Kemble, M.D.

Contents

Foreword

"Treatment Approaches in the Human Services" is the first series of professional texts to be prepared under the general auspices of social work. It is understandable that the editor and authors of this endeavor should be enthusiastic about its quality and prospects. But it is equally understandable that our enthusiasm is tempered with caution and prudence. There is a presumptuousness in attempting to be on the leading edge of thinking and aspiring to break new ground, and our professional experience urges us to be restrained.

The first suggestion for this series came from the editorial staff of The Free Press in the spring of 1975. At that time, the early responses to *Social Work Treatment** were available. It was clear from the responses that, useful as that book appeared to be, there was a wish and a need for more detail on each of the various thought systems covered, especially as regards their direct practice implications. These comments led to a proposal from the Free Press that a series be developed that would expand the content of the individual chapters of *Social Work Treatment* into full-length books with the objective of providing a richer and fuller exposition of each system. This idea is still germane to the series, but with the emergence of new thought systems and theories it has moved beyond the notion of expanding the chapters in

---

* Francis J. Turner, ed., *Social Work Treatment* (New York: Free Press, 1974).

the original collection. New thinking in the helping professions, the diversity of new demands, and the complexity of these demands have increased beyond the expectations of even the harbingers of the knowledge explosion of the early 1970s. No profession can or should stand still, and thus no professional literature can be static. It is our hope that this series will stay continuously current as it takes account of new ideas emerging from practice.

By design, this series has a strong orientation to social work. But it is not designed for social workers alone; it is also intended to be useful to our colleagues in other professions. The point has frequently been made that much of the conceptual base of social work practice has been borrowed and that social work has made few original contributions to other professions. That is no longer true. A principal assumption of this series is that social work must now accept the responsibility for making available to other professions its rich accumulation of theoretical concepts and therapeutic strategies.

The responsibility to share does not presume that professions with a healing and human-development commitment are moving to some commonality of identity and structure. In the next decade, we are probably going to see clearer rather than more obscure professional identities and more rather than less precise professional boundaries, derived not from different knowledge bases but from differential use of shared knowledge. If this prediction is valid, it follows that each profession must develop increased and enriched ways of making available to other professionals its own expanding knowledge of the human condition.

Although the books in this series are written from the viewpoint of the clinician, they will be useful for the student-professional, the senior scholar, and the teacher of professionals as well. On the principle that no dynamic profession can tolerate division among its practitioners, theory builders, and teachers, each book is intended to be a bridging resource between practice and theory development. In directing this series to colleagues whose principal targets of practice are individuals, families, and groups, we take the other essential fields of practice as given. Thus the community-development, social-action, policy, research, and service-delivery roles of the helping professions are not specifically addressed in these books.

One of the risks of living and practicing in an environment characterized by pluralism in professions, practice styles, and theoretical orientations is that one may easily become doctrinaire in defending a particular perspective. Useful and important as is ongoing debate that leads to clarification of similarities and differences, overlaps and gaps in thought systems and theories, the authors of these books have been asked to minimize this function. That is, they are to analyze the conceptual base of their particular topic, identify its theoretical origins, and explain and describe its operationalization in practice, but avoid polemics in behalf of "their" system. Inevitably, some material of this type is needed for comparisons, but the aim is to make the books explicative rather than argumentative.

Although the series has a clear focus and explicit objectives, there is also a strong commitment that it be marked with a quality of development and evolution. It is hoped that we shall be responsive to changes in psychotherapeutic practice and to the needs of colleagues in practice and thus be ready to alter the format of subsequent books as may be necessary.

In a similar way, the ultimate number of books in the series has been left open. Viewing current practice in the late 1970s, it is possible to identify a large number of influential thought systems that need to be addressed. We can only presume that additional perspectives will emerge in the future. These will be addressed as the series continues, as will new developments or reformulations of existing practice perspectives.

The practice of psychotherapy and the wide spectrum of activities that it encompasses is a risky and uncertain endeavor. Clearly, we are just beginning a new era of human knowledge and improved clinical approaches and methods. At one time we were concerned because we knew so little; now we are concerned to use fully the rich progress that has been made in research, practice, and conceptualization. This series is dedicated to that task in the humble hope that it will contribute to man's concern for his fellows.

In recent years practitioners in the helping professions have begun to understand and appreciate the important contributions that cognitive theory can make to practice. While social workers have exhibited considerable interest in this thought system, there has nonetheless been a dearth of social work writing about it. Harold Werner's book is thus an important and timely contribution to the literature and an essential component of this series.

The author argues in the Preface that cognitive therapy is the "third force" in the helping professions along with psychoanalytic and behavioral theory. He also argues that many practitioners have already introduced a cognitive perspective to their practice without having fully built cognitive concepts into their theoretical perspective.

In spite of the oft-repeated criticism that social workers too long practiced from a psychodynamic perspective that stressed understanding and working with the client's unconscious, it is abundantly clear that, in fact, for a long time practice was heavily cognitively oriented and present-focused. An examination of case records of practitioners of a strong psychodynamic persuasion clearly indicates the extent to which reflective consideration of here-and-now problems and logical consideration of alternatives are an important part of their practice. What has been lacking is an acceptance of this and a theoretical basis into which these activities could be placed.

In developing his presentation of cognitive theory, Harold Werner gives an excellent historical summary of the development of this theory and an analysis of its current status and principal authors; this helps to bring the theory into focus for contemporary practitioners.

Because of the emphasis on our cognitive abilities in the search for solutions to problems, it is understandable that cognitive theories strongly support a disciplined approach to practice that includes a commitment to a research-based analysis of practice. The discussion of our responsibility to accountability in this book is important and goes beyond cognitive theory as such with application to all approaches to practice.

This volume clearly will be helpful to those interested in cognitive theory as a basis of practice; but it will also be useful to persons who are seeking to expand their theoretical horizons, whether this be as a form of eclecticism or in a search for linkages between systems as manifested in an interlocking theoretical approach.

FRANCIS J. TURNER

Preface

In 1971, the Community Service Society of New York decided to discontinue casework services to individuals and families and to concentrate exclusively on working with the community as a whole to promote social action and environmental change. It took this step because it had reached the conclusion that social casework was ineffective in dealing with human problems.

In the decade that followed the effectiveness of social casework and of psychotherapy in general has become a major issue. Joel Fischer (1976) in particular played a leading role in raising our consciousness about this subject. He examined the findings of the seventeen available controlled group studies of professional casework effectiveness. Not one of these research studies delivered a shred of evidence that casework was effective in producing positive changes in clients beyond those which could be achieved by nonprofessionals or with no services at all.

While pointing out, however, the startling lack of any research validation of casework effectiveness, Fischer did not conclude, as had the Community Service Society, that casework intervention *in general* did not or could not help people. He noted instead that the casework orientation in the research studies he examined was psychodynamic in one form or another, so that the findings were applicable specifically to psychoanalytically influenced approaches. In 1971 the Community Service Society, one of the nation's leading casework agencies, was the standard bearer of the Freudian-oriented approach.

In a later work, Fischer (1978) called for social casework and (by extension) the other counseling professions to temper their attachment to psychoanalysis and to acquire a new attitude of receptivity to all other available ideas. In his view, the psychoanalytic orientation had stressed *understanding* clients but had provided no techniques for *changing* them. Therefore professionals now had to go further and think about technique building that would result in specific methods for helping people to change. Assembling an individual's history and exploring the causes of his or her current problems were not sufficient, and were often unnecessary, to effect positive changes in a client.

Many of us who work with individuals and families believe that some casework approaches are effective. In struggling for clarity about the issue of effectiveness, it is essential to avoid viewing casework as a single, monolithic entity. In this book, I take the position that there are now three main currents in treatment theory: the psychoanalytic, the behaviorist, and the cognitive. The latter two have shown their greatest growth in the decade of the 1970s. All three can serve as a theoretical basis for the practice of casework, and most treatment approaches fit into one of these three categories.

The main purpose of this book is to help establish cognitive therapy as the recognized "third force" in casework and in psychotherapy in general. Abraham Maslow coined the term "third force" to designate those movements outside of psychoanalysis and behaviorism that, in non-Freudian and non-Watsonian terms, sought to explain human behavior from a cognitive, humanist viewpoint. While this volume is oriented toward the social work field, it is hoped that the discussions in these pages will also be relevant to psychologists, psychiatrists, nurses, educators, pastoral counselors, physicians in general, and students in all these professions. Although the focus will be on individual treatment, cognitive therapy can be used in all modalities, including group and family therapies, and such applications will be pointed out.

At present, cognitive therapy is widely practiced by social workers and other professionals, but it is not often identified as such. This volume places considerable emphasis on achieving recognition for the cognitive approach as a separate, identifiable, definable main current in the treatment of troubled people.

On the contemporary scene, there is much ideological vagueness and confusion among all kinds of practitioners. If the cognitive approach is clearly delineated, professionals will have an opportunity to relate their practice to a third specific framework. In so doing they will be able to see their own practice in fuller perspective. It is hoped that they will gain greater insight into the origins and philosophical implications of the theoretical concepts they utilize, become acquainted with additional ways of looking at human behavior, and be able to determine more precisely the basic allegiance of their theoretical position.

Practice should be guided by theory; otherwise our work with clients and patients is serendipitous, haphazard, and lacking in shape and internal consistency. In addition, if our practice does not have recognizable, repeated characteristics that result from its being based on a clearly defined theory, it is not subject to objective comparison with other approaches and to research validation of its effectiveness. Therefore the attempt of this book to define cognitive theory and therapy is not an academic exercise but an effort to make available a practical tool for those who may wish to use it.

Chapter 1

A Description Of Cognitive Therapy

Cognitive therapy is a process of evaluating clients in terms of limitations and distortions in their consciousness, and then helping to bring their perceptions to a closer approximation of reality. From the cognitive viewpoint, there is no "unconscious" that needs to be brought to consciousness. What clients need to be conscious of is the real nature of themselves, their relationships, and the world around them.

Cognitive theory emphasizes the human qualities in people and regards them as having the ability to fashion their own lives by the force of their thinking, their creativity, and their will. They can modify or deactivate inner drives that interfere with the goals they have set for themselves. In fact, the very thinking that people do about their goals, their evaluations of events, and their judgments about themselves are the primary determinants of their behavior.

A large part of human living consists of continually making judgments about ourselves, other people, events, situations, and the physical world around us. This evaluating, which Albert Ellis (1958) characterizes as sentences we say to ourselves, is a conscious activity that generates both emotion and behavior. [Cognitive therapy focuses on the inappropriate, self-defeating, destructive, and upsetting emotions and behaviors which arise from the inaccurate sentences that people say to themselves. It considers a mentally healthy individual to be one whose perceptions are accurate and who has the ability to act on his accurate understanding of reality. Insight alone is not enough to improve one's mental health unless it is accompanied by the capacity to put it to use in the real world. Cognitive therapy also deals with the client whose perceptions are accurate but who reacts to them with inappropriate responses.

Let us take, for example, a woman or man who overhears a remark by another person. The comment is about our subject, who makes a judgment (evaluation, interpretation) as to its meaning: what was said was positive, friendly, well intentioned, *or* it was negative, hostile, unfair. The accuracy of the perception will determine the appropriateness of the response. Perception is defined as the sensing of an event (in this case through the ears), combined with the evaluation made of that event. Both the sensing and the evaluating are conscious processes. Response consists of the emotions and behaviors that the perception engenders. In this situation, the response could be either a feeling of pleasure and a cordial greeting to the other person *or* a feeling of anger and a heated argument. Cognitive therapy deals with the inappropriate responses that flow out of a client's inaccurate perceptions of his interpersonal transactions: in this case an argument would be inappropriate and destructive if the original remark had actually not been intended as negative, while a friendly overture might result in a rebuff if the other person's true hostility had not been recognized.

As indicated previously, some of the judgments we are continually making concern neither other people nor the external world but ourselves. Some of the most universal limitations and distortions of consciousness that clients present have to do with inaccurate, unrealistic perceptions of themselves. By way of illustration, there is the attractive woman who looks in the mirror and sees herself as ugly. Sensing (in this case visual) combines with an erroneous conclusion to produce an inaccurate perception, which engenders the inappropriate response of poor self-image (emotional) and avoidance of social relationships (behavioral).

Another kind of judgment all human beings make from time to time is how they define success at various stages in their lives. An individual's concept of what constitutes success for him determines some of his goals for that particular period of his life. If a person equates success with having a great deal of money, his goal might be to acquire money quickly in any way possible. He would then behave in ways that he believes would take him towards this goal. These behaviors, if the individual were a store owner, might include selling inferior merchandise at high prices, failing to report part of his income on his tax return, or driving a competitor out of business by unfair tactics. Since his goal is shaping his behavior, this individual's behavior could change only if he altered his concept of success (which would change his goal) or if he held to the same concept of success but adopted a different goal for achieving it—e.g., building a good business reputation and patiently saving his money.

To recapitulate, the cognitist says that the primary determinant of emotion and behavior is thinking. Thinking involves observing with our senses and reaching conclusions about what we observe. These conclusions can be judgments about situations, evaluations of people, self-images, concepts of reality, definitions of success, and formulations of goals. It is these conclusions that generate our day-by-day behavior and the emotions with which we live. It is important to add that we do not adopt goals only in connection with achieving success. We may also evolve goals that will shape our behavior in areas such as protecting ourselves and others, solving a problem, or mastering a new skill.

Motive, a concept with which some theoreticians deal at length, in the cognitive framework is simply the basic reason underlying a certain kind of behavior. It can always be described in the same way. A person's motive in behaving as he or she does is to solve the problems, complete the tasks, or reach the goals brought into existence by his or her personal perceptions of reality.

Finally, the cognitist offers a definition of emotions which regards them as conscious phenomena. In the cognitive view, an emotion is the feeling an individual experiences after perceiving an event (sensing plus evaluating) and reacting with a set of involuntary physiological responses. This concept was elucidated by the writer in a previous work as follows:

> As an example, the face of Mr. Fernandez becomes flushed and his heart begins to pound whenever anyone makes a disparaging remark about his Puerto Rican background. Here we have an objective description of an individual's emotion of anger. He judges the incident to be a hostile act, and this estimate triggers a set of involuntary physiological responses. This combination of evaluation (deciding what the offensive statement means) and physical sensation (flushing and heart pounding) is the content of all emotions.
>
> What we are saying, then, is that an emotion arises out of an event (act, incident, or object) of which a person becomes aware through doing it, seeing it, hearing it or hearing about it, touching it, tasting it, or smelling it. When the event registers on one or more of his senses, the individual makes a judgment as to what the event means to him, if anything. Should the event have little or no significance for him, no somatic response will take place and he will move on to something else. In such case, we would conclude that there was no emotion around this particular event, which might have been, for example, the placing of a routine letter in the mail box. On the other hand, under different circumstances, mailing a letter might give rise to a strong emotion, as when one is applying for a very important job and has doubts as to whether his letter of application will be impressive. The mailing of a letter is now a crucial event. The individual believes his future is at stake. As he opens the mail box, he worries that the letter will be inadequate, he

wonders if he should rewrite it, yet promptness in applying for the position is vital and he dreads the prospect of doing the letter over. Ambivalent and uneasy, he finally thrusts the letter in, thinking as he does so that the mailing of this letter may be a mistake. Accompanying this evaluation is a set of involuntary physiological responses in the form of sweating and trembling. The emotion of fear surrounds the event.

By our definition, there are two component parts in an emotion: an estimate of what an event means to us, and a felt somatic response. Judging what we become aware of and experiencing physiological reactions are both fully conscious activities. It is for this reason that we hold emotion to be an exclusively conscious phenomenon. [Werner, 1965, pp. 31–32]

It should be emphasized that one of the component parts of an emotion is a *felt* somatic response. The cognitive definition was formulated in this way to make it practical and usable. It could be argued that we make some somatic response, no matter how slight, to every stimulus in our environment and are therefore experiencing emotions every minute of the day. By considering that the existence of an emotion depends on the existence of a felt physiological reaction, we establish a cut-off point which denies that an emotion is being experienced when the surrounding event has so little meaning for us that our bodies do not react in any way we can feel.

Emotions vary in strength and in type. The stronger the physiological reaction, the stronger the emotion. The type of emotion is not determined by the type of somatic response, since an increased heartbeat and tingling sensation could be associated, for example, with both joy and fear. In one case, the precipitating event might be a decision to get married; in another, being called into the boss's office. What does determine the type of emotion is the individual's evaluation of the precipitating event as positive or negative, beautiful or ugly, favorable or unfavorable, reassuring or threatening. Emotion is therefore a psychosomatic entity—its nature is determined by both the thinking and feeling elements of which it is composed.

Cognitive theory, which, as we have said, insists on regarding emotions as exclusively conscious phenomena, views the psychoanalytic concept of "unconscious guilt" or "unconscious anger" as a contradiction in terms. It finds definitions by Adler, Rado, and May more useful. Adler concluded: "The unconscious is nothing other than that which we have been unable to formulate in clear concepts" (Ansbacher and Ansbacher, 1956, p. 232). Rado described the "unconscious" as a "non-reporting (in contrast to the conscious mind which is reporting) organization of causative links between processes of which we are aware" (Rado, 1956, p. 182). May wrote:

> The "unconscious", then, is not to be thought of as a reservoir of impulses, thoughts, wishes which are culturally unacceptable; I define it rather as those potentialities for knowing and experiencing which the individual cannot or will not actualize. [May, 1960, p. 688]

The cognitist does not see a substantive "unconscious" as the controlling force of our mental lives. One can be unconscious (unaware) of certain facts, of the impression one is making on others, of the origins of current ideas and behavior, of one's own potentialities, or of a thought one has forgotten or deliberately put out of mind. In the cognitive view, however, material which is out of awareness does not exert any influence over our behavior.

There are reciprocal relationships among perception, emotions, goals, and behavior. These relationships may be summed up as follows:

1. Change in perception alters emotions, goals, and behavior;
2. Change in goal is especially influential in altering behavior;

3. New activities and new kinds of behavior alter perception.

Cognitive treatment techniques make direct use of these interrelationships. The cognitist will challenge the client whose perceptions of self, others, and society are not accurate. Evidence supporting more realistic appraisals will be introduced whenever necessary. When the client's problems are the consequences of antisocial or self-destructive goals, the worker will point out the connection between the client's distress and his choice of goals. The worker then has the therapeutic task of helping the client to reorient himself with a different set of goals. When inaccurate perceptions do not yield to discussion between worker and client, they will often change when the client, encouraged to engage in a new activity which he previously feared, carries out such activity to a satisfying end. His distorted perceptions about the dangers around him or his lack of competence are modified by life itself.

The use of behavior to alter perception stands in marked contrast to the traditional emphasis on helping the client gain "insight" (accurate perception) through discussion as a necessary first step *before* behavioral change can occur. Glasser, one of the cognitive theorists who calls his treatment technique "reality therapy," believes that behavior is much more important than feelings. He contends that feelings will change when behavior changes, that they do not change merely by being discussed. In Glasser's (1965) view, the therapist has the task of educating clients to adopt behavior that will fulfill basic needs they have not yet satisfied. The emphasis should not be on the clients' attitudes and emotions, but on what they are doing at present and what they plan for the future. Consciousness-altering activity is also part of the "rational-emotive psychotherapy" practiced by Ellis, who gives his clients "homework" to do between interviews. This might involve participating in a social activity about which the client has been apprehensive, confronting a spouse with a grievance one has feared to raise, or taking a job for which one feels inadequate. Successful self-assertion is effective in diminishing unfounded negative emotions (Ellis, 1962).

Figure 1.1 portrays in simple pictorial form the relationships, sometimes reciprocal, among the real world, sensing, thinking, involuntary physiological reactions, and behavior. As events come into the client's awareness through being sensed by his physical organs, he evaluates their meaning to him, such judging being greatly affected, colored, or distorted by the prism of his life experiences and by his own personality. Perception is the combination of sensing and thinking. Emotions are the combination of thinking and the involuntary physiological reactions that thinking engenders. Thinking is the primary producer of behavior, which can be strengthened or weakened by involuntary physiological reactions taking place at the same time. For example, an individual on a ski slope sees an avalanche starting at the top of the mountain. He judges, on the basis of past experiences, that he is in immediate danger. This thought, however, also triggers off involuntary physiological reactions that immobilize him (he "freezes up"). The combination is the emotion of fear. His thinking calls for escape behavior, but the coexisting somatic response interferes (temporarily, we hope).

Most of the processes depicted in the diagram move from left to right. As has been suggested, however, while thinking is the primary determinant of behavior, new behaviors undertaken under the influence of another person with different perceptions (i.e., the therapist or a friend) can become feedback which alters or corrects the client's original thinking. The arrow connecting "thinking" and "behaviors," therefore, points in both directions.

On more than one occasion we have referred to thinking as the *primary* determinant of behavior. The diagram indicates a *secondary* source of behavior, the conditioned reflex, a process which bypasses all thinking activity. Physiologically

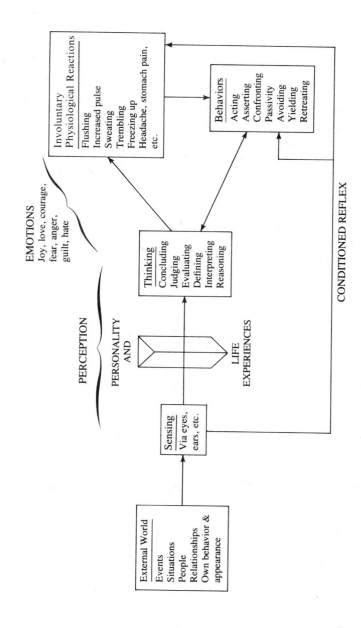

FIGURE 1.1 The interrelationship of perceptions, emotions, behaviors, and involuntary physiological reactions.

speaking, what happens is that certain stimuli, linked to certain behavioral and somatic responses by a traumatic or vivid experience or by repetition, acquire the ability to trigger off behavior without the mediation of thinking. An automatic physiological phenomenon, known as a conditioned reflex, gets built into the autonomic nervous system so that the sensing of a particular stimulus instantaneously evokes the same behavior every time. No judging, evaluating, or interpreting is involved. The higher cortical centers of the brain are bypassed.

A phobia of dogs illustrates how a conditioned reflex develops after a traumatic experience. A very impressionable young child is bitten by a dog, or perhaps the victim is an adult who gets bitten under very frightening circumstances or more than once. Evaluating what has happened, such individuals may subsequently perceive *all* dogs as dangerous and to be avoided, with the sight or sound of any dog immediately triggering some kind of escape behavior (crossing the street, going back inside the house). If this stimulus-response bond is not dissolved through the helpful interference of another person or a counteracting life experience (encounter with a friendly dog, the gift of a puppy), it is reinforced by repetition and becomes an automatic behavior, a conditioned reflex.

We are granting that, in a conditioned reflex, the mere sensing of a particular stimulus automatically generates the same behavior each time, this process taking place without the mediation of thought. Nevertheless the cognitist maintains that thinking is still the primary determinant of all behavior. In the example cited, the avoidance of dogs originally came into existence as the result of a person's thinking about an event. Finally, as mentioned above, somatic responses can become part of a conditioned reflex so that the stimulus not only triggers the same behavior each time but also the same involuntary physiological reaction.

Conditioned reflexes are not always a response to threatening and emotionally charged incidents. The set of reflexes that is activated every time we drive a car develops through repetition of a series of tasks which we deliberately decide to master. The various automatic responses we develop in the form of conditioned reflexes by free choice include, in addition to driving a car, various grooming activities (shaving, hairsetting), routines for getting dressed, playing a musical instrument, using a typewriter, engaging in sports, and countless others. When our conditioned reflexes satisfy our needs (e.g., we read music well or hit a tennis ball accurately), they make our lives easier. When a task can be performed properly in an automatic fashion, it is not necessary to learn it all over again each time we face it. In Chapter 3, there is a discussion of the overall relationship of cognitive therapy to behavior therapy, which is based on the conditioned reflex.

If most of the professionals who practice cognitive therapy in part or all of their work do not identify it as such, how can it be recognized? Whether identified or not, a cognitive approach is being applied when a worker/counselor/therapist does some of the following things:

1. Relates to the client on the basis of his behavior and his stated thoughts, emotions and goals, without postulating unconscious forces;
2. Makes a diagnosis in terms of the distortions or limitations in the client's thinking;
3. Looks for the client's strengths rather than his pathology and puts those strengths to use;
4. Guides the client into trying selected experiences which may alter his inaccurate perceptions;
5. Recognizes that each client's behavior is shaped by his personal goals rather than by universal biological drives;

6. Works to achieve the changes the client wants by expanding his consciousness of self, others, and the world around him;

7. Requires the client to take responsibility for his behavior, not allowing the past or the "unconscious" to excuse present conduct.

As can be seen, the cognitive practitioner does not postulate unconscious emotions, conflicts, or ideas. He bears in mind that the uniquely human characteristics are language and the ability to think and reason. He makes use of these unique characteristics in the way he conducts his treatment. The client is asked to put into words what he has been saying to himself about significant events and problems. He is encouraged to describe his emotions, his goals in life, and his current behavior. What the client says combined with what the worker observes is considered to be a valid basis upon which to develop a treatment plan. A treatment plan is always a clearly stated and mutually agreed upon venture of worker and client. As treatment progresses, the client will be making basic decisions about his future. It is one of the responsibilities of the worker to be sure that the client has all the facts and concepts necessary to make judgments that correspond to reality. In this connection, it is vital for the worker him- or herself to have both feet planted firmly in reality. Otherwise, the worker will not be able to tell which of the client's behaviors, emotions, and decisions are appropriate and which are not. This means that the worker must have an accurate perception of the client's life situation, that is, where he is coming from, and must keep fully abreast of newly published information and explanations about human behavior.

Chapter 2

History and Current Status

History

The reader will see that some of the characteristics of cognitive theory include clarity, simplicity, and a down-to-earth approach. Despite these common sense aspects, however, it is not a naive or simplistic theory and has been developing for seventy years.

Although the Greek philosopher Epictetus observed back around 100 A.D. that men are not disturbed by things but by their perceptions of things, we can say that cognitive theory really began in Vienna around 1911, when Alfred Adler and Sigmund Freud went their separate ways after a close association of many years. Fundamental differences arose between them, and Adler proceeded to develop his own conceptual framework, which he named "individual psychology." Adlerian theory was in disagreement with Freud's division of the psyche into sections and Freud's concept of the continual war between the id and the superego. Adler saw the human personality as a unified whole never in conflict with itself, a view which later came to be known as the "holistic" approach. To Adler, conflicts in people were not within themselves but with the world around them and resulted from antisocial or distorted thinking. Today we realize that conflicts can also arise out of an individual's resistance to people or environments he regards as oppressive.

Adler seems to have been the original proponent of the cognitive approach by virtue of his contention that each person's behavior was shaped by his notions of what constituted success and by the goals he set up to achieve it. We have here, in elementary form, the main tenet of cognitive theory: thinking shapes behavior. In the 1920s and 1930s, Adler's ideas were widely accepted in many parts of Europe and also had some following in the United States. For about twenty years after his death in 1937, there was a decline in interest, but since the publication in 1956 of a comprehensive collection of excerpts from his writings, edited by Heinz and Rowena Ansbacher, interest has been increasing steadily again.

Adler placed great emphasis on the uniqueness of each human being, which accounts for his designation of his theories as an "individual psychology." He was interested in the nuances which made one person different from another. He resisted the psychoanalytic practice of insisting that certain experiences and characteristics were universal and inherent in everyone, such as the Oedipal or Electral conflict, the primacy of the sex drive, and inborn aggression. He always focused on a person's embeddedness in his society. He saw the sex drive as just one of several that could influence behavior. Adler denied the universality of the Oedipal or Electral conflict; while granting that children's hostilities and attachments to parents were sometimes sexually motivated, he believed that in most cases they were consequences of a child's efforts to secure a more favored position for himself in the family. He did not believe that anxiety had exclusively sexual origins. While sexual impulses might be threatening in some cases, anxiety was more often triggered by demands, problems, and failures in everyday living.

As for the concept of inborn aggression, it was Adler himself who first formulated it during his early association with the Vienna Psychoanalytic Society. Later, he abandoned it and is reported to have said: "I enriched psychoanalysis by the aggressive drive. I gladly make them [Freud's followers] a present of it." He went on to reach a conclusion diametrically opposed to Freud's view that each person is born "a wolf unto other men." Adler's final formulation was that "man is not born good or evil, but he can be trained in either direction." He asserted that people can be taught "social interest," by which he meant a community feeling, a desire to live cooperatively with others, a sense of responsibility to society. For him, individuals who exhibited aggressive or destructive behavior were lacking "social interest." Cognitists today agree with Adler that aggression is not an instinctual drive requiring continuous satisfaction. They have extended his formulation so that aggressive behavior, in addition to being triggered by selfish goals or greed (lack of social interest), is seen also as a reaction to deprivation of rights or dignity, or as a defense against an anticipated attack.

The decade of the 1950s saw the appearance of other writings which made contributions in varying degrees to the substance of cognitive theory. Joseph Wortis was perhaps the first to use the term "rational psychotherapy," a synonym for cognitive therapy (1953, p. 81). Joseph Furst, in a work published in 1954, proposed that neurosis be viewed as a distortion or limitation of consciousness, a concept that is the essence of cognitive theory. The year 1955 witnessed the first issue of *Psychotherapy,* the journal of the Robbins Institute in New York City, which was headed by Bernard Robbins and made up of psychiatrists who had received orthodox psychoanalytic training but were moving away from Freud. An article in this publication entitled "An Integrated Psychotherapeutic Program" took the position that cure is change, cure is the development of rational consciousness, which is not a knowledge of the "unconscious" but an accurate awareness of one's real nature as a person, the natural and social environment, and one's connection with the out-

side world. In 1956, the American Psychological Asssocia-
tion heard a paper on rational psychotherapy for the first
time at one of its annual meetings. In this presentation,
Albert Ellis described emotion as a "strongly evaluative kind
of thinking," a result of the sentences we say to ourselves. Irrational or unrealistic thought produced distorted and disturbed emotions and behavior, and it was the task of the
therapist to show his clients that their internalized sentences
were unrealistic and that they had the ability to control their
emotions by telling themselves more rational sentences and
trying new experiences and actions (Ellis, 1958).

Between 1960 and 1970, the earlier literature on cognitive
therapy was augmented by two important books by Ellis, *A
Guide to Rational Living* (coauthored with Robert A.
Harper) (1961) and *Reason and Emotion in Psychotherapy*
(1962), by William Glasser's *Reality Therapy* (1965), and by
this writer's *A Rational Approach to Social Casework* (1965)
and *New Understandings of Human Behavior* (1970). Abraham Maslow, in various writings, made it clear that he be-
longed in the cognitive camp. He maintained that man's
thinking was important and that he was not controlled by his
instinctual drives or his habits as other animals were. He regarded whatever innate tendencies man had as mostly constructive rather than destructive, referring to these tendencies
as a need for self-actualization, a need "to become everything that one is capable of becoming." Maslow believed
that a healthy individual's motivation was stronger than
most instinctual drives. He concluded that the power of these
drives had been overestimated, and reclassified them from
"instincts" to "instinctoid impulses" (1970, pp. 77–95).
Leon Salzman, during this same period, also placed himself
within the cognitive approach with significant contributions
to the understanding of the obsessive-compulsive personality, the paranoid state, and masochism.

Salzman's ideas merit a brief summary at this point. The
Freudian view had come to regard obsessions or compulsions

as rituals to deal with "unconscious" sexual guilt and "unconscious" wishes intolerable to the individual's consciousness. Salzman approached these as the products of an individual's current perceptions of reality. He saw the compulsive person as someone with excessive feelings of insecurity which required absolute guarantees before action could be pursued. Such insecurity could develop from all kinds of life experiences and environmental stresses, not only from fear of losing control of sexual or aggressive urges. The compulsive individual, unable to take the ordinary risks and chances implicit in normal daily living, develops rituals to use as a guarantee against risk. By performing the ritual a certain way or a specific number of times, the individual believes he is following a proven, automatic procedure that takes care of a particular problem. He thereby eliminates the doubt that comes from making a choice of action each time. Thus, one person tries a doorknob a dozen times to assure himself that the door is really locked, while another washes his hands frequently in a particular fashion to make sure he is free of germs or toxic substances (Salzman, 1973).

In regard to the paranoid state, Salzman took the position that its primary origin was in an extremely deflated self-esteem. This was quite different from the Freudian conception of paranoid symptoms as invariably the consequences of a failure to repress a homosexual tendency. The poor self-image underlying paranoid behavior, in Salzman's view, could in some cases be caused by sexual pathology, but he did not see sexual pathology as its main cause in the majority of cases. He outlined the development of paranoid behavior as follows: feelings of deflated esteem can arise from many different sources, sexual and nonsexual; an individual may try to overcome these feelings of worthlessness by grandiose behavior which antagonizes the environment; anxiety-producing rebuffs from the environment can provoke the organization of a self-protective delusional structure, i.e., a paranoid state (Salzman, 1960a).

Finally, Salzman approached the problem of masochism not as "unconscious guilt seeking for punishment" but as an attempt at mastery, an adjustive maneuver designed to deal with certain personal and social conditions. People remain in unhappy marriages not out of a desire to be punished but because they perceive such a course as preferable to facing the world alone. Others remain in interpersonal situations of great suffering because they have no hope of gaining attention or sympathy except through being helpless or powerless. Salzman pointed out that, although masochism demonstrates a kind of behavior which appears to be punishment seeking, this behavior can actually be reward seeking (Salzman, 1960b).

Current Status

Since 1971 the literature on cognitive therapy has continued to grow. The followers of Adler, who pioneered the cognitive approach, are seeing Adlerian societies expand and increase nationally and internationally, aided by institutes in various cities and annual conferences. For over thirty-five years, they have been publishing the *Journal of Individual Psychology,* an excellent source of clear, practical articles on understanding and helping troubled people through Adlerian methods. Ellis, through his Institute for Rational Living, his many books, conferences, and numerous appearances on radio and television, has promoted rational-emotive therapy, his brand of cognitive treatment, on a national scale. His organization publishes a journal called *Rational Living.* Glasser has, to a lesser degree, done the same thing with his reality therapy.

A list of other books about cognitive theory and practice published in the past ten years (1971–1981) should begin with

Techniques for Behavior Change. Edited by Arthur G. Nikelly (1971), who also wrote some of the chapters, it is a collection of writings about Adlerian theory and its practical applications to treatment. It simplifies Adler's principal concepts and brings them up to date. Because of its clarity and brevity, it can serve as one of the basic textbooks for social workers and other professionals who want a practical introduction to the cognitive approach. The book's basic premise is that maladjustment stems from an incorrect evaluation of oneself and others, from excessive striving and mistaken goals, from discouragement, and from an inadequate interest in cooperation with others.

Maxie C. Maultsby, Jr. published *Help Yourself to Happiness* in 1975. In this work, he reinforced previous writings by himself and others on the importance of utilizing mental imagery in cognitive treatment. A close associate of Albert Ellis, Maultsby has his clients use what he calls "rational emotive imagery" to practice correct thinking, feeling, and acting. The main purpose of this book is to serve as a guide for "rational self-counseling."

The second half of the 1970s witnessed the appearance of Aaron Beck's *Cognitive Therapy and the Emotional Disorders* (1976). This is one of the definitive works on the subject, giving an overall view and having no affiliation with any particular group within the cognitive orbit. Dr. Beck, a leading psychiatrist who was originally trained as a psychoanalyst, pulls together the ideas and formulations of many who preceded him. He sets down a body of principles and the cognitive therapeutic techniques appropriate for each of the major emotional disorders: depression, anxiety, phobias, obsessions, and conversion reactions. His basic premises are that "there is a conscious thought between an external event and a particular emotional response"; thought shapes emotion and behavior; and the task of therapy is to reshape the erroneous beliefs which produce inappropriate emotions and behavior. He contends that the concept of "free-floating anxiety" is a fallacy since anxiety is the consequence of a specific thought.

The reader will observe that, all through the years, books about cognitive therapy have been produced exclusively by psychiatrists and psychologists, with the single exception of this writer, who is a clinical social worker. It is therefore encouraging to note the publication in 1981 of *Social Learning and Change: A Cognitive Approach to Human Services* by Dr. Howard Goldstein, Professor of Social Work at Case Western Reserve University. In his view, learning involves acquisition of the knowledge tools we need to manage the contingencies of living effectively, e.g., information, guidance, and opportunities to try out new courses of action. Learning also calls for the reshaping of our essential beliefs about the nature of our personal reality. The personal reality of each of us is composed of our cognitions: what we *know* we know, what we *know* we believe, what we *know* we value, and what we *know* we are. Change in behavior can take place if we are able to modify our accustomed premises. Conversely, if we can work out new forms of adaptive behavior, changes in our conception of our world will follow. Basing himself on a formulation by Perry London, Goldstein divides his book into three sections, each devoted to a different element of his subject. The first section comprises an anthropological philosophy as a foundation for his theory and method of change, with considerable attention to the historical derivations of modern social and psychological thought. The second presents a general theory of human behavior. The third translates this philosophy and theory into operational strategies of learning and change.

To complete this brief examination of the current status of cognitive therapy, the three leading social work journals in the United States were reviewed, beginning with their January 1970 issues *(Social Work, Social Casework, Social Service Review)*. The intent of the survey (1970–1980) was to determine how much significance these periodicals have been attributing to cognitive theory and practice as evidenced by the frequency and content of articles related in some way to this topic.

For those readers who are interested in earlier social work literature, one of the author's previous writings discusses articles appearing in social work journals in the 1960s and early 1970s which reported the use of cognitive elements in practice, but without identifying them as such (Werner, 1979). Those who would like to read articles about non-Freudian concepts of human behavior published in psychiatric and psychological journals from 1960 to 1968 will find them collected in the author's *New Understandings of Human Behavior* (1970).

The survey of the three social work journals reveals that in 1970, 1971, and 1972 they published a total of only three articles which discussed or advocated some element of a cognitive approach. (These three articles will not be quoted here inasmuch as they were quoted in the author's previous work cited above.) Norman Epstein (1970), without identifying it as such, called for a cognitive orientation in brief therapy groups with parents. White (1970) favored an experiential approach in doing casework with reluctant welfare clients. Such an approach was predicated on the belief that people achieve better emotional health through heightened consciousness of their current behavior. Siporin (1972) urged social workers to adopt a situational perspective in their efforts to help the client, maintaining that it was the individual's perception of his situation, his situational definition or consciousness, that influenced his actions and responses.

In 1973, there were no articles relating directly to cognitive treatment. In 1974, Orten and Weis presented a comparison of strategies and techniques used in four forms of therapeutic intervention. Strategies discussed were analytic, behavioral, environmental, and rational. The rational-emotive therapy of Albert Ellis was used as a representative example of the last named, which is equivalent to the cognitive approach (Orten and Weis, 1974). There were no other articles that year about cognitive practice.

In 1975, Thomas, Etcheverry, and Keller reported on the questionnaire responses of 140 individuals engaged in direct practice. These respondents were asked about the practice methods they used. One method of treatment that emerged was described as "humanistic" and characterized as "non-behavioral evocative methods," but this did not turn out to be any kind of clearly defined cognitive therapy with which the reader could compare his own practice. Maultsby (1975) described how to diagnose and treat neurotic adolescents within a framework of rational-emotive therapy. Saleeby (1975) clearly and succinctly outlined a humanist perspective on how people function, showing that there is a close connection between a humanist philosophy and a cognitive approach to treatment. (Saleeby's ideas will be summarized in the next chapter.) Snyder (1975), a supervisor of therapy in an alcoholism treatment program, discussed cognitive approaches in the treatment of alcoholism. She identified cognitive approaches by that name and encouraged their use in work with alcoholics. Quoting this author's observation (Werner, 1979, p. 266) that addicted persons are outside the scope of cognitive treatment until they are *first* brought under control by medical, pharmaceutical, or behavior modification means, she asserted that cognitive therapy may be employed *concurrently* with these means. She saw the alcoholic client as being able to assume responsibility for his thinking, motives, and behavior and in need of the help to change his lifestyle which the cognitive approach provides.

Also in 1975, Bennett made a plea for the restoration of personality theory to the curricula of social work schools, from which it had been largely discarded because of a renewed emphasis on social action in practice. In essence, personality theory deals with why individuals behave as they do. In advocating that personality theory should be taught in depth in schools of social work, Bennett made reference to a statement in this writer's 1965 work (p. 156), which was the first book by a social worker to expound a cognitive approach. The statement was that "the conditions under which people live determine their thinking, which in turn determines their behavior." Bennett regarded this comment as a "behavioristic, mechanistic, simplistic, and truly reductionist explanation of human behavior" which did not take into account "individual differences occurring in the same social environment between people living under similar conditions." She thought that this formulation led to the erroneous conclusion that all problems would disappear if social workers saw to it that society met the basic needs of its citizens. She also believed that this concept discouraged any interest in personality theory and the concern of such theory with differences in individual development.

The cognitist will reiterate that the conditions under which people live *do* determine their thinking, but this in no way implies that a particular environment or society influences every individual in the same manner or to the same degree. The cognitive approach, as far back as Adler at the beginning of the century, has always affirmed the uniqueness and psychosocial nature of each individual, and it has not accepted classical behavior theory's concept of the Stimulus-Response Bond as a sufficient explanation of human behavior. As Ralph Waldo Emerson expressed it, "The cause of anything is everything." A person's thinking and the behavior it generates are products of the conditions under which he lives, modified by the personality he has become and the experiences he has encountered. Neither this writer nor cognitive therapists in general have ever taken the position that, in a society which provides everyone with sufficient medical care, housing, education, employment, and civil rights, all problems in thinking and behavior will automatically disappear. Even in the healthiest and most benign societies, individuals will have difficulties in relating to other people or will make poor decisions, such as marrying the wrong spouse or taking the wrong job. In cognitive treatment, as is described in Chapter 6, the therapist is very much concerned with taking the kind of personal history and making the kind of assessment that will reveal each client's individual personality development.

In 1976, Epstein again advocated cognitive techniques in brief therapy without naming them as such:

> A brief therapy program for children and parents needs to tackle the myth that children (as well as parents) are the victims of compelling unconscious forces and can neither control nor take responsibility for their behavior. In spite of the lack of substantive research, speculation concerning unconscious forces has survived, and has often taken the form of theological disputation. A brief therapy program views the child and the parent as being able to give expression to their beliefs and expectations about themselves and each other, as well as to evaluate the congruence with reality of those beliefs and expectations. . . .
>
> A basic goal, involving the child, is to help stimulate interest in examining the range of self-defeating, immature behaviors that are mired in misperceptions of the self and others. . . . The participants are urged not to seek rationalizations of current behavior through repeated explorations of the past. Utilizing the here and now focus, parent and child are encouraged to view the relationship as being composed of ingredients that are subject to conscious control and manipulation by the participants in the relationship. [Pp. 318–319]

Also in 1976, Silver reported on a program of outpatient group treatment for male sexual offenders, describing it as based largely on the principles of guided group interaction and behavior modification. Called the Sexual Deviance Program (SDP), it appears to contain a large element of cognitive therapy. The primary focus is on each client's current interpersonal behavior. The goal of the program is the control and understanding of deviant sexual conduct. One method of teaching control is by the use of imagery to create a "cognitive interference." The client is helped to construct a mental scene in which he suffers severe consequences because of deviant sexual behavior, and through practice to call up this image as an aversive stimulus whenever he has a deviant impulse. Other objectives of the program include learning to accept responsibility for one's behavior, expanding sexual knowledge and dispelling sexual myths, and increasing awareness of one's current situation. Members get a chance to enhance their self-esteem and to alter inaccurate perceptions of themselves by taking turns directing the group and receiving feedback from each other on their strengths, potentials, and limitations, and on the universality of their problems. Periodically, female professionals and volunteers join the men for sessions or gatherings to give the clients opportunity to build social skills with the opposite sex, test out new behaviors, and modify their thinking through new experiences and role-playing activities.

In 1977, De Lo and Green wrote about a technique which they called a cognitive transactional approach. They used this approach to improve interracial communication. The procedure consisted of making verbal presentations in all types of workshops and discussion groups of a series of deficient transactions between blacks and whites. In these transactions one or both individuals were put down or hurt. These examples were presented to give the audience a new experience which might modify inaccurate belief systems by stimulating cognition and discussion and leading participants to generalize to other transactional experiences in their lives. De Lo and Green suggested that this model of intervention could be applied to other majority-minority group interactions such as those between men and women, nondisabled and disabled, and "WASPS" and ethnic groups.

De Lo and Green (1977) based their technique on the theory of personal constructs:

George A. Kelly points out that the individual uses a cognitive process to develop personal constructs that account for the organization and direction of behavior. The end product—his behavior—is dependent upon the manner in which the individual conceptualizes his experiences. [P. 295]

They went on to say that, once a personal construct system is developed, the individual tends to seek information and choose behavior that support these constructs. There is a strong vested interest in maintaining personal constructs. Transactions between people are influenced by the cognitive set of the participants. In the matter of transracial communication, it may be assumed that blacks and whites, with their different histories, approach each other with totally different sets of constructs which they wish to validate at the expense of the other. Often, they approach each other with cognitive sets (inaccurate stereotypes, unjustified fears, etc.) that produce mutually harmful transactions.

In 1978, Lantz published a landmark article on "Cognitive Theory and Social Casework" in which he stated that "The primary concept held by cognitive practitioners is that most human emotion is the direct result of what people think, tell themselves, assume, or believe about themselves and their social situations" (p. 361). He went on to discuss six treatment procedures, some of them already familiar casework techniques, which can be used with a cognitive orientation to help a client change misconceptions that create dysfunctional emotions and behavior. These included using the treatment relationship, clarifying communication, explanation, imagery, experiential learning, and the therapeutic bind.

In the *treatment relationship,* the respect and support provided by the worker can help the client to change misconceptions about his own worth and potential. The treatment relationship also offers an opportunity to examine any distorted perceptions about people which the client projects onto the worker. *Clarifying communication* refers to aiding the client to understand the implications and effects of what he does through a "cognitive review" of his words and actions in interpersonal situations. *Explanation* is a process of teaching clients how emotions work, how to discover any inaccurate perceptions they may have, and how to work out strategies for overcoming inappropriate emotions. *Imagery,* which has not received much attention in the casework literature, grew out of the behavior modification approach and is a treatment procedure easily adapted for use with a cognitive orientation. This is, however, a technically complex procedure for which the therapist will need training; essentially, it involves teaching the client deep muscle relaxation and then having him visualize both threatening and happy scenes. The purpose of this technique is to show the client the relationship between thought and emotional response, and then have him practice associating a happy image with an act or situation that is causing him unrealistic apprehension. Often, the client is then able to face the feared situation.

Experiential learning makes use of the human tendency to eliminate any cognitive dissonance, a discrepancy between thought and behavior, that develops. For example, the author of this book has set up a treatment situation (therapy group) or assigned a "homework" task (attending a party) for clients who were afraid of social activities with other people. Any confidence, self-esteem, or success arising out of this new experience contributes to developing a discrepancy between thinking of social activity as threatening and enjoying such activity, with the result that the thinking changes. In addition to group therapy and task assignments, Lantz (1978) lists other techniques based on experiential learning that the cognitist can employ: assertiveness training, role prescription, psychodrama, modeling, and role playing. Finally, the *therapeutic bind* is a treatment procedure that can be used in two ways to help clients change irrational ideas. The first form of therapeutic bind is paradoxical intention or prescribing the symptom. The second form is a double bind: the worker gives the client a directive which results in challenging his misperceptions because, whether he carries it out or not, he is behaving in a way which he previously did not recognize or think possible.

Lantz concluded that cognitive theory had generally been

ignored in the casework literature and hoped that his presentation would result in more systematic use of cognitive theory in the practice of social casework. However, two other articles appearing in social work journals in 1978, while mentioning cognitive theory in passing, gave no recognition to it as a major alternative to psychoanalysis and behaviorism or as a separate, main current in treatment. Siporin, whose previous writings contained large elements of a cognitive approach, wrote that the conflict over the psychoanalytic model of therapy resulted in a fairly successful public campaign for the adoption of behavior modification and experimentation with various other new approaches. Among these new approaches he listed rational-emotive and cognitive as separate entities, perpetuating confusion by not recognizing cognitive as the generic term, and made no further mention of the cognitive approach (p. 424). Jayaratne (1978) reported on his national survey of clinical social workers to determine their choices of clinical orientation. Definitions of the various theoretical orientations were not provided in the questionnaire. Listed as separate entities were psychoanalytic, neo-Freudian, Rogerian, transactional analysis, gestalt, behavior theory, existential, humanistic, rational-emotive and reality therapy. Again there was a failure to realize that the last three belong in the overall category of cognitive theory, and further confusion was demonstrated by the fact that respondents frequently combined "psychoanalytic" and "humanistic," or "psychoanalytic" and "reality" approaches.

In 1979, Sigmund Freud's granddaughter, Sophie Freud Loewenstein, questioned the psychoanalytic practice of attributing behavior to the inner characteristics acquired in one's early development or to deficits in early development. She focused on the situation and the communications taking place within it, seeing behavior as a reaction to what was currently going on. She took the position that different people and events will cause the same person in the same situation to behave in a different way. Her views on some basic issues were compatible with those of the cognitive approach, but she did not recognize or identify them as such. Loewenstein concluded:

> It would be best for caseworkers to accept situation and communication theories as the *major* conceptual frameworks for casework practice. Caseworkers deal with serious social problems and an interactional, situational approach provides a more hopeful philosophy than ego psychology. The medical model, with its emphasis on inner space and diagnosis, may have become politically tainted and misleading when applied to human behavior. . . . Casework is social interaction that utilizes a variety of helping processes; some of these discussed here are: changing the clients' immediate or broader situational context; informing and educating them; cognitive restructuring (of guilt for example) and providing meaning to clients' behavior; prescribing their symptoms and giving creative advice; providing an audience and consensual validation for clients who need to bear witness; and, above all, providing affirmation in every encounter between worker and client. It is not expected that these new approaches would modify the casework method in important ways; they are rather a case of updating theory to match actual practice. [1979, p. 29]

In 1980, Zacks proposed a general outline of an educational program for groups of midlifers, aged 35 to 45, to help them develop problem-solving techniques for problems typical of their age group:

> The proposed program is cognitively oriented; it focuses on developing a rational approach to dealing with personal difficulties. Hence, the objective of the program is to sharpen and perfect the ability of individuals to resolve their midlife conflicts by enhancing the learning of new and correcting old problem-solving techniques. . . . It is intended for people in the range of the "normal", people who are capable of rational thinking and acting and of learning from their own as well as others' experiences. [Pp. 232–233]

The program proposed by Zacks consisted of two parts: the first was composed of a number of sessions devoted to a presentation by the group leader of research findings on adult development and midlife, of the various steps of the problem-solving process, and of other didactic topics. The second part of the series of ten weekly sessions would concentrate on actual work to solve personal midlife problems brought up by the group members. The group leader would also be responsible for creating linkages between individual participants and community resources.

Also in 1980, Combs examined the theory, method, and clinical outcomes of cognitive therapy as applied by Aaron Beck to the treatment of depression. Combs contended that the theory had problems: its explanations rested on inferred variables, such as thoughts and feelings, which could not be observed directly; and in regard to causality, the fact that depressed and nondepressed people differed in their cognitions was not proof that cognitions led to depression. It could also be argued that the experience of being depressed caused individuals to begin to think differently.

Combs went on to review the relatively small number of existing experimental studies of the effectiveness of cognitive therapy in treating depression, concluding that it showed promise, especially in combination with other modalities. Most studies did not, however, show a maintenance of positive results at follow-up. Recommendations were made as to some of the areas that needed special attention in future research on the cognitive treatment of depression: the type of client most likely to benefit from cognitive techniques; the most effective combinations of cognitive techniques; the most effective combinations of cognitive approaches and other approaches; and extended follow-up testing.

Combs (1980, p. 366) concluded:

> Although there are deficits in the research supporting Beck's cognitive therapy in the treatment of depression, it has been shown to be an effective treatment component in

some instances. Further research must address several problems, with particular attention to long-term maintenance of results.

Finally, during the first half of 1980, Walter Miller suggested that the medical model has had a detrimental influence on the profession of social work. In offering alternative models, he proposed a humanistic approach that emphasized the expansion of the client's consciousness, which is the keystone of a cognitive orientation. Miller did not, however, identify this approach as "cognitive":

> People base their decisions on information and feedback from systems, and a person's very being at any one time may be considered to be the totality of all this information. . . . With every action or decision a person redefines his or her own being—and for that definition the person must be solely responsible.
>
> This author proposes that caseworkers view human decision-making in a human way. . . . The practice of social work should be based on a human, ethical intent to make the maximum number of choices available to the profession's clients.
>
> Many human actions, such as breathing or sweating, are fairly automatic. But many others involve a selection among choices provided by the environment. A human makes such choices on the basis of information received—and this choice changes his or her being. The proposal presented here contends that a caseworker cannot take responsibility for making a client's decisions. The worker can, however, affect such decisions by limiting or expanding the client's choices or by changing the other information the client receives.
>
> A caseworker who respects the humanity of his or her clients will supply them with as many choices and as much information as possible. It is conscious or potentially conscious decision-making that concerns caseworkers. [Miller, 1980, pp. 284–285]

Miller concluded that caseworkers can also expand an individual's choices by causing the environment to provide more choices or by helping to change institutions of social control. This would be in addition to informing the client of choices that already exist.

The foregoing review of articles published in three social work journals, from January 1970 through July 1980, does not give a complete picture of how cognitive theory has fared in social work literature. There have been articles in other social work journals. In addition, all through the years psychological and psychiatric journals have been paying some attention to the subject, perhaps more than social work publications. It is hoped, however, that the limited focus of this review will still give the reader some sense of how much awareness, interest, and support cognitive theory has been receiving in the last decade from social work editors, educators, and practitioners.

It is of interest to note that a journal called *Cognitive Therapy and Research* began publishing in 1977. Under its stimulus, we can look forward to a regular flow of objective studies of the effectiveness of the cognitive approach, with the result that shortcomings can be pinpointed and practice improved. Some of the clinical outcome studies published in this journal are reported in Chapter 10. Our immediate concern in the next chapter, however, will not be the outcome of cognitive practice, but the philosophical underpinnings of the theory on which it is based.

Chapter 3

The Significance of a Humanistic Approach: Applications to Life

Having described cognitive therapy and the personality theory on which it is based, we proceed now to identify the philosophical underpinnings of that theory. In subsequent chapters, we shall discuss in detail the specific treatment techniques used by cognitists to help their clients change.

Cognitive theory flows naturally out of a humanist philosophy. We have referred to cognitive theory and therapy as the "third force," the third main current in the treatment of troubled people. The term "third force" can also be used as a synonym for that primary determinant of behavior which is neither unconscious biologically determined inner drives (psychoanalysis) nor externally conditioned habits (behaviorism). In a paper about Adler, Ansbacher spelled this out very clearly:

> Today the entire movement of humanistic and existential psychology and psychotherapy is founded on this "third force", namely, the self-determination of the individual, as opposed to the other two determining forces: Freud's psychogenetic determinism and the environmental determinism of behaviorism. While Adler was far from denying

the importance of biological determinants or environment, he insisted that the individual is not passively shaped by them but "uses" them in accordance with his style of life. [Ansbacher, 1970, p. 779]

Humanism is the attitude that man's behavior is most accurately and most fully understood in terms of his special human characteristic, one that is not shared by other animals. That special characteristic is language, which makes it possible to think, to think about thinking (metathinking), and to speak, reason, remember, solve problems, invent, and make choices. Freudianism and behaviorism, on the other hand, both stress the animal nature of man, viewing his conduct as determined respectively by unconscious instinctual drives or by a network of fixed learned responses to external stimuli. In either of these views, man's cognitive activity, his thinking and judging, does not significantly influence his behavior, so that we are left with a perspective on man that ignores the unique characteristic and the special abilities which differentiate him from all other animals. Saleebey pursues this point further:

> To accept the humanist view of human nature is to accept the belief that human beings differ from the rest of the animal world, in at least one respect: They are the creators of meaning. Whereas animals, to a greater or lesser degree, are built into the world instinctually and are assured of a highly probable integration with their immediate object world, humans, lacking refined instinctual equipment, must symbolically build themselves into such a world. The human task is to manufacture inner and outer reality out of transactions with the object world; the world itself has no intrinsic meaning. Humans strive to create meanings, with which they construe self and world, that can be sustained, from which can be derived conviction, and which are loyal to the urges and possibilities of the body. [Saleebey, 1975, pp. 472–473]

Saleebey regards the power of conceptual thought, the ability to symbolize, and, thus, the powers of propositional language and abstraction as distinctly human capacities which are dramatically different from anything observable in animals. Because of their conceptual and symbolic powers, humans have ethical responsibilities centering on the problems and consequences of choice:

> Human beings are the only animals who need, and have the capacity to construct, a symbolically constituted sense of self—a consciousness of self and being—and who have the potential to be in the world both objectively and subjectively. . . . Man is a functioning whole. The whole that he is can not be understood except as a whole. To separate any part from the whole . . . is to change the character of both part and whole since the nature of the self is synergistic. . . . Disorder and dysfunction in man are manifested by inappropriate, painful, or unacceptable behavior, thoughts, and feelings. These always emerge within the symbolic context of the individual's thinking about himself and are related to motive, meaning, memory, or morals. . . . The process of changing behavior involves insight into the dynamic interplay between behavior, thought, and feeling. . . . Change comes from understanding, cognitive control, or a reformulation of the symbolic self and, thus, the redirection of action. [Saleebey, 1975, pp. 469, 470, 471]

For Ellis, humanism "seems to mean the study of the person, the individual as a whole (as opposed to the study of his discrete traits and performances)." Humanistic psychology, he says,

> completely accepts people with their human limitations; it particularly focuses upon and employs their experiences and their values; it emphasizes their ability to create and direct their own destinies; and it views them as holistic, goal-directed individuals who are important in their own right, just because they are alive. [Ellis, 1973, p. 3]

Ellis contends that man's "high-level ability to think—and especially his ability to think about his thinking—is probably his most unique and most 'human' quality." To stand up against the forces in the world that dehumanize him, man had better make full use of these abilities. Humans can usually choose to make or not to make themselves seriously disturbed. While biological and early environmental factors are important, man has an enormous amount of potential control over what he feels and does, because he can consciously intervene between what is happening in his life and how he reacts to events. Those therapies that stress the potentialities of cognitive control over dysfunctional emotional processes are in many respects the most humanistic means of personality change, usually being man-centered, creativity-oriented, and relevant to the maximum actualization of human potential. Ellis points out that, while lower animals may be importantly conditioned and deconditioned by externally applied reinforcement and extinction, man seems to be the only creature who can literally recondition or retrain himself by changing his basic ideas. He also holds that "man's behavior, although to some degree determined and limited by his biological nature and his history, is considerably less determined than the orthodox Freudians or behaviorists seem to think it is" (Ellis, 1973, p. 10).

In brief, humanism views man as a creature who, having acquired language and the ability to think both abstractly and creatively, largely determines his own behavior. Some of the sources of his conduct are his judgments, choices, and goals. His existence is shaped by his own human thoughts and the tendency of most human beings to strive for competence. He is not controlled by demons, unconscious drives, or divine power.

Philosophically, the cognitive therapist is a humanist. His identification with humanism leads him to do certain things and to avoid doing certain things with his clients.

If the cognitive therapist believes in the humanness of his clients and seeks to help them through making use of their human qualities, he will also utilize those same qualities in himself. He will bear in mind that each individual (including himself) is an original who can think in his own way, create new ideas, express his emotions in words, exercise control over impulses, choose among various courses of action, and both commit and correct errors in perception. Such a view of man calls for approaching each individual with an open mind and endeavoring to understand him in his own terms as one of a kind. It is inconsistent with such a philosophy to undertake the treatment of any client with a prior conviction that all behaviors have the same specific origin and that all people are traumatized by the same experiences.

Within a humanistic framework, errors in perception will be seen in terms of their relatedness to human society rather than as a consequence of unconscious conflict. Individuals to whom society has not given opportunity for an adequate education may, out of pure ignorance, evaluate events and people inaccurately. Traditional folk superstitions lead us astray. We may adopt stereotyped notions after their endless repetition in newspapers, magazines, movies, and television. Parents and relatives transmit their misperceptions to us or fail to correct our own perceptual errors when they begin. What the important people in our lives think about us, whether valid or not, becomes part of us. We are under great pressure to think the way the majority believes although the conclusions of majorities are often wrong. The convictions of our economic or social or religious group become our own. Finally, traumatic atypical experiences are so vivid that we sometimes make unfounded generalizations from them.

It is always understood that in a small percentage of cases unrealistic thinking is a consequence of an organic brain abnormality. The fact that mind is matter in motion—i.e., a physiological phenomenon—is one of the prime characteristics of human beings. While we do not yet have all the answers about the schizophrenias and other psychoses, it is quite likely that their genesis eventually will prove to be a combination of chemical predisposition and emotional trauma. Meanwhile, the disordered perceptions of the psychotic are most effectively modified by medication.

A therapist's identification with humanism calls for him to recognize his own susceptibility to perceptual errors in working with clients. He cannot claim that his advocacy of a particular theory of personality and treatment renders him immune to such errors. The past literature of all the helping disciplines is replete with theories, teachings, and ideas that were published with great conviction and subsequently rescinded or modified. It is the responsibility of the mental health professional to see to it that this healthy process of continual reassessment goes on, and to contribute to it by being acutely aware that therapists, like all other people, are constantly absorbing the propaganda of the previous generation. Vigilance, self-discipline, and keeping up with the latest knowledge in the field are necessary so that the therapist can meet each new client with a minimum of invalid preconceptions.

To illustrate, one misconception in the field of psychotherapy has been the assumption that infantile autism is caused by coldness and rejection on the part of the parents. Leo Kanner, who in 1943 was the first to designate autism as a distinct illness, at no time pointed to the parents as the primary postnatal sources of pathogenicity. Instead, he ventured the opinion that "We must assume that these children have come into the world with an innate inability to form the usual, biologically provided affective contact with people" (Kanner, n.d., p. 27). A tendency developed, however, in the United States to view autism as a developmental anomaly exclusively due to maternal emotional determinants. Twenty-five years later, Kanner stated:

> It is recognized by all observers, except for the dwindling number of those impeded by doctrinaire allegiances, that autism is not primarily an acquired, or "man-made" disease. The fact that many of the parents are rather detached people has been confirmed frequently enough, but this observation cannot be translated summarily into a direct cause-and-effect etiologic relationship, an assumption

sometimes ascribed to me via pathways of gross misquotation. Making parents feel guilty of responsibility for their child's autism is not only erroneous, but cruelly adds insult to injury. [Kanner, n.d., pp. 30–31]

Whittaker (1976) reached a similar conclusion in regard to both autism and learning disabilities, noting that there was a widespread belief in the "family etiology hypothesis," an assumption that a child's problem usually is either directly caused or unconsciously influenced by the pathology or shortcomings of the parents. He quoted a standard psychiatry textbook published in the mid-1950s which took the position that the majority of emotional problems in children are probably created by emotional problems of their parents. Whittaker, after a review of recent research, asserted that there appeared to be no evidence in support of this belief:

> It is not the total rejection of the family etiology hypothesis that is sought here; clearly, troubled parents can bring about troubled children. What the author questions is its blanket application to all families of children with problems. . . . it now appears altogether likely that at least some of the "pathology" exhibited by parents of troubled children is responsive to rather than causative of their child's disturbance. Perhaps the most damaging consequence of this predisposition is that it causes social work professionals to grossly underutilize their most valuable natural resource in child treatment: the parents themselves. Parents are often the best experts on their troubled child. [Whittaker, 1976, pp. 91, 94]

The tendency to blame parents for their children's problems extends to many other kinds of difficulties. Fisher, referring to the child guidance field, mentions one claim that "much needless blame is placed on parents without offering them a chance to learn to become better parents. Too often the parent's only contribution is to take the child to his therapy hour, from which the parent is excluded. He is not to know what his child and his child's therapist are doing, and

he is given no opportunity to learn how to better himself"
(Fisher, 1973, p. 534).

On the issue of responsibility for a child's behavior, a
humanist perspective insists that children are just as capable
as adults of thinking independently, exercising self-control,
choosing among various courses of action, and making their
own perceptual errors. Consequently, the humanist/
cognitive therapist will not take an a priori position that the
parent(s) must be the principal cause of a child's problem. It
frequently happens that, despite responsible behavior and
support from parents, a child, on his own initiative or influenced by factors outside the home, will make poor
judgments, yield to impulses, choose a destructive course of
action, or misinterpret events around him. In such cases, the
child himself should be held accountable for his difficulties.

Another important perceptual error of psychotherapists,
which has only recently begun to be corrected, is the misin-
terpretation of the behavior of battered women. A combination of sexist attitudes and recourse to unconscious dynamics
produced a limited approach to the entire problem because
the matter of family violence was not examined in its human
and social context. The victim was seen as unconsciously pro-
voking abuse because she enjoyed and had a psychological
need for it; therefore, the source of the violence was within
her. The reluctance of most women to leave such marriages
was assumed to verify this hypothesis. No attempt was made
to account for the perpetrator's aggression or for his wife's
submission in terms of their respective perceptions. Recent
writings by Carlson (1977), Star (1978), and O'Donel-
Browne (1979) deal with marital violence as transactions between human beings which reflect strongly conditioned patterns of thought, and thereby support a humanistic approach
to the subject.

Viewed humanistically, the physical battering of a wife by
her husband is the end result of his indoctrination by society
in such a manner that, under stress, he perceives himself as

having "permission" to allay fear of failure by the use of violence. Her continuance in the home is less expressive of a basic sadomasochism than it is the result of the evaluation she makes of herself and her total situation. Synthesizing some of the ideas of Carlson, Star, and O'Donel-Browne, we can begin to understand marital violence in human and social terms. What follows is that kind of humanistic perspective.

For hundreds of years, society has taught men that their status should be higher than that of women; that men who are not dominant and physically more powerful than women are inadequate and unmasculine; and that wives and children are a man's property, against whom it is perfectly proper, when necessary, to use force to control them. When this indoctrination by society combines with one or more stressful situations that threaten his image of himself, and if he perceives the woman as the one who makes him feel inadequate, a man may resort to physical abuse. The violence is his way of stopping the woman from reinforcing his sense of failure. He cannot communicate in any other way: he has never learned to verbalize his emotions, has never tried, or lacks the capacity to do so. The man may be even more predisposed to this kind of "solution" if he has witnessed violence between his own parents.

Stressful situations that can trigger off an episode of battering include some of the following:

1. Man has a job inferior to that of his wife, or makes less money, or loses his job;
2. Woman commands more respect from their children, is the obvious leader of the family, or solves family problems more effectively;
3. Woman is more successful socially in the community, has more status with neighbors, makes a better impression;
4. Woman is more intelligent, better educated, knows more than her husband;

5. There are disagreements between the couple regarding money, how to raise the children, or sex;
6. The man drinks or takes drugs, which weakens his normal controls. This is the catalyst, however, not the cause of the violent episode;
7. Woman asserts herself in a dispute, decides to give up a previously passive role, or takes on a new role (job, etc.) outside the home.

Women remain in a battering situation for various reasons. They may fear vicious retaliation if they call the police, leave, or seek other help. Some women, after continued physical abuse, become overwhelmed by feelings of hopelessness and depression. Since the outbursts of violence are often unpredictable and unexpected, they cannot control their immediate situations and lose faith in their own competence. Attempts to change their fates seem pointless, and they end up paralyzed and immobile. Of course, economic considerations are a serious obstacle to any plan by a woman to take her children and try to manage on her own. Even though, however, day-to-day survival as a separated woman would be possible for them, many women still choose to remain in abusive situations. They may believe that the first black eye is a one-time occurrence that will not be repeated. Most battered women underplay rather than overplay the violent episodes, the denial representing a refusal to acknowledge the potential seriousness of the situation.

Reared to believe that it is *their* job to make the marriage work, many women assume full responsibility if things go wrong. Abused women readily accept blame projected toward them by their assailants, even for vicious attacks which they passively endure. Some are ashamed to be seen in public with bruises, believing that this reflects on them rather than on the man. As the new field of victimology is discovering, the victim often feels more guilty than the aggressor. Battered women, before learning otherwise in a protective shelter, have misconceptions about marriage, thinking that most women get beaten and that marriage makes the woman the property of the man. Such ignorance is in part a consequence of social isolation: battered women, because of shame and other reasons, tend to have only a small circle of relatives and acquaintances upon whom they may draw for counsel and emotional support.

Instead of the damaging and inaccurate stereotype that battered women are masochistic and provoke the abuse they receive, a humanistic approach supports those who focus on passivity and low self-esteem as the creators of such victims. Abused women tend to show timidity, withdrawal, and apprehension—signs of passivity rather than of masochism. They have very poor images of themselves: after years of negative feedback, they come to believe that they are incompetent, unattractive, and intellectually inferior. Many believe that they will face devastating loneliness if they leave their present relationship because no other man is likely to become interested in them. Despite its destructive aspects, the existing living arrangement gives the illusion of some kind of human relationship, the abusive man is not always abusive, and an occasional beating may be a price they are willing to pay to maintain the unit and avoid the risk of poverty or loneliness. Finally, in respect to provocative behavior by battered women, some victims do engage in screaming, emotional outbursts, verbal criticism, or sarcastic remarks. But this kind of behavior has to be considered in context. It is generally a reaction to perpetrated violence or an attempt to retaliate against their assailant, rather than the original cause of the man's aggression.

Treating the psychological problems of the aged is another area of psychotherapy in which misconceptions have been prevalent. Again, in our view, this has occurred because of a nonhumanistic attitude which approached older people as a stereotyped category rather than as greatly varied individuals. Stensky (1975) refers to a statement by a gerontologist that the differences among older people are much greater than the differences among younger people because they have had more time to undergo dissimilar experiences.

Stensky challenges some of the inaccurate thinking about old age, including the notion that old age is chronological and begins on a specific date. She regards this notion as manifestly absurd in view of the fact that people mature at differing rates and that the arrival of a particular birthday does not wipe out the knowledge, skills, and habits accumulated during all the preceding years. One does not become a completely different human being in a single day.

Another myth is that older people choose to disengage themselves from active involvement with the currents of living. On the contrary, what is astonishing is the degree of their involvement in consumer groups, public demonstrations, and voting, despite the tendency of other citizens and public officials to denigrate their opinions and provide grossly inadequate programs of assistance for those in need. They participate even though their strength is greatly taxed to maintain themselves in an inhospitable environment. The proportion of "senior citizens" qualified to vote who do so is the highest percentage of all groups of voters in the United States. Stensky maintains that where social interaction does decline, the change is due largely to the withdrawal of society from the old, rather than the reverse.

The classic, stereotyped view of old age is that the older person has lost the capacity for growth and creativity, can no longer learn and does not wish to, and is not able to adjust to changes. Everyone knows, however, of the continued participation and valuable contributions in the arts and sciences made by great men and women in their seventies, eighties, and even nineties. Rigid ideas that almost all older people suffer from organic changes which severely impair thinking, learning, memory, and clarity simply do not hold up. Shoham (1978), referring to estimates that 50 percent of the institutionalized geriatric population and 30 percent of older people living at home suffer from organic brain syndrome (OBS), cautions against unwarranted conclusions:

> The feeling that treating the psychological problems of the aged is a hopeless task is probably the major reason why a body of skills and knowledge in this area has been late in developing. . . . There is considerable evidence that OBS patients, like the rest of us, do not use the full brain capacity available to them. Much of their confusion and disorientation appears to be reaction formation to isolation and social neglect rather than a result of organic disease. A great deal of the memory loss that is supposedly merely a consequence of brain changes is quite selective and could represent purposeful withdrawal from a painful environment. Senility itself has been defined by some as a form of emotional breakdown in older people resulting from anxiety. Studies seem to show that there is no one-to-one relationship between the degree of brain tissue deterioration as demonstrated by postmortem examination and the patient's functional history. All these factors would tend to point to the importance of influences other than brain damage on the level of functioning. [Shoham, 1978, pp. 178, 179]

Shoham suggests that other, nonorganic influences on the functioning of older people include the individual's personality and established patterns of coping with loss. Also very important are the meaning to a person of a situation or problem and the emotions experienced regarding such events. How one deals with illness, whether organic or functional, and adjusts to change are not exclusively determined by one's physical condition. It is believed that about 50 percent of all psychiatric disturbances of the aged are functional and characterized largely by depression and anxiety, which can be relieved by psychotherapeutic help. The crucial therapeutic and humanistic imperative is to regard every older person, no matter what his or her condition, as treatable to some degree, and to avoid stripping the aged of every role except that of "patient." Stensky (1975) asserts that "the ability to change has little to do with one's age and more to do with one's life-long patterns of coping—and . . . even these patterns are amenable to change and growth" (p. 5). Shoham notes that "Environmental manipulation, by mustering all available resources, both physical and psychological, can help maximize coping potential."

We have presented some examples of mistaken notions about clients that have been held by psychotherapists, have suggested different formulations based largely on a humanist perspective, and have insisted that none of us is protected from such errors by the treatment ideology with which we identify. We now examine the implications of a humanist perspective in regard to the therapist's use of his own humanness, a concept that is receiving increasing attention.

Kenneth Reid states:

> Like the client, the worker brings to the helping relationship his own humanness. In spite of his training, he is a human being first and a professional person second. It has been said that the worker is just like the client but more so. He needs social companionship, recognition, prestige, and security, and he needs to be liked. It is this humanness that provides the ability to enter the client's life and to assist him in the growth process. [Reid, 1977, p. 601]

Bill Powell (1979) encourages the therapist to enter the client's life in working with acting-out adolescent delinquents. In his own practice he will demonstrate strength in confronting a client, use profanity when it will break down barriers, refuse to accept manipulation, and be very blunt. In addition, he will reach out into the adolescent's existence by removing artificial walls (there is no desk between them in the interview room), touching (hand on the shoulder, etc.), taking the client out for a hamburger, making home visits (this is not beneath a professional), and accompanying the young person to court, school, or employment office when he or she cannot face this alone. Humor and informality are an important part of his approach.

For the therapist in general, using his own human qualities in working with a client raises some important issues. Does he wish to be opaque or transparent? Will revelation of his own humanness affect his "neutrality" as a helping person? What happens to transference reactions?

The therapist who wishes to maintain himself as opaque has reached the conclusion that he does not want the client to see into him. Therefore, he will not discuss his own emotions or experiences, even though they are relevant to the client's problem and might be informative or supportive. A counselor who himself is divorced would not reveal this to a client going through the agonies of a separation. On the other hand, a therapist who believes that his own experiences can clarify or reassure and who believes that his own emotions, when openly expressed, can disinhibit the client and form a bond between them, will not object to becoming more transparent.

One argument against the therapist's revelation of his own humanness has been that such revelation would make it difficult for the professional to maintain a neutral role. A humanistic philosophy questions whether neutrality is desirable or even possible. Psychiatrist Irving Markowitz (1975) insists that the therapist always imposes his values on the patient, even unintentionally. In fact, the patient often searches out the therapist's values because he wants to identify with them. The only way to avoid such influence on the patient is to be so blank and so neutral as to represent nothing, which in itself is a value position. Markowitz takes the completely humanist position that the therapist should be aware of the strong influence he exerts, should struggle to minimize the tendency to impose his values on patients, and should acknowledge that he is struggling.

The major force against self-revelation by the therapist has been orthodox psychoanalysis, which took this position in order to make possible the development in the patient of a transference neurosis, one of the keystones of the Freudian method. A therapist who remains completely opaque encourages the patient to project onto him perceptions and emotions carried over from significant others in the patient's life. The analyst's interpretation of distorted views of himself and inappropriate feelings expressed by the patient (the transference neurosis) is considered a crucial part of the treatment.

The humanist/cognitive therapist regards the encouragement of a transference neurosis as contrary to his basic approach to people, which is to promote the most accurate perceptions of reality that are possible. Instead of hoping that the client will see him in a distorted fashion if he is sufficiently blank and aloof, the humanistic therapist strives for a different objective. By discussing his own experiences, emotions, weaknesses, mistakes, and personal traits, he tries to make it possible for the client to be himself, reveal problems and limitations, risk taking off his protective mask, and trust another human being. Knowing what the therapist is really like can set the client free. If the therapist is just like himself but more so, the client can take a chance and face his own humanity and lack of perfection. Obviously, self-revelation by the therapist should be carried out in a highly disciplined and selective fashion, used only when it will help the client and never indulged in as merely private catharsis for the professional. In those treatment situations where the client's perceptions of the therapist become or remain distorted despite the latter's efforts to be an open human being, such phenomena are dealt with in humanistic terms, not as unconscious projections but as limitations of consciousness.

A humanist perspective on people and the cognitive theory of personality that flows out of it result in a particular set of conclusions about the nature of man. The brief statement of the nature of man which follows synthesizes the ideas of all the writers thus far presented in this book, making use in addition of Otto Rank's concept of will and contributions from learning theory and existentialism. A discussion of the relationship of Rankian ideas, learning theory, and existential concepts to cognitive theory will be found in the next chapter.

The Nature of Man*

For the humanist/cognitist, a person's behavior is mainly determined not by unconscious forces but by his thinking and willing. He evaluates himself, others, and the world around him; sets up goals to achieve; and behaves in ways he thinks will attain his objectives and otherwise give him maximum satisfaction. The strength of an individual's will and the direction in which it is applied affect the amount of effort he expends and the progress he makes toward his goals. He has the ability to control and deactivate instinctual drives which interfere with his purposes. He normally feels and acts according to the thoughts he presently holds concerning significant factors in his environment.

People have to make choices all their lives: between dependence on others and independence; between clinging and separating; between conformity and originality; between accepting and challenging limits; between goals on the destructive and on the useful side of life; between avoiding and facing all the implications of their existence.

Emotional distress can develop in various ways. A man's goals may be destructive or antisocial, in which case the lifestyle he evolves to reach these goals will bring pressure, rejection, or retaliation from his society. If an individual is afraid to reveal his authentic self for fear of being found imperfect by others, he erects defensive structures behind which to hide what he really is, becoming anxious and draining his emotional energy in the process. Emotional strain may be experienced in making any of the crucial choices listed in the preceding paragraph. In other cases, individuals become upset as a result of blaming themselves too severely for

* The text of this section originally appeared in *New Understandings of Human Behavior,* ed. Harold D. Werner. Copyright © 1970 by Association Press. Used by permission of Association Press/Follett Publishing Company.

mistakes they commit just by virtue of being human. Some of us suffer acutely when significant people do not approve of us or when we encounter disagreement in the world at large. Some of us become disturbed when we are unable to give love, receive love, or behave so as to feel worthwhile to others and to ourselves. There are all kinds of realistic and unrealistic fears and guilt feelings which prevent people from enjoying a measure of inner peace. Finally, strongly conditioned responses which a person cannot stop even though he knows they are inappropriate can cause great distress.

The humanist/cognitive conception of man's nature views him as not born either good or evil but trainable in either direction. He is not seen as inherently aggressive; cooperation with a society in which he believes does not repress his true nature but develops it. Man is creative, possesses an innate purpose to grow, and has a basic tendency to strive for competence and a sense of completion. His sex drive is not primary but is just one of several drives. Attachments or hostilities to parents, neurosis, and anxiety do not inevitably trace back to sexuality and are more often reactions to all types of life situations. Each person is unique, differing in some ways from all other persons, and comprehensible only in his own terms. Diagnoses and labels at most can contribute only a partial understanding of an individual.

Chapter 4

Indications, Limitations, and Comparisons

Cognitive therapy is appropriate for most so-called "emotional disorders," which perhaps should be renamed "problems of living." These include anxiety, depression, phobias, marital problems, parent-child difficulties, lack of confidence, trouble in making friends or feeling socially accepted, academic and behavior problems in school, conduct unacceptable to the community, conflicts between adults and their parents, obsessive-compulsive behavior, and unmanageable feelings of guilt, worthlessness, or anger. All of them are approached by the cognitive therapist as problems of limitation or distortion of consciousness.

Neurosis

Some of the aforementioned "problems of living" fit into the category of neurosis. The cognitist defines neurosis as a way of living based on unrealistic guilt, fear, or anger, the individual being saturated with anxiety. Since many of the people who seek treatment are neurotic, it is of major importance for therapists of all persuasions to be clear in their own minds as to what a neurosis is. The cognitive approach pro-

51

vides a simple, clear concept of neurosis which facilitates the efforts of the therapist to devise techniques to help the client change, since we are defining neurosis as a specific error in perception. While the Freudian regards neurosis as anxiety and the defenses against it, with the source of the anxiety in the unconscious, the cognitist views the neurotic's anxiety as the consequence of a particular entrenched misconception of reality.

Anxiety

Anxiety in general is a state of mental apprehension combined with somatic reactions such as rapid heartbeat or stomach cramp. Cognitive therapists believe that anxiety is always the consequence of a conscious perception.

In the cognitive framework, however, not all anxiety is generated by inaccurate perception. Thorne (1963) suggests that anxiety is triggered by either a fancied or an actual failure in any important aspect of one's life, constituting a severe threat to security because most human beings strive for competence. Krauss (1967) looks upon anxiety as the dread of some future event that will prove the individual worthless or defeat him. Sarbin (1964) regards anxiety as a condition of cognitive strain, defined as large increases in cognitive activity when a person cannot place a new situation or object in proper perspective, cannot find his place in society, or cannot evaluate the way he performs his life tasks. Understood in these terms, nonneurotic anxiety is amenable to cognitive treatment techniques: (1) encouraging the client to try out new experiences which may bring a sense of success, the best antidote for anxiety; (2) working with the client to change his goals and/or behavior so that the future event he dreads will not materialize; (3) helping the client to develop skill in comprehending and categorizing new events, coming to terms with his world, and rating himself objectively.

Depression

Cammer (1969, pp. 36–80) divides depression into three types: (1) depression directly reactive to loss (of a loved one, a high-status job, community ties, a valued friendship, popularity, etc.); (2) endogenous depression, the product of internal chemical changes associated with childbirth, menopause, aging, drug toxicity, glandular disorders, injuries, infections, the aftermath of surgery, or other physical events; and (3) neurotic depression. In my own practice, I consider neurotic depression to be the consequence of an *inaccurate* conclusion that one is worthless, permanently trapped in an upsetting situation, has no chance for a happier future, or will never overcome guilt about a past event.

The first type of depressed person needs emotional support during a natural period of mourning that has to take place, and the depression will eventually dissipate if the individual avoids drawing any mistaken self-denigrating conclusions about his responsibility for the loss. The cognitive therapist can help in this regard. Treatment of the person with endogenous depression, on the other hand, is largely a medical matter, although educating the patient about the true nature of his condition, a cognitive technique, is a necessary psychotherapeutic component that can be very reassuring. For neurotic depression, the third type, cognitive therapy is the treatment of choice because, as Beck maintains, the psychological disorder revolves around a cognitive problem:

> Depressed patients generally provide essential information in spontaneous statements such as: "I'm sad because I'm worthless"; "I have no future"; "I've lost everything"; "My family is gone"; "I have nobody"; "Life has nothing for me." It is relatively easy to detect the dominant theme in the statements of the moderately or severely depressed patient. He regards himself as lacking some element or attribute that he considers essential for his happiness: com-

petence in attaining his goals, attractiveness to other people, closeness to family or friends, tangible possessions, good health, status or position. . . . The depressed patient shows specific distortions. He has a negative view of his world, a negative concept of himself, and a negative appraisal of his future: the cognitive triad. The distorted evaluations concern shrinkage of his domain, and lead to sadness. . . . The term "loser" captures the flavor of the depressive's appraisal of himself and his experience. [Beck, 1976, pp. 105–106]

Phobias

In dealing with phobias, the cognitive therapist is treating a person who repeats strongly conditioned avoidance behavior in response to a specific stimulus. Originally the consequence of the client's perception of a new event, the stimulus-response bond has become through repetition an automatic physiological process which now bypasses the thinking centers of the brain. If the fear is exaggerated or unwarranted, the therapist will attempt to help the client understand, through discussion and actual experience, that either the original situation was mistakenly evaluated from the very beginning, or the original perception was valid then but is not valid any longer. Should the client be unable to curtail phobic behavior on the basis of this new knowledge, as is often the case, the therapist will need to employ behavior-modification techniques or refer the client to another professional who does. In those instances where the client recognizes the irrationality of the phobia but cannot control it, the neurotic behavior is influenced more by physiology than by cognition. In such cases the indications are not for cognitive techniques but for procedures in the behavior-modification repertoire, which deal with behavior on a physiological level.

Persons who cannot recognize that their fears are unjustified or whose fears are indeed based on fact can be helped by the cognitive therapist to evaluate their situation in a realistic fashion and make changes in their lifestyles which will avoid contact with the objects or circumstances that distress them.

Intrafamily Problems

Cognitive therapy approaches marital problems and parent-child difficulties, either in individual sessions or in groups, as manifestations of various kinds of perceptual errors. Spouses can have unrealistic expectations of each other or misinterpret each other's behavior or intent. Parents may expect more from a child than he can produce, the child may see his privileges and responsibilities within the family in a different way than they do: such discrepancies breed tension, anger, and defiance. When conflicts are between adult chilren and aging parents, cognitive therapy is useful because it will deal with the generation gap as insufficient appreciation by those involved of each other's needs, fears, insecurities, and values.

Acting-Out Behavior

A large proportion of mental health work is devoted to academic and behavior problems exhibited by children in school, and to antisocial conduct in the community manifested by persons of all ages. The cognitist will explore the life history of such individuals to understand the lifestyle they have developed, their concepts of success, the goals they are pursuing, and their self-image. The premise is that although it may be self-defeating and against their own interest as seen by society, individuals engage in troublesome behavior because they think it serves their purposes. In cognitive treatment, the therapist will try to demonstrate to the client, preferably through actual experience, that changes in goals and behavior will accomplish more of what the client really wants for himself.

Other Problems of Living

The relevance of cognitive therapy to other problems of living has been touched upon earlier in this volume. These include lack of confidence and social acceptance, obsessive-compulsive behavior, and feelings of guilt, worthlessness, and anger. In all instances the therapist will want to determine the nature of the perceptions that have brought these behaviors and these emotions into being. If the perceptions are erroneous, the therapeutic task is to help the client see himself and his world more accurately. If the perceptions are valid and the client has reason to lack confidence, feel insecure, or consider himself guilty, therapist and client will work together so that the client can grow in strength and competence, change aspects of himself and his environment, and accept what cannot be altered. Only in this way can the sources of self-defeating behavior and disturbing emotions be eliminated.

Limitations

Cognitive therapy requires in the client sufficient language development, speaking ability, and capacity for reasoning to enable him to verbalize thoughts, emotions, memories, needs, fears, and experiences; recognize his problems; and think about solutions. This requirement generally rules out schizophrenic and other psychotic individuals who cannot distinguish what is real from what is imaginary, the severely mentally retarded, those with incapacitating organic brain damage, very young children, and those substance abusers whose addictions render them incapable of consistent reality contact.

In addition, the nonmedical cognitive therapist, like all other nonmedical psychotherapists, should learn about and be constantly on the alert for medical conditions such as hypoglycemia whose symptoms mimic those of the psychological disorders. Neither cognitive therapy nor any other school of psychotherapy is indicated for the person whose primary need is for medication and/or medical treatment. In fact, it could be dangerous and keep a client from crucial medical attention if a therapist treats him for an emotional disturbance when his atypical behavior is actually the result of organic pathology such as a brain tumor.

Bockar (1976, pp. 1–10) discusses some of the medical conditions that masquerade as emotional problems, mainly in the form of anxiety. She includes among these hyperthyroidism, hyperventilation, chronic kidney disease, postconcussion syndrome, brain tumors, and the aforementioned hypoglycemia. No nonmedical psychotherapist, regardless of ideology, has the right to assume that a client's problem is completely emotional or psychogenic. Since the mind is matter in motion, the possibility of an organic basis for each client's presenting problem must always be kept in mind and ruled out by a recent medical examination, consultation with a physician, and/or familiarity with relevant literature by Bockar and others. These writings orient the nonphysician to the problems and dangers inherent in the evaluation of new clients and offer guidelines that may help to prevent mistakes.

Stuart (1979, p. 434), referring to "information therapies," suggests that therapeutic success depends upon four factors: the accuracy of the therapist's understanding of the client's thoughts and feelings; how persuasive the therapist is in encouraging changes in these processes; the willingness and ability of the client to act on the basis of his new perceptions; and the willingness of key people in the client's environment to accept or reinforce his changed behavior. Applied to cognitive therapy, this represents a fair statement of additional limitations which the practitioner should keep in mind.

Relationships to Other Schools of Thought

PSYCHOANALYSIS AND EGO PSYCHOLOGY

As was apparent in the preceding chapters, cognitive therapy and psychoanalysis are at opposite ends of the ideological spectrum. The cognitist views thought as the primary determinant of behavior and emotions, while the Freudian therapist believes that unconscious processes are primary in the psychic life of each individual. Cognitists approach each person as unique and able to create his or her own destiny; the Freudian's premise is that all conflicts and hang-ups date from early childhood and are similar in nature for everyone, regardless of his or her place in society. For the analytically oriented practitioner, sexual libido is considered the main dynamic force in human behavior, neurosis is always a defense against one's sexual drives, and most aspects of a person's conduct are manifestations or sublimations of the sex urge. The cognitive therapist takes the position that the sex drive is just one of several that a human being has to integrate, and it should not automatically be assumed to underlie a particular problem.

Classic psychoanalytic theory was the dominant influence

on American social work and psychotherapy in general for twenty years until the mid-1940s. The Great Depression and World War II made it clear that preoccupation with the unconscious was ineffective in helping people to deal with the massive pressures and anxieties generated by the world around them. Part of the psychoanalytic establishment shifted to a new subdivision of Freudian theory called ego psychology. Freed, a social worker, explains this shift very clearly:

> Freudian theory overemphasized internal, instinctual forces and psychic conflicts and underemphasized the significance of the social, cultural, and interpersonal environment in molding personality. Ego psychology, in contrast, deals with both the internal and external forces that impinge on the growing human personality. It stresses the adaptive and coping mechanisms of the individual and the individual's efforts to change and grow. In ego psychology, the human being is seen as an open system that interacts with the various systems around it. It reflects a shift away from the view that man is a conflict-ridden internal system struggling to contain his instincts. Instead, it assumes that people are born with a conflict-free autonomous ego sphere.
>
> With regard to ego psychology generally, while caseworkers take unconscious phenomena into account in diagnosis and in designing treatment, they concentrate on enhancing ego functioning and interpersonal relations. [Freed, 1977, pp. 217, 218]

The new emphasis was on the nonconflicted ego functioning of the client. The adoption of this new focus by social workers was testimony to the fact that social work intuitively had moved back to working with the consciousness of people. The conceptualization of consciousness as "a conflict-free autonomous ego sphere" whose ultimate sources were still in the unconscious was an attempt to preserve the Freudian terminology and framework. Nevertheless, this represented a partial recognition of Adler's view that personality is a holistic phenomenon, that human beings function as a unit. Thus, an element of the cognitive orientation has become part of ego psychology.

LEARNING THEORY

Learning theory, in which we can include the ideas of John B. Watson, Pavlov, and the contemporary behaviorists, is used in cognitive therapy when a client recognizes the inappropriateness of his behavior and/or emotions but is unable to change them by his own efforts and the exercise of will and determination.

> Watson pioneered in presenting the viewpoint that almost all behavior and emotions are learned reactions to events or stimuli in the environment or inside the body, not responses to unconscious psychic forces, and become habitual by unplanned repetition or deliberate conditioning (training). Except in the case of infants, he thought these reactions usually involved a combination of limb and body movements, some form of language activity, and changes in internal organs. He rejected the concept of consciousness, however, on grounds that it was too subjective and vague.
>
> Pavlov began his labors earlier than Watson, but for about two decades beginning in 1912 their work went on simultaneously. Pavlov's laboratory experiments were with animals, while Watson used both animal and human subjects. Pavlov concentrated on investigating the physiological activity of the cerebral cortex as the key to understanding conditioned reflexes. Watson confined himself principally to studying overt behavioral phenomena. [Werner, 1965, pp. 105-106]

The modern practitioner of behavior modification, drawing on these earlier theories about learning and the conditioned reflex, has developed a variety of techniques for helping people to modify or replace strongly conditioned behaviors which do not respond to discussion or reasoning. These may be behaviors that are regarded as inappropriate or self-defeating or unacceptable, either by the clients themselves (e.g., phobias) or by the systems of which they are a part (e.g., resistance to eating by patients in a mental hospital). The premise, as Salter (1964) phrased it, is that "Psychological events are physiological events, and conditioning is the modification of tissue by experience" (p. 23). A behavior modification approach is therefore needed to make changes on the physiological level both for clients who want to change but whose entrenched reaction patterns are beyond their cognitive control, and for those who themselves seek no alteration in the status quo because of self-centered goals, poor mastery of impulses, severe mental retardation, or serious mental illness.

The cognitive therapist fully supports the use of a learning theory (behavior modification) approach under the circumstances described. This includes techniques such as assertiveness training, operant conditioning, behavioral contracts, deep muscle relaxation, desensitization, thought stoppage, aversive conditioning, positive imagery, and modeling. Behavior modification has been effectively used in institutions for severely retarded and mentally ill adults, in classrooms and camps for emotionally disturbed and neurologically impaired children, and in correctional facilities for youth and adults, as well as in individual, marital, and family counseling for the general population.

There is a vast divergence between classical Watsonian behaviorism and cognitive therapy. Watson brushed aside any consideration of thinking and emotion in working out his theories about human behavior because in his view man was just another animal, and since thought and feeling were not objectively measurable, they were irrelevant in the formulation of behavioral dynamics. The humanist/cognitive conception of human beings as having unique characteristics that set them apart from other animals was completely alien to Watson. Pavlov, on the other hand, made it a point to differentiate between man and other animals. Students and coworkers in his laboratory paid a monetary fine for formulating in human terms any findings from experiments with animals.

The modern behaviorist, however, has broadened Watson's narrow perspective, and in the past decade learning theory has moved closer to cognitive theory. In discussing this trend, Jacobs has commented:

> John B. Watson in the 1920's published his famous book "Behaviorism" in which he advocated ignoring intrapsychic material in favor of studying only observable behavior. The first behaviorists were interested only in the stimulus and response; they weren't concerned with what went on between. The contemporary behavior therapist rejects this point of view, however, and he is definitely interested in what takes place between the stimulus and the response. Obviously man is a thinking animal, and to ignore his cognitions or his thinking may be to ignore what is most important to his cure. The contemporary behaviorist considers a person's cognitions and his self reports as behavior. A host of behavioral techniques deal not only with the client's thinking but with his imagery and fantasies. Some of the best cognitive therapy today is being done by behaviorists. [Jacobs, 1971, p. 6]

Lazarus (1977, pp. 550–554), a principal figure in present-day behavior therapy, confirmed that while orthodox behaviorists remained opposed to the idea that behavior can be influenced by cognitions, the field of behavior therapy was currently becoming increasingly "cognitive." He regarded the stimulus-response "learning theory" basis of behavior therapy as passé, claiming that a distinctly cognitive orientation now prevailed which did not deny consciousness and recognized that conditioning was produced through the operation of higher mental processes.

FUNCTIONAL THEORY

Functional theory is based on the ideas of Otto Rank and insists, as does cognitive theory, on the primary importance of consciousness. Smalley (1967) tells us that the push toward growth and fulfillment is primary in human beings: the innate purpose in each of us is to grow. This conception is shared by Adler, Maslow, and others in the cognitive category. Otto Rank himself was especially interested in the will, which he considered to be a significant component of consciousness. Functionalists believe their task is to help the client use his will positively toward his own self-chosen ends. The cognitive practitioner has in mind a similar concept when he helps the client to understand his situation, assert himself, and confront whatever needs to be faced. Rank maintained that individuals are understood through their present experiences, where their whole reaction pattern, past and present, is apparent. The cognitive practitioner uses the same kind of "here-and-now" approach.

For Rank (1936), will and consciousness were primary. We remember what we *will* to remember. We will unconsciousness to escape facing the present. Cognitive theory, with its view that the *content* of people's behavior is usually based on what they think, recognizes that the *intensity* of their acts depends on the strength of their will. Adler, for example, ascribed much importance to the cultivation of courage in the client.

Rank placed considerable emphasis on the process of choosing between alternatives, a conscious act which every person carries out repeatedly throughout a lifetime. We make choices all the time between depending on others and trying to exist on our own, between self-centered and social goals, between refusing and accepting help, between playing it safe by not making waves and daring to be true to ourselves, between avoiding the truth and facing the truth, between accepting limits and challenging limits.

The subject of limits was given special attention by Jessie Taft, one of the pioneers in the application of Rankian ideas to social work, who augmented Rank's original theories by adding the concept of agency function. The agency was given a central place in functional social work practice by being used as the arena where the client could struggle toward growth through his interaction with the organization's limits of time and service. The worker informs the client of what services the agency offers and the specific procedures for making use of these services. The client can accept, reject, or try to change these limits, but must eventually face the reality that the agency function will remain firm and that he is to decide what parts of it he can make use of. If the client discovers that he does not want anything from the service being offered, he can choose to discontinue. According to Yelaja (1979, p. 134), "In choosing to accept the limitations of the agency's service, the client identifies with the social purpose the agency represents and so discovers, rediscovers, or confirms his ability to deal responsibly with reality in the pursuit of his own particular ends."

The cognitist can agree that a client's perceptions of reality become more accurate when he comes to grips with the limits of an agency's function. It is apparent, however, that a large number of agencies, because of financial, administrative, and/or philosophical lacks, do not function in ways that are appropriate to the needs of their clients. Yielding to the structure of an inadequate social agency will not promote growth in clients.

Yelaja (1979), a contemporary proponent of the functionalist view in social work practice, sees conflict as inherent in the development of the human organism, but, in common with Adler and the cognitive approach in general, he does not locate conflict within the individual. Conflict takes place between the individual and others and with society (p. 132).

EXISTENTIAL THEORY

Existentialism is a philosophy which is rooted in personal experience. It defines a person as his actions, behavior, and choices and does not give much value to clinical diagnosis, which, it is believed, misses what is unique about a particular client. Emphasis is on the client's here-and-now lifestyle; how he got that way is of questionable significance. Treatment focuses on the goals the client chooses for himself. People are regarded as having an inherent drive to create their own authentic lifestyle by using their ability to make choices, take responsibility, and learn from disillusionment and personal suffering.

Cognitists and existentialists share the same humanist perspective: people have the ability to choose how they live and they are responsible for the consequences of their choices. Krill (1979) elaborates on this point:

> The existentialists disagree with those who hold man to be either essentially an impulse-driven animal or a social animal of learned conditioning. Both of these ideas deny man what is, for the existentialists, his source of dignity: the absolute value of his individual uniqueness. Man discovers his uniqueness through the way he relates to his own subjective experience of life. Sartre points out that this subjectivity is man's freedom; it is something that is there; it cannot be escaped from or avoided; one can only deny one's own responsibility for choices made within this freedom. From the existential view, psychoanalytic theory is sometimes misused by encouraging man's denial of responsibility on the basis of impulsive forces; similarly, sociological and learning theory may be misused by excusing man on the basis of totally determining social forces. [P. 148]

Each must assume the burden of responsibility for his own freely chosen perspective and the associated consequences of his actions. To be a man is to assert one's uniqueness, knowing that one does not have an absolute knowledge of truth and that one may hurt others or oneself; one's efforts will often end in mistakes or failure. One must assert this uniqueness again and again—choosing courage or cowardice and knowing that suffering is often inevitable as one's perspective conflicts with the limits of life. [P. 150]

In existential thinking, one can move from a life of self-deception to one of authenticity by giving up defensive beliefs and manipulations which have been used to create the illusion of security. An important task of the existential therapist is to help a client experience disillusionment with those various security efforts that block his own growth. Disillusionment may engender feelings of great despair but, as Krill puts it, "On the far side of such despair arise the possibilities of new values and beliefs" (p. 153). The existential approach challenges those of the client's values which interfere with his needs and with his growth, helping him substitute more realistic, human values and encouraging actions that will activate the new values chosen by the client. It is opposed to any therapeutic practices that seek to adjust clients to family and social norms, or to those prognostic norms stemming from the rigid use of diagnostic categories.

Krill, a leading advocate of existential social work, has pointed out the necessity of dialogue for the client and the importance of openness in the therapist:

Man does not grow from within himself alone. His emergence happens in responsive relation to his surroundings. He creates his own meaning in response to situations, and these meanings become the basis for choices and actions. . . . His own growth has to do with the continued reassessment of personal meanings, and he depends upon feedback from his environment (particularly human responses) for this reassessment activity. [P. 154]

(The therapist) shares some of his own struggles, disillusionment and experiences wherein he, too, sought growth in the face of pain . . . . we see that the therapist sees his own unique world view as an important experience to share with his client—not in a "go and do likewise" spirit, but rather showing himself as a fellow traveler on the rocky road of human existence. [P. 158]

According to Van Kaam (1966), the existential viewpoint holds that the essential difference between one individual and another is the degree of readiness which each has developed to be open to whatever he encounters in his environment. The whole life of a person is built upon the decision he makes either to face or to avoid the truth about himself—e.g., his weaknesses and limitations. Only when an individual opens himself to all of significant reality and to the many modes of his existence can he understand his authentic self and fulfill his potentials and responsibilities.

Hora, in explaining existential psychotherapy, states that complete understanding of one's mode of being tends to bring about a changed attitude toward life. Change occurs when a person can see the totality of his situation. Hora contends that "change is the result of expanding consciousness" (1962, p. 37).

In sum, the existential therapist and the cognitive therapist share many convictions: the uniqueness of each human being; man's ability to create his own meanings and destiny; personal meanings as the basis for choices and actions; the responsibility of each person for his behavior; the importance of openness in the therapist; the embeddedness of man in his society; and the dependence of change on expanding the client's consciousness of himself and his world.

Chapter 5

The Introductory Phase of Individual Treatment

This chapter and Chapters 6 and 7 will describe the actual practice of cognitive therapy with individuals, as conducted by the writer. While different cognitive practitioners will of course vary from one another in personal style, emphases, ways of explaining and interpreting, and choice of techniques, the treatment process outlined below is completely consistent with the basic premises of the cognitive orientation.

How the therapist introduces himself and his treatment approach

The cognitive therapist, who is a humanist by philosophy, makes it clear from the beginning of treatment that he has no intention of playing a god-like role. He points out that the possibility that he will be able to help derives not from superior intelligence and not from knowing the client better than the client knows himself but rather from his professional training, experience in treating other people, and capacity to view the client's life objectively. He states that the greatest expert on the client or on the client's children is the client, and that he will depend on what the client tells him for the information necessary to commence the treatment process.

The therapist insists that there is nothing sinister or mysterious about the forces underlying the client's problems. If the client and the therapist can work closely together and be completely open with each other in an atmosphere of trust, it is possible to discover the real nature of the problem and to work out a plan for overcoming it. The therapist states his willingness to accept the obligation of being as helpful as he can be in the shortest possible time and of being entirely honest. In turn, he expects the client to take full responsibility for his past, present, and future behavior. He will not permit the client to project blame or to attribute socially unacceptable acts to an unhappy childhood, insensitive parents, poverty, discrimination, or his "unconscious." The therapist takes the position that the client has considerable control over the direction his life will take by virtue of the choices he makes every day. At the same time, it is recognized that the various systems of which we are a part render us powerless in many areas, and the therapist states his commitment to changing those aspects of the environment which are detrimental to human growth or dignity.

The practitioner explains to the client that words like "good" or "bad," "right" or "wrong," "moral" or "immoral" will not be used in the treatment interviews. Rather than use such terms to characterize the client's actions, the therapist will ask the client to evaluate his behavior as constructive or destructive, helping others or hurting others, facilitating or blocking his progress toward his own goals.

The therapist's role

The therapist describes himself as the partner of the client, ready to work with the client toward mutually agreed upon goals. It is the client's responsibility to decide which problem or problems should be worked on first. It is the therapist's responsibility to point out any goals that he cannot support because they are either not feasible or not in the client's best interest. One aspect of the therapist's role is to engage the client in a dialogue about the choice of goals when there is a disagreement, and to continue this dialogue until the issue is resolved by the client's acceptance of a modification in goals or by the therapist's yielding to the client's persuasion that the original goals are appropriate. Out of this consensus comes an oral or written contract that treatment will focus on the attainment of the mutually acceptable objectives. The setting of goals gives shape to the treatment process, which cannot begin in earnest until this is accomplished.

The therapist informs the client that he has no intention of telling him what to do about the various situations confronting him. Rather, he sees the therapeutic role as one of making sure that the client looks at his problems from all possible viewpoints and is aware of all the choices that are open to him. The therapist's role is then to help the client to develop the strength and courage and skill to take the actions that he himself concludes are necessary. When working with parents, for example, the practitioner emphasizes that he will in no way attempt to instruct them on how to raise their children. Instead, he will assist the parents to evaluate as objectively as possible the value and effectiveness of their particular style of child management, encourage them to make whatever changes are indicated by this assessment, but again leave the choice of action to them.

A large part of therapy consists of helping the client to face the truth about himself and his situation. The importance of this aspect of the therapist's role cannnot be overestimated, especially in regard to self-deception. While it is necessary to deal with deliberate evasions or distortions by the client, it is more difficult and perhaps more crucial to work with those who, in order to avoid pain or guilt, convince themselves that the facts are other than they really are.

They do this by acknowledging all the things which bolster their preferred self-image while ignoring or minimizing those things which would lead them to other conclusions about themselves.

Finally, part of the therapist's role is to function as an educator, teaching the client why people become upset or behave in self-defeating ways; how such emotions and behavior are shaped by inaccurate perceptions; how to determine when their behavior is rational; and how the treatment process will help them to make the changes they themselves desire. The sources of emotional distress and maladaptive behavior have been summarized at the end of Chapter 3 in the section titled "The Nature of Man." The diagram in Chapter 1 can serve as a starting point for a discussion of the relationships among perception, emotion, and behavior.

Maultsby has worked out a succinct definition of rational behavior:

> Both physical and emotional behavior is rational when it obeys at least three of these five rules:
> (1) It's based on objective reality or the known relevant facts of a life situation.
> (2) It enables people to protect their lives.
> (3) It enables people to achieve their goals most quickly.
> (4) It enables people to keep out of significant trouble with other people.
> (5) It enables people to prevent or quickly eliminate significant personal emotional conflict. [Maultsby, 1975, p. 8]

In order to have the client feel that he is an active partner in the treatment process, to take the mysticism out of therapy, and help the client understand what lies ahead, the therapist explains how the cognitive approach works. Basing their analyses on the concept that thinking shapes behavior, therapist and client together will evaluate the latter's reality perceptions. The client will be helped to modify those evaluations of himself, other people, events, and relationships that are inaccurate. He will be encouraged to replace impractical or self-defeating goals with more appropriate ones. Problem-causing or unsatisfying behaviors arising out of faulty perceptions will be identified and alternate ways of acting will be explored. In each case, it is only after the client himself recognizes a deficit in his perception, goal, or behavior and chooses to change it that the therapist can proceed. The next step is, through cooperative effort, to construct and strengthen a new perception, goal, or behavior pattern by means of discussion, trying it out in real life, role playing, and/or mental rehearsal (emotive imagery). (Role playing and imagery will be examined in Chapter 7.)

The client's role

The therapist, in addition to clarifying his own role in the treatment process, talks to the client at the very beginning of therapy about the client's part in their joint endeavor. The therapist wants to come up with a clear agreement, whether oral or written, as to the client's responsibilities. Such a stance on the part of the professional delivers the message that the client is not being regarded as the helpless, passive recipient of a "cure" but rather as a person who has strength of his own and the ability to think. He will be expected to contribute fully to the problem-solving process and to his own growth. Nothing will be done *to* him, everything will be done *with* him. In working with children, this matter is brought up in a simpler and less formal way, but the same principle applies.

The therapist will expect dependability from the client in connection with keeping appointments, arriving on time, paying fees, and carrying out mutually agreed upon home-work assignments. As far as children are concerned, the responsibility for keeping appointments, getting to the therapist on time, and paying fees may have to be transferred to an adult in the family. The therapist is obligated to confront any client who is irresponsible about completing an accepted task. If the client has committed himself to a particular goal in treatment or to making a particular change, the therapist insists that he persevere despite obstacles or discouragement. The rationale for this is that the client's role is to keep his commitments and the practitioner's role is to maintain him on the right track, reminding him of what needs to be done to attain his chosen objective and applying pressure when necessary. The therapist experiences no discomfort in so doing because he is only insisting that the client carry out what he has freely chosen to do. In every facet of his relationship with the client the therapist is meticulous about his own dependability, punctuality, and fulfillment of promises, thus modeling the self-discipline that he expects from the client.

Answering questions the client may ask

After hearing the therapist's description of a cognitive approach, the client may ask about unconscious forces in the mental life of human beings, since Freudian concepts are familiar to so many people in our culture. The cognitist replies that he does not regard an "unconscious" as the determinant of our emotions and behavior. He grants that we can be unconscious (i.e., unaware) of many things about ourselves (see p. 6), but takes the position that material outside our awareness does not influence our behavior until we become conscious of it through recognizing or remembering it.

Clients sometimes claim that they feel depressed, anxious, angry, guilty, or nervous without knowing why. They wonder if this does not prove that the source of these emotions is in their "unconscious." The therapist presents the concept of emotion as an exclusively conscious phenomenon. He asks the client what sentences he is currently saying to himself and tries to show the client that his feelings are the product of these sentences, which are verbalizations of how he perceives reality. Thus, for example, depression can be shown to be associated with the client's view of himself as worthless; anxiety with a fear of losing control of oneself in a public place; anger with lack of appreciation from one's spouse; guilt with inattention to one's aging parents; and nervousness with a general lack of confidence.

Some clients believe that accepting the need for psychotherapy is equivalent to admitting that they are crazy. The therapist takes the position that people are crazy only when they cannot distinguish what is real from what is imaginary. Since most of his clients will not be in this category, he can tell them that coming to him does not mean that they are sick but that they have problems in living. When the therapist does work with an individual who is intermittently psychotic but amenable to psychotherapy during periods of rationality, any question about being crazy will be answered in the affirmative, in keeping with the cognitist's commitment to help his client see reality as accurately as possible.

Clients are often concerned that engaging in psychotherapy carries a stigma. In some circles, going to a "shrink" is the "in" thing, and the psychoanalytic movement in this country has influenced many people to believe that treatment of many years' duration may be necessary and desirable. Despite this, a large proportion of the general population is still probably prejudiced against those who seek out professional psychological help. The therapist openly discusses this truth with the client. He then makes the point that, in his view, the client's decision to come for help was an act of strength and courage rather than a confession of weakness. He notes that undoubtedly a large number of the client's neighbors and acquaintances have personal problems which they keep locked up within themselves. The faces these people present to the world may be masks that conceal considerable emotional distress or unhappiness, so that in spite of any stigmatization, the client is actually taking better care of his interests than they are of theirs.

A client may question how a cognitive approach, which emphasizes a direct, down-to-earth attack on his problems and eschews a lengthy exploration of his past, can be expected to help him accomplish fairly rapid changes in feelings and behaviors that have existed for a long time. This question is frequently raised because the therapist, when explaining how he operates, reveals a sense of urgency about the client's problems and the intention of contributing to the relief of his suffering as soon as possible. The therapist contends that since behavior is shaped by thinking, change in thinking begins to affect behavior without delay. Resistive behavior patterns entrenched by reinforcement of long duration may not change easily, but the therapist will work closely with the client to weaken such behavior patterns by using them less and less and also to replace them with new, more satisfying ways of acting and feeling. The therapist states that although he may see the client only once a week, the bulk of treatment and change takes place between sessions as the client practices new ways of acting and feeling and tries out new experiences that may further modify his previous perceptions. Consequently, although the client is only face to face with the therapist one hour a week, if he carries out his homework assignments he is intimately engaged in a therapeutic process every waking minute between formal interviews.

In regard to the general issue of frequency and length of treatment, the therapist arbitrarily arranges to see the client once a week. This allows the therapist to work with the maximum number of troubled people that is consistent with maintaining a sense of continuity and impact within each relationship. Should a crisis or emergency arise which the client believes necessitates extra sessions, the therapist accommodates him for a limited period of time. Care is taken not to provide more help or less help than the client requires to survive, grow, and solve problems. Since the nonpsychotic client is not considered sick, he does not need to be "cured." The cognitive therapist encourages the client to try to manage on his own as soon as perceptions and behaviors and emotions related to the problem areas have become more appropriate and more satisfying. The understanding is that the door is never closed, that the client can always return, and that therapy sequences of limited duration as needed are preferable to an open-ended treatment process that can turn clients into perpetual patients. At the same time, the cognitive therapist will engage in long-term treatment with those who truly need it.

The cognitist/humanist has no difficulty dealing with personal questions that clients may ask. He is willing to be open about his own humanity to further the goals of treatment, to help the client see the therapist realistically as another human being, to extract from his own life examples of behavior that may be instructive, and to make clear that the client is not alone in possessing problems and shortcomings.

Clients may ask about the therapist's training, where he lives, his marital status, number and ages of children, his experience in the field, and so forth. These are legitimate questions and represent an effort on the part of the client to know the therapist, to determine what they share in common, and to acquire information for deciding whether or not the therapist merits his confidence. In this latter connection, older clients may voice doubts about a younger therapist's ability to help them when he or she is not married, has no children, or has not been out of school long enough to know much about "real life." One reply to this is that therapeutic effectiveness does not depend only on the practitioner's own life experiences: even a young therapist has worked with other people presenting similar problems, has systematically studied about the various social and physiological and psychological difficulties that befall human beings, and has been trained to evaluate and treat such difficulties in an objective fashion. A therapist does not need to know more about "life" than the client does in order to be helpful. He or she can make a significant contribution by being objective and not emotionally caught up in the client's difficulties; from this vantage point he or she can suggest alternate interpretations and choices. Social workers and other professionals, regardless of their age, can be very knowledgeable about the network of social agencies in their community which can augment the services provided by the therapist.

In those cases where the client is not comfortable with the therapist for any reason—age, gender, amount or nature of professional experience, cultural or racial background, personal style, and so on—the therapist has to make a choice. He discusses the matter openly with the client and then either arranges for another therapist or encourages the client to work with him a while longer on the basis that the client's discomfort is part of the problem he himself wants to overcome. Transfer to another therapist is indicated when there appears to be little possibility that the client can ultimately form a relaxed, trusting relationship with the professional.

Confidentiality and record keeping

The therapist pledges confidentiality to the client. This means that nothing of what is discussed in the weekly treatment hour will be conveyed to anyone else without the client's permission. The therapist keeps an ongoing written account of their face-to-face sessions, relevant phone calls, and contacts with other individuals and agencies. These records are primarily to remind the therapist of important facts in the client's situation, agreements and homework assignments made in previous sessions, issues which the client has asked to discuss in future interviews, and the overall shape and pattern of the treatment process. The last-named item refers to the subjects brought up in the weekly sessions and what happens to them: are they faced or avoided, are problems solved or continued? Also part of the shape and pattern of treatment are punctuality and consistency of attendance, progress or lack of progress toward mutually agreed upon goals, and changes in perceptions, behaviors, and emotions.

There is no reason to deny any client access to his own records should he request this. While no part of his file is shared with anyone else without his permission, he himself is entitled to see what is being written about him at any time. Aside from ethical considerations, there can be great therapeutic value in discussing with him the patterns of progress, thinking, behavior, and emotions that emerge from the records over a period of time. In addition, it may contribute to more accurate reality perceptions on the client's part should he become aware of any discrepancies between his view of himself and the way the therapist evaluates him. Some practitioners find it very useful to have the client write his own summary of treatment or progress for inclusion in the record, for he is thus compelled to stand back and look at himself and his situation with some objectivity. Furthermore, since the file contains an evaluation of the client by the therapist, the inclusion of a written appraisal of the therapist by the client is not out of order and also has therapeutic possibilities: distance between therapist and client is reduced, and the therapist can model healthy attitudes about accepting criticism and recognizing shortcomings.

Clients do not usually ask to see their case records or to include their own written evaluations of self or therapist. Nevertheless, the potential benefits from such a request are kept in mind. Federal laws now mandate access to case records when requested by clients of federal agencies, educational institutions, and certain other organizations receiving federal funds. Some states have passed similar legislation.

Having stressed his commitment to confidentiality, the therapist makes it a point to let the client know that there is one exception. If the client exhibits or talks about behavior which endangers his own or another's safety, health, or welfare, the therapist may communicate this information to the next of kin, other professionals, or the authorities—to whomever seems most appropriate. The therapist explains that his rationale for such a policy is his concern for the human being in front of him, and for the community to which they both belong. A teen-ager who reveals that he or she, without the parents' knowledge, went out drinking with peers and was brought home by an inebriated driver may not be guaranteed confidentiality by the therapist. In such cases the therapist first tries to persuade the client to be the one to inform the parents about what is going on but, failing this, the therapist may take the responsibility himself. Likewise, the spouse and/or physician of an adult who appears suicidal or abuses prescribed medications may be contacted by the therapist. If someone is granted probation or parole on condition that he regularly come for therapeutic sessions, the therapist is obliged to report any missed appointments to the probation or parole officer.

Adolescents are particularly reluctant to confide in a professional without an assurance of confidentiality as far as their parents are concerned. For this reason, when the treatment plan includes consultation with the parents, it is often desirable to assign a second therapist to the adults and to assure the young person that confidentiality will be preserved, subject to exceptions like the example discussed above. A second therapist for the parents is indicated when the child client, regardless of age, is uncomfortable with the idea that his own therapist will also be the person who sees his mother or father. In such an arrangement, while the content of the child's interviews with his or her therapist is not revealed to the parent by the second therapist, the two therapists keep in close communication about the case. The second therapist does inform the parent in a general way about what the child's therapist and the child are doing and how the parent can help. When indicated, the child's worker tries to obtain the child's permission for the second worker to bring key problems, questions, and complaints to the parent's attention. With the child's consent, occasional joint sessions including all four people can also be very productive.

Very young children are generally not concerned about confidentiality, but any child who raises the issue is promised that his confidences will be kept within specified limitations. Discussions with a young child about confidentiality are not undertaken unless initiated by the child himself, and then only on a simple level.

It has been this writer's experience that spelling out the limits of confidentiality to both adolescents and adults seldom inhibits their revelations to the therapist once rapport is established.

Homework

Homework assignments, which have been mentioned previously, can be one of the therapist's most effective means of helping the client to change self-defeating behavior and distressing emotions. Given the interplay among perception, behavior, and emotion as described in Chapter 1, the cognitive therapist looks for opportunities to alter faulty client perceptions by assigning the client to engage in activities and experiences which will correct his inaccurate evaluations of himself, other people, and events around him. Successful participation in a previously feared situation begins to change the client's views about the world, other people, and himself. As he perceives things in a different way, his emotional response changes: if a person, object, or situation no longer seems as threatening, negative emotions will decrease.

Success tends to augment self-confidence and a willingness to try similar new situations. Further positive experiences reinforce the growing confidence and the recently begun changes in perceptions and emotions.

The key word in all this is "success." The therapist takes great care to choose homework assignments that have a maximum chance of success. The client can survive an occasional failure but if he is steered into experiences that repeatedly do not work out, the result may be devastating.

Roberta, a woman in her fifties, had a phobia of shopping in big stores. She feared that, amid large numbers of people, she would have difficulty in breathing, faint, or start to scream. None of these things had ever happened, but she could not shake this image from her mind. She was encouraged to go into a supermarket despite her fears and to take her sister along with her for security. The therapist expressed confidence in her ability to carry this out without any difficulty as she had done all her adult life until the previous year. After the assignment was successfully completed a couple of times in the company of her sister, Roberta was asked to go shopping alone at a specified time on a particular day. The therapist would be available in his office at that hour, and the client could telephone him from the store if she became anxious. Roberta followed through on this homework, calling the therapist from the store for a little emotional support. She was subsequently able to go shopping alone without her sister and without telephoning for reassurance and soon afterwards, she was able to generalize these gains and to go alone into buses and into a large restaurant, places she had been avoiding.

In addition to prescribing the homework assignments, the therapist in this case had earlier developed a strong rapport with Roberta in which his firmly expressed confidence in her was a major component. Also, previous discussions about the widespread occurrence of phobias such as hers and their maintenance by strong images of negative outcomes took away some of her feelings of isolation and some of the sinister implications. The main thrust of treatment focused on helping her to overcome the sense of helplessness and inadequacy which had been recently engendered by some severe family problems combined with constant criticism from her husband.

Summary

We have described how the cognitive treatment approach is introduced to the client and how the "ground rules" are spelled out. The reader has been told how certain questions commonly raised by new clients are answered. Various principles that will guide the therapist and some of the techniques he may use during the ongoing phase of treatment have also been discussed. Preceding that, however, is the evaluation phase, which is the subject of the next chapter.

Chapter 6

The Evaluation Phase of Individual Treatment

Diagnosis asks the question: what is the problem? Cognitive theory implies that the answer should be given in terms of clients' goals, perceptions of reality, and lifestyles. This means that the cognitively oriented worker tries to determine whether the clients' goals are constructive or destructive, what distortions or limitations there are in their evaluations and judgments, and what is the nature of their lifestyles. In order to accomplish this, the worker will be interested in the kind of psychosocial history which provides material in these areas.

For some practitioners, evaluation is different from diagnosis and asks what are the client's strengths and weaknesses? This writer will use the single term "evaluation" to denote the process of seeking answers to both questions.

The cognitive therapist, after obtaining enough data to identify the client's problem tentatively (i.e., make a diagnosis), has a choice of the way in which he will formulate his findings. Under the influence of existential ideas, he may decide that a diagnostic label will not help much in the treatment of a particular individual, and he will describe the problem by describing the client's goals, perceptual distortions, and lifestyle. In other cases, and especially if he is a psychiatrist, the therapist may consider it important or necessary to come up with a formal psychiatric diagnosis, using a term and code number from the DSM-III. When it is necessary, the choice of medication to be prescribed may depend upon a precise classification of the client. Research studies or the accurate compilation of statistics may require DSM-III diagnoses to ensure a uniform data base. Government agencies and private insurance carriers ask for formal diagnoses as a condition for reimbursement of services rendered to a client.

The cognitist seeks to discover the nature of the client's problem by asking him directly, listening to his past history, and observing his behavior during interviews and, when possible, in his own lifespace. At no time does the therapist take the position that the client does not know his problem because it exists on an "unconscious" level. The client has come for help in the first place precisely because something specific, which he can name, is troubling him. (In the case of a child, it may be something specific that is troubling the adults in the family.) The older child or adult may not be aware of the origins of the problem, his own part in creating it, or its connection with other aspects of his life, but he can and does tell the therapist that he wants something to change—himself, other people, or his situation. Therapy can begin from there.

Evaluating a new client

The first step in evaluating a new client is to ask him to state his major problem or problems. He is then encouraged to give a brief account of his past life, including hospitalizations for both physical and mental difficulties, previous psychotherapy, and a review of all medications to date. The therapist questions him about any significant illnesses he has had and his current state of health. Written permission is requested for contacting physicians and other professionals when information from them is needed to fill in any gaps in the total picture. It is important to know about children's attitudes and performance in school, and about the employment history and experiences of adults. When the client is a child under eighteen years of age, much or most of the above information is obtained from a parent. Many practitioners, both in social agencies and in private practice, use preprinted face sheets or questionnaires, and these data are recorded on those forms either by the therapist or by an intake worker during the first interview, or by the client himself at home before coming to his initial session.

Both during and after the gathering of background information, the therapist observes the client carefully in order to ascertain what psychiatrists call his "mental status." This is the sum total of the client's use of speech; orientation to time, place, and other persons; specific emotions; continuous mood; mannerisms; memory; intelligence; thought processes; insight; and judgment. The therapist directs the conversation as needed in ways that will elicit these characteristics from the client.

Through collecting data and directly observing the client, the therapist arrives at tentative answers to the questions originally posed: what is the problem, and what are the client's strengths and weaknesses? This working evaluation is always subject to revision as treatment proceeds and additional information and awareness come to the therapist. Obviously the process of taking a history and observing the client as just described is common to many psychotherapeutic approaches and has no special connection with cognitive theory. The cognitist, however, makes use of his findings in ways that other approaches do not. Prior to that he encourages the client in the recounting of his history to focus a great deal on three aspects in which other treatment theories show little interest: the aforementioned goals, perceptions, and lifestyle.

In that part of the history taking which focuses on the client's goals, the cognitive worker can use the projective technique of Early Recollections (ER), which, incidentally, has the advantage of being economical in terms of time and cost. The client is simply asked to think back as far as he can and state his earliest childhood memory. In direct discussion with the client about his goals, the therapist tries to ascertain who are the principal opponents in his life and whether the goals represent an attempt to compensate for a lack or an inferiority feeling. Nikelly and Verger (1971, p. 55) believe that ER's can help the therapist understand the client's purposes, repetitive patterns of behaving, and the unity of his life.

In regard to perception, the therapist pays close attention to the client's judgments about himself, others, and his world. The gathering of the psychosocial history includes queries about the family atmosphere, which can be a prime cause not only of maladjustment but of perceptual distortions and limitations. Dewey (1971) has worked out the following classifications of family atmosphere: rejective, authoritarian, martyrdom, inconsistent, suppressive, hopeless, indulgent, pitying, high standards, materialistic, competitive, disparaging, and inharmonious.

Another cause of distorted perceptions of reality is what Adler called "private logic," a faulty *process* of thinking which leads to inaccurate conclusions. In taking the history, the worker is alert to any evidences of a faulty private logic. Still other factors in distorted perceptions for which the cognitive therapist probes include severely traumatic experiences, the client's ordinal position in the family (first, middle, last, only child), physical unattractiveness or handicap at any time, and what being a male or female of a certain color, nationality, and religion has meant to the client within his particular family and surrounding environment.

Lifestyle, a third basis for cognitive diagnosis, is the way the client goes about his quest for personal significance, his pattern of living, his "style of acting, thinking and perceiving" (Adler, 1979). Nikelly (1971, p. 31), in discussing psychotherapy from the Adlerian point of view, states: "Instead of deciphering unconscious wishes and motives, as the psychoanalyst would do, the therapist looks for the basic pattern by which the client moves through life." The psychosocial history should include sufficient clues from the past so that the therapist, by combining these data about past behavior with his own observations of the client's current behavior, can reach an assessment of the client's lifestyle. Some varieties of lifestyle are: pampered, withdrawn, self-sacrificing, controlling, inadequate, joyful, obsequious, and altruistic.

Kurt Adler believes that the assessment of goals and lifestyle is as important in treating schizophrenic individuals as it is in working with those who have a stable contact with reality:

> It is one of the basic tenets of Individual Psychology (Adlerian theory—H.D.W.) that every expression of a human being always serves a purpose. This must, of course, be also true for delusions and hallucinations. In order to understand what they mean to the patient, one has to ask what their purpose is, what they are aiming at, what the patient wants to achieve with them. The usual question of "where they come from" is relatively unimportant. After delusions and/or hallucinations have abated, the therapist together with the patient will have to discuss for what purpose the patient had created the delusions or hallucinations and what he had hoped to gain from them. Even after a complete recovery of a patient from his acute episode, it is still very important to find out, with the patient, for what purpose he had caused his breakdown and his delusions or hallucinations. Only insight into all that will give him the ability to develop a real understanding and insight into his life style and make him able to avoid resorting to a breakdown as an escape from difficulties the next time he is confronted with them. [Adler, 1979, p. 160]

When observing the behavior of a new client in the interview setting, the practitioner bears in mind that his own presence adds another and possibly distorting factor to the total picture. We are all familiar with the child, extremely disruptive in the home, school, or community, who is completely cooperative and responsive in the office of a professional who gives him attention, respect, and freedom of expression. Consequently, making the effort to observe the client in his own lifespace (classroom in school, family meal at home, etc.) can sometimes provide the therapist with a new dimension of understanding.

Christopher—A case example of cognitive evaluation

To sum up the cognitive evaluation process with a new client, we can follow a cognitive practitioner as he takes a psychosocial history on Christopher, a single man in his thirties.

Christopher states that he is coming for help because he feels tense, overwhelmed, and anxious. After explaining his treatment philosophy and method and answering any questions, the therapist asks the client for a brief history. He may suggest that the client tell his early recollections. He will probe for indications as to the client's chief opponents in life. He will find out Christopher's current goals, which mirror his conception of success. He will try to determine whether or not any of these goals may have developed out of a strong need to compensate for a specific lack or a specific kind of inferiority feeling. As the history taking proceeds, the therapist will obtain data about the family atmosphere, any handicaps the client has suffered, his ordinal position [order of birth in a family], traumatic events, and any problems created by gender, race, or other ethnic characteristics. Finally, the therapist will evaluate the soundness of the client's private logic.

In this case, the therapist obtains a picture of a man who, because of a sickly childhood, fell behind in school and never matched the educational achievements of his four siblings, among whom he was the middle child. (The middle child often lacks the status of the oldest and the attention given to the youngest.) His parents, who overvalued both college education and material possessions, did not conceal their disappointment and Christopher developed feelings of failure and inferiority. His earliest recollection was of being left behind for misbehaving while all his siblings were taken on a special family trip. Because of the family atmosphere, he came to equate success with monetary wealth and he set up for himself the compensatory goal of making lots of money in business in any way he could. His private logic permitted bending or breaking the law, taking advantage of associates, cheating customers, and using people for his own purposes. Anyone who stood in his way was his opponent. He used the fact that he was a member of the majority ethnic and religious group in the community to beat out business competitors by appeals to bigotry. His manipulating lifestyle finally became clear to a significant number of people, who began to challenge him, block him, and retaliate with all kinds of pressures. He sought professional help when he could no longer cope with his increasing anxiety, which was triggered by the threat to one of his essential values—business success.

The diagnostic impression of this client is that of a very tense individual with antisocial goals whose manipulating lifestyle has finally evoked societal retaliation which he cannot handle. Impelled by an urgent need to overcome his feelings of inferiority through the attainment of a family-approved type of success, Christopher has a limited and distorted perception of himself and his situation which has led to equating self-worth and success with the accumulation of wealth by any means possible. Cognitive treatment will include helping the client to adopt a more constructive lifestyle by having him reevaluate his goals. The reevaluation of goals, however, can take place only when, through the treatment process, the client alters his perceptions of his world so as to approximate reality more closely. Change in goals will lead to a change in behavior, including discontinuation of actions that provoke hostility in others.

As noted earlier, the cognitive therapist may wish or need to come up with a formal psychiatric diagnosis in addition to, or instead of, this diagnostic impression rendered in cognitive terms.

Referring to DSM-III, he can then offer the following diagnosis: Generalized Anxiety Disorder (300.02).

Communicating evaluations to the client

No evaluation of a client by a therapist has any value unless it is transmitted to the client. The therapist shares his thoughts about the client and his situation at least three times during the course of treatment. The first time this process takes place is near the beginning of the relationship, but not before the therapist has introduced himself and his treatment approach, taken a history, observed the client, and established some rapport with the person he is trying to help. Clients really cannot hear or accept what a therapist says until he has first atttained credibility and status in their eyes. The extent to which these are attained depends upon how effectively the therapist carries out the various steps in the introductory phase as described in Chapter 5, and also upon how positively each client rates him in regard to empathy, warmth, and genuineness.

In the first evaluation, the therapist conveys his ideas about the nature of the problem, the positives and negatives in the situation, and how the client might begin to overcome the distress and move toward the goals which he himself has identified. As mentioned in the previous chapter, the client specifies his goals and priorities. If these appear feasible to the therapist, he is obligated to support the client's efforts to move in his chosen direction. In working with children, the therapist more often than not communicates the three evaluations to the parent(s) but, depending on the child's age and maturity, he is also able in many instances to convey some of his impressions to the young client directly.

A second evaluation may be offered to the client when treatment is well under way and either the client himself wants some feedback on his progress or the therapist wants to use it to encourage the client or to make him aware of insufficient movement.

A final evaluation is given at the termination of treatment, regardless of the nature of the ending. Because of his reality orientation, the cognitive therapist feels responsible for helping the client to see himself and his situation at the time of termination as accurately as possible. Different types of treatment endings will be discussed in the next chapter.

In returning now to the first evaluation, it should be pointed out that this can also be the occasion for discussing a written contract if such is called for by the situation or desired by either client or therapist. A written contract binds both parties to reality by setting down a mutually agreed upon formulation of the problem(s) at the start of treatment, what responsibilities each will undertake, and what goals the client will try to reach in a specified time period. Later on, this contract becomes a useful instrument for comparing changed behavior with original behavior, reminding all concerned of the tasks to which they committed themselves, and measuring progress toward the client's own stated goals.

Even when there is no written contract, discussion between client and therapist about the nature of the presenting problem(s), what each will do to promote change, and the client's objectives results in a treatment plan that gives shape to both the evaluation phase and the treatment process as a whole.

Chapter 7

The Ongoing and Termination Phases of Individual Treatment

The content of ongoing interviews

The cognitive therapist uses ongoing treatment interviews to review with the client his current situation; to catch up on what has happened since the previous session; to see whether homework assignments have been done; to listen to the client express his feelings, fears, and accomplishments; to identify the next problem to be tackled; and to work with the client on a plan for the coming week. If something particularly upsetting or satisfying has taken place recently, the recounting of these details and the ventilation of associated emotions are given precedence.

In some cases, the immediate objective is not primarily a change in the client's interpersonal behavior or in his external situation. Instead, the goal may be a change within the individual: overcoming indecisiveness, improving self-image, breaking out of a depression, or clarifying identity. In such instances, the ongoing sessions still cover the same subject matter but the target problem and the plan to overcome it may remain the same for several weeks.

As indicated earlier, the therapist does not deny his own value system but struggles constantly to avoid or to minimize imposing it on the client. He answers information-seeking questions directly. He keeps up to date on the community's network of social agencies and refers the client to the appropriate one whenever he manifests a need for a concrete service which is not available in the therapist's own organization. The combination of psychotherapy plus concrete services represents the highest level of professional help that can be given.

The therapist does not make decisions for the client or tell him what to do, but he tries to be sure that the client has sufficient information about facts, differing viewpoints, and possible choices to come up with a sound decision. The cognitist makes a particular effort to bolster the client's confidence, whenever possible, by recalling the client's own statements about past successes. While conveying to the client his belief in the uniqueness of each human being and his respect for that uniqueness, the practitioner also takes pains to relieve any undue anxiety or panic by informing the client of the frequency and universality of his problems.

The use of confrontation

There are people whose bluntness and directness inflict cruel wounds on others, and yet they want credit for "telling it like it is." The cognitive therapist believes in confrontation, but only in the service of therapy, to help and not to hurt. Since his aim is to enable his client to see reality as accurately as possible, there are occasions when confrontation is indicated. We define confrontation as bringing a client face to face with the truth by means of some direct action on the part of the therapist.

The therapist, for example, may be working with the

mother of a young boy. She complains that the child is cranky, restless, and disobedient and avoids any closeness with her. She comes across as an irritating personality who talks endlessly in a disorganized fashion, is extremely self-centered and full of self-pity, and lacks any trace of humor. After careful deliberation, the therapist tells her that he thinks he can understand part of her son's behavior, because he himself feels very edgy and uncomfortable in her presence only a short time after meeting her. If he, the therapist, is "turned off" as the result of a relatively brief contact, he can imagine the feelings of a child who lives with her day after day. The therapist goes on to say that he knows the mother wants to help her child and for this reason he has confronted her with what she may be contributing to the problem.

The mother is taken aback by the therapist's comments, but recognizes their constructive intent and possible validity. At the next session she is ready to examine her own behavior more closely and to consider making changes in herself.

The therapist's relationship with another client, a female adult, is not going well. The client does not seem relaxed, her conversation is guarded, and there is no sense of rapport. The therapist is white, the client is black. During the third interview, the therapist confronts her with his view of the situation. This enables the client to talk about her uneasiness with a *male* therapist and her distrust and hostility toward a *white* therapist. Having reviewed his notes on the first two sessions without recognizing any major errors in dealing with the client, the therapist proposes that she come to him for a few more sessions to see if they cannot remove some of the barriers between them. She declines the suggestion; the prospect of working with a white male even for a trial period is too much for her to handle. She requests transfer to a black female therapist in the agency, and this is arranged.

In this case, failure to confront the client with her resistance to the therapist early in the treatment sequence would probably have resulted in her dropping out, with no guarantee that she would seek or find assistance elsewhere. As a consequence of the confrontation, she was transferred to another worker in the same agency. While she never worked out her difficulties with the original therapist directly with him, they did receive attention in her sessions with the second professional.

The use of dreams

Freud regarded dreams as "the royal road to the unconscious," with a purpose of their own. That purpose was to keep the dreamer asleep by disguising the threatening, frightening material from the unconscious which made its way into the consciousness of the sleeping individual. If the dream did not distort its imagery, the dreamer would be shocked into wakefulness.

The cognitive therapist makes use of dreams whenever they will facilitate treatment, but as a form of consciousness rather than as the product of unconscious mechanisms. This conception has been given much support by Montague Ullman (1955, pp. 30–60), who suggested that the phenomenon of dreams be reinvestigated using a different approach from that of Freud. Freud regarded dreaming as a purely mental process governed by the unconscious. Ullman proposed studying dreams in physiological terms first, then fitting the psychological aspects into place on a physiological framework which he constructed from the discoveries made by Pavlov about the cerebral cortex and its activity. Some of the conclusions that Ullman reached as a result of investigating dreams with his alternative approach were summarized by this author in another work:

> [Ullman] believes that primarily we dream about problems or situations that we have not mastered in our waking ex-

istence. These unsolved problems and situations have been acting as stimuli to our cortical centers during the day and will not cease to do so until they have been mastered. When we are asleep at night, they continue to impinge on our consciousness, but those parts of the brain associated with the secondary signalling system are inactive and not available for selecting, organizing, and systematizing the imagery that is produced. It is for this reason that the dream content is often distorted, illogical, or contradictory. Dreaming occurs only in a transitional state between being awake and deeply asleep where there is partial inhibition of higher cortical activity. Falling into a deeper sleep is the result of the spread of inhibition over both signalling systems, in which circumstance dreaming cannot take place. Excitation of the primary signalling system beyond a certain point results in the activation of both signalling systems and waking up. The impact of the dream itself may set in motion the arousal process, or the ringing of the alarm-clock bell, or a need to go to the bathroom. In any case, it is not how well the dream masks repressed material that determines whether or not the sleeper awakes, but tissue needs. If the body's need for rest is stronger than the disturbing stimulus, he will not awake. If his body is well-rested, relatively weak stimuli will arouse him. [Werner, 1965, pp. 117–118]

It should be explained that the first signalling system refers to the direct impressions of reality received through the senses which man experiences in common with other animals. The secondary signalling system, found only in humans, is composed of the words and language that we attach to these sensory impressions. The words and language serve as signals of the first signals. "According to Pavlov, the conditioned associations in the cerebral cortex of a human being are formed chiefly by speech stimuli" (Kabanov, 1955, p. 232).

Since the cognitist does not believe in the existence of an "unconscious" that needs to be brought to consciousness, any attention he pays to the client's dreams is not to find clues to unconscious material. Rather, as in the case of Patricia, he uses the client's description of her dreams to clarify feelings and attitudes which she has not yet been able to put into words.

Patricia is an attractive married woman in her early twenties. Although she had been dating another man, her parents pushed her into meeting the man who became her husband. Patricia tells the therapist that she feels guilty about not making up her own mind and, in effect, permitting her parents to select her husband for her. There was a whirlwind marriage followed by a quick pregnancy. At this time, her son is two years old. There is little physical intimacy in the marriage, which is agreeable to Patricia. Sometimes the baby gets on her nerves and she has thoughts of just taking off and leaving her husband and child. She thinks she would have married the first man if her parents had left her alone and not kept influencing her to get serious about her husband. In fact, all her life her parents have made her feel that she is stupid and has poor judgment. Her husband, who is very kind to her, also ignores her opinions. She has indicated to her husband that she now has little feeling for him, and apparently he recognizes and accepts this. They have even talked about separation. She has tried hard to love her husband deeply, but when he comes home from a trip she cannot give him a very enthusiastic welcome. They are more like brother and sister. She thinks she would like not to be married.

On her own initiative, Patricia tells the therapist some of her dreams. In one of them, she is at a gathering of several couples and gets into an argument with a woman friend. She loses her temper and becomes violently angry, but does not feel any guilt. This is the exact opposite of what occurs in her waking life, where she is very uneasy about asserting herself. The therapist suggests that guilt about self-assertion in her real existence is a problem she has not yet solved but would like very much to master.

Patricia discusses the content of other recent dreams. She is married to her husband but he literally fades out of the picture. She is single again and is dating several different men. She and her husband are at a church at someone else's wedding; he scolds her and as he does he fades away. She sits down in a booth in her street clothes and has her photograph taken; the picture that comes out of the machine shows her in a wedding dress, her face is old and lined, she is forty years of age.

It is not hard for the client to understand how these dreams reflect her wish to be single again and her resentment of her husband's criticism. She has difficulty, however, with the implications of the scene where her photograph is being taken. The therapist guesses that she seems to be equating marriage with the loss of her girlhood and the end of youth, and she agrees that she does feel this way about marriage.

The use of humor

Spontaneous humor, not given much attention in the professional literature, can have many uses and values in the therapeutic process. The cognitist, an advocate of putting both the client and himself in touch with their own humanness, has no difficulty in recognizing with Dewane (1978, p. 509) that "a sense of humor is one dimension of personality." The following summary of some of the ways in which the cognitive therapist uses humor in therapy is based largely on ideas formulated by Dewane (1978, pp. 508–510).

The presence or absence of a sense of humor in the client in response to what takes place in therapy gives the therapist a clue to his cognitive functioning. In this sense, the nature and amount of humor expressed serves as an informal projective test, an indicator of possible cultural influences on the client's behavior, a measure of sophistication and socialization, and a key to the individual's emotional strength or fragility. As Dewane phrases it, "The level of a person's ego strength can be measured by his or her ability to deal with humor. The ability to laugh at one's self may be one indication of an integrated personality" (p. 508). Most important of all, the client's use of or response to humor may reveal disorders of mood or thought.

The cognitive therapist uses humor to break the ice during the first interview and to communicate his own warmth and good will toward the client. In general, as treatment proceeds, the cognitive therapist employs a light, good-natured touch at those times when it cannot be construed by the client as disrespect or insensitivity to his worry or suffering. The presence of a sense of humor in the therapist's serious discussion of the client's problems serves as a metacommunication, a message about the main message. Through humor the therapist says that the client's situation is not hopeless and that the therapist has some confidence about being able to help. Through humor the therapist is also defining their relationship as one of human beings working together for a common cause, rather than one between a person coming to be cured and a distant, austere being who will cure him.

Like the practice of self-revelation by the therapist, the practice of humor by the therapist involves the risk of coming across to the client as a less than perfect and very human creature. The cognitist accepts this risk because of the benefit to the client, who, face to face with the therapist's humanness, may feel more free to express his own.

Humor, employed either by client or therapist, can make discussions about unpleasant or difficult matters easier to carry through. A light touch eases tension for all concerned when the therapist has to point out the client's failure to attempt his homework assignment. A rather overwhelming problem may seem a little less hopeless if the therapist can help the client find a hitherto unrecognized humorous aspect.

Finally, humor can be used by fearful, withdrawn people as a vehicle for practicing assertion. Fifteen-year-old Albert has had a communication problem all his life. As a young child, he did not speak and was diagnosed as autistic. He attended special schools and over the years gradually came out of his shell but is still far behind his age group in academic achievement and the ability to communicate easily with others. In their treatment sessions, Albert and the therapist play cards and talk about things regarding which the boy has little information, such as life in other countries. Albert enjoys these relaxed, nonthreatening conversations which the therapist encourages because they expand Albert's consciousness, require him to talk, give him more knowledge of the world, and foster a perception of himself as someone whom the therapist treats as an equal. In both the card games and the conversations, Albert is given a model of assertive expression by the therapist, who jokes, banters, and delivers mock insults. Because he feels safe in the therapeutic relationship, and because his verbalizations are cloaked in humor, Albert is able to return the jokes, the banter, and the friendly insults. For the first time in his life he is asserting himself without fear. Later the school reports with delight that he punched a bully who was badgering him on the playground.

Strengthening will

Rollo May refers to will as the capacity to organize one's self so that movement in a particular direction or toward a certain goal can take place. The cognitist agrees with the followers of Otto Rank that the quality of a person's life depends upon the strength or weakness of his will and the goals to which he chooses to apply it. The *content* of a person's behavior depends upon his thinking; the *intensity* of his behavior depends upon the strength of his will.

Human existence is circumscribed by all kinds of rules and limits that we impose upon ourselves or that are imposed upon us by other people or the systems of which we are a part. All our lives, every human being continually makes choices as to which restrictions we will accept and against which limits we will exert our will. On one level, life can be regarded as an experience in challenging and accepting the will of others, with every individual finding for himself a proper combination of the two. A *rational* yielding to limits may require as much strength of will as struggling against them, especially if in the process of yielding one gives up things of value and importance. Furthermore, "surrendering" to rules and regulations may be a sign of true maturity, in that one is putting aside personal gratification for the social good and displaying "social interest." The cognitive therapist helps to strengthen the client's will for both challenge and submission, the choice each time belonging to the client. Depending on the circumstances, the decision of a citizen to accept the iimitations decreed by his society is not necessarily detrimental to his emotional development.

Freud thought otherwise. In *Civilization and its Discontents,* he contended:

> it is impossible to overlook the extent to which civilization is built up upon a renunciation of instinct, how much it presupposes precisely the non-satisfaction (by suppression, repression or some other means?) of powerful instincts. . . It is not easy to understand how it can become possible to deprive an instinct of satisfaction. Nor is doing so without danger. [Freud, 1962, p. 44]

Freud made it clear in this same work that the powerful instincts to which he was referring were sexuality and aggressivity. According to him, it was hard for man to be happy in a civilization that compelled him to restrict his sexual life and his "inclination to aggression." Freud's overall view of civilization was that the more civilized a society became and the more sacrifice of instinctual drives it demanded, the more neurotic its people became in response to the greater conflict between those drives and societal prohibitions.

The cognitist has a much more optimistic view of civilization and its effects upon the individual. Society is not static and over a period of time excessive restrictions on personal behavior can disappear. A prime example of this phenomenon is the current sexual revolution, which has done away with so many of the taboos which Freud saw as making people guilt-ridden, frustrated, and neurotic. In fact, the pendulum may have swung completely to the other side, as witness the widespread complaint that our culture is now too "permissive." In addition, since the cognitist regards aggression not as an innate "inclination" but as a potential capacity that needs to be activated by circumstances, he does not worry that society's laws against violence are bottling up a natural drive that must be continually satisfied.

From the larger perspective, then, the cognitive therapist views the strengthening of the client's will as a basic aim, regardless of the use to which it will be put, because a firm will supplies the organizing force necessary to change one's life. Should the will be employed in the service of conforming to rules and regulations because compliance is perceived by the client as being in his own best interest or as a contribution to community stability, the therapist does not view this as neurotic or unhealthy. Conversely, the therapist supports protests by the client against the status quo and challenges to the establishment's rules if the client's perceptions of unfairness, ineffectiveness, or unsuitability appear to be accurate. The practitioner does not encourage submission to unfair or humiliating situations because the client wants to avoid "making waves," but neither does he reinforce a client's tendency to violate rules for antisocial purposes or the satisfaction of momentary impulses.

Cultivating courage

The subject of courage is seldom discussed in the literature on the theory and practice of psychotherapy. This is unfortunate, because the acquisition of courage by the client often makes possible new movement toward facing his problems and taking action to solve them. In regard to the client, we define courage as the willingness to endure pain in order to grow. In regard to the therapist, we define courage as the willingness to endure tension in order to help the client grow. Following in the tradition of Alfred Adler, one of the few to note the importance of cultivating courage in the client, the cognitive therapist incorporates the building of courage into his treatment style.

Warren is a single man of thirty who works as a scientist in a large corporation. Although he has ample opportunity to meet women his own age on the job, he has great difficulty getting through even the first steps of a casual encounter—i.e., being introduced and making light conversation. Despite strong heterosexual desires, meeting any female who is attractive to him triggers off an anxiety-provoking reaction. Brought up by a mother who behaved seductively toward him and at the same time made him feel guilty about his emerging sexual feelings, he has become an adult who cannot be comfortable with his own sexuality. Having seen or become superficially acquainted with someone of the opposite sex whom he would like to know better, he finds the prospect of an extended chat or asking her to lunch frightening and immobilizing. Any sexual fantasies he may have engender an overwhelming sense of guilt, which combines with the irrational notion that this woman is a surrogate for his mother. The result is a highly neurotic conditioned response of panic and avoidance.

The therapist and the client painstakingly work together to reach an agreement finally that the client's perceptions about his own guilt and about the relationship of other women to his mother are not accurate. The origins of these misperceptions are explored and identified. This insight, however, is not sufficient to overcome the problem, which, in the cognitist's view, can be mastered only by weakening of the client's conditioned neurotic response through the practice of nonneurotic behavior with women. The therapist's next task, therefore, is the cultivation in the client of the courage to take the risk and endure the fear involved in making successful social contact with women and possibly asking them for a date.

In another case, the therapist is dealing with a man who is very disturbed by the contemporary behavior of adolescents in general. He is particularly unhappy over the fact that his sixteen-year-old daughter, musically talented and doing well in school, goes out on weekly dates. He continually talks about how different things were when he was a child and girls did not date regularly until they were much older. This man has become so preoccupied with this issue that he looks for every opportunity to find an excuse to "ground" his daughter so that she cannot go out on weekends. He listens in on her phone calls and checks up on her whereabouts when she is out with friends, convinced that she is headed for serious trouble. The girl has become very tense and unhappy at home and so has her mother, who shares some of the father's fears but also senses that he is overreacting. The therapist decides to confront the father with some of the excesses in his behavior, not in terms of "right" or "wrong," but in terms of the great tension in the home and what can be done to alleviate it. The therapist anticipates that the upcoming session may not be pleasant but is willing to accept the strain. As it turns out, the therapist does find himself on the receiving end of great hostility from this client, who characterizes him as one of those "do-gooder social workers" who encourage parents to be overpermissive and lax in the enforcement of discipline.

Facilitating self-assertion

The cultivation of courage in the client is usually undertaken for the purpose of facilitating self-assertion when this is a problem for him. Assertion can mean any of the following:

1. Carrying out a task which is necessary for growth but is frightening or painful;
2. Expressing feelings or opinions to someone who is reluctant to listen;
3. Issuing a "declaration of independence" to someone who is attempting complete domination and control;

4. Demanding the return of freedoms and rights unjustly curtailed by another person or a system;
5. Requesting recognition for achievements, a promotion at work, a salary raise;
6. Taking action to terminate an unsatisfying relationship;
7. Taking action to stop being victimized by another's aggression.

The cognitive therapist teaches or encourages assertion but not aggression and makes a careful distinction between the two. Assertion is standing up for one's own views, expressing emotions and needs, and behaving in ways that advance one's own interests without any intention of attacking or harming someone else. Aggression involves an attack—physical, verbal, or emotional—against another person with intent to hurt, embarrass, or demoralize that individual and/or to destroy his or her ability to continue behavior not acceptable to the aggressor. It must be said that, in the kind of world we live in, self-assertive behavior which starts off with no aim of attacking anyone sometimes becomes aggressive in self-defense when the other person forcibly tries to prevent the self-expression of the asserting individual.

The therapist takes pains to point out the difference between assertion and aggression to all his clients. Making this distinction can be very helpful to parents of disobedient children, who often aggravate the situation by responding with aggression (attack) against the youngsters instead of self-assertion. Some parents need to be taught how to express anger and frustration to the child regarding his defiance without crossing over into the area of retaliatory aggression: humiliating and insulting the child; threatening to send him away; withdrawing basic acceptance; or voicing regret that he was ever born. It is generally better for parents to state their unwillingness to accept the acting-out behavior and, without attacking the child, announce and carry out a disciplinary plan.

Encouraging consistency

One of the greatest contributions a therapist can make during the treatment process is to educate clients as to the value of consistency. This refers both to patience and perseverance as the client struggles toward his own chosen goals and to maintaining a firm disciplinary policy in the management of his children. Consistency also calls for predictability and dependability in one's social relationships with peers.

In applying the principle of consistency to carrying out a disciplinary plan for a noncooperating child, we bear in mind that punishment and discipline are not the same. Punishment is usually the immediate physical action an adult takes to bring a specific situation under control—e.g., spanking a small child who runs into the street or depriving an older child of his allowance for failing to do his chores. Discipline is a long-term process of teaching a child responsible behavior so that he eventually controls himself.

To implement a new disciplinary plan, the therapist discusses with parents the importance of spelling out the rules to the child in advance. Privileges, restrictions, and penalties should be clear and simple. Parents should not promise or threaten anything which they cannot or will not carry out. Respect for parental authority cannot be increased if the child's perception of the adult is of a person who breaks promises or threatens a great deal but can be easily circumvented or pressured to back down. No matter to which parent the child comes, it is crucial that he experience the same handling. Parents are not to disagree in front of the child. Should the youngster violate one of the new rules under circumstances which do not permit a parent to impose a penalty or restriction on the spot and make sure that it is carried out, the parent is to inform the child that the transgression was observed and that it is the adult's decision, not the child's, to delay the consequences until a later time.

An effective disciplinary plan tends to be one that enables the child to understand precisely what his responsibilities are and what consequences will result from specific kinds of behavior. Its chances for success will be enhanced if it is administered in a completely consistent manner and with a touch of humor. There is no value in parents' saying no to a child's requests simply in order to assert their authority. Within the disciplinary plan, positive child-parent relationships can grow if the adults say yes whenever possible. Refusals should be confined to those requests that are not possible for practical or financial reasons or that would endanger the child's health, safety, or general welfare.

In dealing with intrafamily problems, the cognitive therapist places major emphasis on parental consistency, which directly influences how clearly the child perceives his role in the family. The wide diversity of family lifestyles in our culture results in every possible degree of "tightness": from families where the children have great freedom of movement and choice to families that exercise tight control over all aspects of the child's life until he leaves the home. Experience suggests that most children with problems come from homes with inconsistent controls rather than from homes where the children know where they stand, even though the home atmosphere may be rather permissive or rather strict.

Fostering social interest

Social interest is a term coined by Alfred Adler to describe an attitude of cooperation with others for the common good. It is a significant factor in the cognitive framework today, because the extent of a client's social interest strongly influences his choice of goals, and his goals shape his behavior.

It is not possible to exhort anyone to exhibit social interest. The cognitive therapist does not confront his client with his lack of this quality, nor does he attempt to convince him of the advantages of acquiring it. Since it is an attitude, a way of looking at the world, it comes into being within an individual only by developing out of that person's own experiences. It can be fostered early in life by adults in the home and teachers in the school who exemplify social interest by what they do and say, but many individuals do not encounter such models in their life situations, or the influence of their models is weaker than that of opposing forces in the world around them.

People usually behave in ways that they believe serve their own needs or bring them closer to their goals. A thirteen-year-old boy who is a product of a broken home from which he derived no emotional support or sense of worth is developing a pattern of delinquent behavior. He brandishes a knife at another boy to impress him with his toughness, steals from stores, and at home strikes his mother and kicks a hole in the wall. Lacking social interest, he has nothing in his life to deter him from impulsive attempts to overcome his sense of powerlessness. His third appearance at Juvenile Court is followed by a stay of several days in a detention facility, which frightens him. Out of this experience arises the beginning of a willingness to cooperate with societal expectations, based on fear of consequences. As he controls his aggressive behavior, he enjoys the absence of community pressure and conflict with his mother, which in turn tends to reinforce his new-found social interest. The role of the cognitive therapist is to make the client as aware as possible of the connection between his increased contentment and his willingness to exercise self-control.

Thus, the role of the cognitive therapist in fostering social interest is an indirect one. When circumstances compel a client to substitute cooperation for defiance, the practitioner points out the practical benefits, the payoff, resulting from the change. The actual development of social interest, however, if it occurs at all, can emerge only from the client's own recognition that cooperative behavior yields him a greater payoff than antisocial conduct. When there are no circumstances at work to precipitate the client's abandonment of destructive behavior on his own initiative, the cognitive therapist tries to persuade the client to behave differently as an experiment that may yield him a greater payoff than he is now receiving. Social interest cannot be advocated as an end in itself. Like happiness, it cannot be acquired directly but is the result of other things falling into place.

Role playing

Like other practitioners, the cognitist uses role playing whenever it will prepare the client more effectively than discussion to deal with situations in real life. Since therapy is a temporary substitute and a rehearsal for the client's true existence in the world, what is learned in the treatment process should approximate real life as closely as possible.

Role playing gives the client an opportunity to rehearse in safety an anxiety-provoking confrontation that he is now ready to risk. In other cases, therapist and client can take turns at playing the different roles that might be called for at a social gathering, when the client is deficient in social skills and party manners. Sometimes the therapist becomes the client and the client becomes a significant other in his life, the reversal enabling the client to observe how the therapist views him and requiring the client to get inside another person and delineate him. A large number of variations is possible.

Role playing fits in very well with the cognitist's emphasis on the client's perceptions as the basis of his behavior. As the client plays out a particular role, the therapist picks up clues to distortions and limitations in his conceptions of himself, other people, and his personal environment. Role playing also helps the professional to rate the client's intelligence, sophistication, store of knowledge, perceptiveness, and response to pressure.

Prescribing imagery

Just as role playing serves as physical and verbal rehearsal, the client's deliberate production of specified images serves as mental and emotional rehearsal. This technique of asking the client to visualize a certain scene and give it a positive ending is a behavior-modification device which the cognitive therapist is very willing to use. Its value in treatment is that it can help to undermine misperceptions by the client which prevent him from attempting a growth-producing experience. Furthermore, it can weaken the association between a threatening situation and a conditioned upsetting emotional response that is not appropriate.

Arthur, a bright young man employed by a large corporation as a financial analyst, has many innovative ideas which could improve the fiscal efficiency of some of the company's departments. Presenting these suggestions at a staff meeting could conceivably enhance his status and win attention and promotion from his superiors. Arthur, however, never asks for the floor to present any of this material. In his mind he always imagines that such an action will be badly received, make him look like a fool, and engender resistance or hostility. The therapist has him relax during a treatment session, close his eyes, and imagine a scene where he discusses his ideas at a company meeting and receives enthusiastic praise from a vice-president. This procedure is repeated during subsequent interviews as well as assigned as homework between sessions. In addition, there are role-playing activities during the sessions in which the client delivers his talk to his colleagues and both client and therapist play various other parts: executives and coworkers who respond either positively or negatively to what they have heard. Client and therapist also have frank discussions about the possible risks and benefits that could result from the client's making his new proposals.

Finally, Arthur makes his own decision to take the plunge and present his suggestions for some changes in company procedures.

The prescribed imagery technique has helped to free him from his previous automatic anxiety reaction to any thought of presenting his ideas at a company meeting, because his tendency to assume a negative outcome has been undermined.

According to Maultsby (1975, p. 88), people do not see and react to actual external events but to the image of them that the brain makes in the neocortex. The brain does not automatically distinguish between images it makes of real external events and images it makes from the imagination or memory of old happenings. One can react to one's memory or imagined image of an event with as much intensity of emotion as to the actual event itself. For example, an individual can become very upset by a radio report of a tragic accident. Maultsby has his clients use what he calls "rational emotive imagery" to practice "correct" thinking, feeling, and acting. In his view, it is the brain's mental image, from whatever source, that controls emotional and physical reactions. He will therefore instruct people to imagine that they are systematically and repeatedly acting effectively and feeling calm in anxiety-provoking situations.

Arnold Lazarus (1976, pp. 37–38) describes imagery as various "mental pictures" that exert an influence upon our lives. He recommends using imagery as an aid in assessing a client's problems. He himself asks clients to picture three things in their mind: their childhood home, a tour from room to room in this childhood home, and a special safe place. He then probes for details, information about other people involved, and associated feelings. In general, Lazarus ascribes great importance to imagery:

> It must be stressed that image formation is a crucial component of thinking. In other words, cognitive processes involve various levels of construct formation, abstract reasoning, intentions, plans, decisions, expectancies, values, belief systems, internalized rules, and mental imagery—innumerable events, scenes, people, and places drawn from past ex-

perience. Any cognitive schema that ignores imagery is bound to be incomplete. [Lazarus, 1976, p. 90]

Blocks and bottlenecks

While the cognitive therapist fully understands the extent to which powerful emotions can immobilize a client or cause him to "freeze up" during a treatment interview, he handles such obstacles to the therapeutic process as problems in perception when they occur with adults. The woman who sees herself as trapped in a destructive marriage often blocks in facing up to the situation and creates a bottleneck in the treatment process by her inability to make a decision. Martha is a case in point.

Martha tells the therapist that life with her husband is intolerable. He is violent and abusive, shows no affection to herself or their two children, and tightly controls all the finances, barely giving her enough money to manage the household. She cannot go on like this any longer. The therapist wonders why she does not leave. Martha explains that, not having worked for several years, she has no confidence in her ability to find work and earn enough to support herself and the children. She is sure her husband will resist making any support payments and, in fact, fears his rage should she attempt to take the children and leave. The therapist comments that under the circumstances she may have to accept her situation for now and gradually prepare for making a break in the future. Martha insists that she cannot endure the marriage any longer and thereby creates an impasse in the treatment process: she sees herself as unable either to accept her situation or to change it, feels overwhelmed, and blocks at the therapist's suggestions for taking action on her own behalf. Actually she is hoping that the therapist will come up with an alternative solution that will not require her to make one of the two basic choices.

The therapist then helps the client to expand her perceptions about the current circumstances. If having a part-time job would make it possible for her to accept her situation for the present, the therapist encourages her to think in this direction, discusses how she might go about obtaining employment and day care for the children, and attempts to secure her agreement to take specific practical steps. It should be noted here that a basic principle of cognitive therapy with all clients is that nothing relieves anxiety as effectively as doing something specific. In connection with separating from her husband, another way that the therapist can contribute to expanding Martha's consciousness is to suggest that she consider living arrangements for the children other than staying with her, which might make such a move more feasible. He also informs her about agencies that can protect her safety.

In general, when there are blocks and bottlenecks in working with adolescents and adults, the cognitive therapist focuses on how the client's view of the situation has led him to conclude that he is trapped. The therapist and client then labor together to reevaluate the situation, with the objective of discovering possible ways out of the impasse not previously perceived by the client.

In those cases where the client realistically cannot make a constructive move for the time being, the therapist helps the client to face this. It is then the therapist's responsibility to reinforce the client's ability to hold on by encouraging his involvement in some activity, either serious or recreational, that will bring satisfaction and lessen feelings of frustration and inadequacy.

Half the battle in therapy is won when clients are able, in a courageous manner, to examine themselves and their behavior honestly and to recognize weaknesses and mistakes. Clients who cannot do this, who cannot take responsibility for their contribution to the problem, who need to place the entire blame on someone else, create another type of roadblock against therapeutic progress. The therapist needs to help such persons find the courage to grow, the willingness to face the pain associated with accepting one's humanness and one's human errors. It is at this point that a display of openness by the therapist through recounting examples of his own weaknesses and mistakes can have an effective impact.

Sometimes a client blocks and is unable to discuss a past event because it was so traumatic that the resulting fear or panic or guilt is still present to a high degree. The therapist does not press for immediate resolution of this impasse, which is different from the bottleneck created by indecision over difficult choices or by unwillingness or inability to recognize one's own mistakes. He waits for the time when the client's growing self-confidence and/or confidence in the therapist enables him to decide for himself to deal with this sensitive material. If such a decision does not materialize and coming to grips with the past event is essential for progress, the nonmedical cognitive therapist considers referral to a psychiatrist or other professional who can employ pharmacological or hypnotic techniques, or to a behaviorist practitioner who can try intensive relaxation and desensitization procedures.

Teodoro comes to see the therapist on orders from the court as a condition of being placed on probation. A married man with several children, he was found guilty of assault and battery against his wife during a fit of rage over some relatively minor matter. Referral for psychotherapy was made in the belief that Teodoro needed an opportunity to ventilate an inordinate amount of anger and work out more constructive ways of managing it in the future. In this case, the block to treatment arises out of Teodoro's vast sense of humiliation. Although there is no doubt that he committed physical violence against his wife, his perception and his private logic convince him that he has been victimized by the justice system and that his pride has been affronted. He was offered the alternatives of counseling or incarceration, so his attendance at the weekly therapeutic sessions is his grudging choice of the lesser of two evils. He lets the therapist know at the outset that he is coming under protest and has no intention of revealing his innermost feelings. They belong to him and he cannot possibly trust anyone sufficiently to reveal them.

The therapist deals with this kind of blocking by shifting gears. Client and therapist discover a mutual interest in opera and foreign languages, and the therapist maintains communication by focusing on these for a while. The client is also willing to talk about problems on the job and his youth in another country. At intervals, he tells the therapist that he is aware of what the therapist is doing—namely, shifting gears and eliciting his feelings in an indirect way. Teodoro also recognizes that despite his resolve to reveal nothing about his inner self, the therapist is learning to know him.

Blocking in young children usually assumes a different form. Sometimes it results from the child's insufficient mastery of language to find words for his anxieties and needs and resentments. Often a child who can verbalize nevertheless deliberately blocks therapeutic efforts by repeatedly insisting "I don't know" or "I don't care" when asked to explain his behavior or when advised that certain behavior may have unpleasant consequences. In either case, the cognitive therapist quickly shifts to nonverbal transactions and, in common with practitioners of most persuasions, provides the child with an opportunity to communicate through the use of play equipment, dolls, and puppets. For the youngster who is intimidated by a strange adult, it is often effective for the therapist to take the child out of doors to play baseball, throw a frisbee, or go for a walk. In this less artificial context, the child can arrive at an accurate perception of the therapist's good will and helpful intent more quickly, so that the blocking is overcome with less delay.

Traps for the therapist

The basic principle of cognitive theory that behavior is shaped primarily by perception applies not only to the client but also to the therapist. The cognitive practitioner always bears in mind that his reactions, attitudes, activities, verbalizations, and strategies during each treatment session reflect the way he "reads" the client at any particular moment. It is therefore very important for the therapist continually to review and reexamine his perceptions of the client, immediately modifying or changing them in the interests of greater accuracy when new data or insights call for such alterations. As part of this process, the therapist also tries to be on the alert for traps the client may set.

Some clients, doubting their own potential for functioning independently, try to prolong treatment beyond the point actually necessary. They maximize their helplessness and minimize their competencies, simultaneously insisting that they need the wisdom and security provided by the therapist for a while longer. The practitioner needs to be on guard against such seductions. The cognitist uses what Frances Scherz referred to as the concept of "sequential treatment": therapy is focused on a specific problem or set of problems, and when the client appears to have been helped sufficiently to manage on his own, he is encouraged to do so until another situation arises which he cannot handle alone. Enabling the client to let go may require diligent effort by the therapist to build up the client's courage and to remind him of past evidence of his adequacy. As a rule of thumb, the therapist does not offer less help than the client needs to master his problems, but neither does he offer more.

There are some clients who, having failed to reach certain objectives in their lives, defend themselves against the pain of a poor self-image by concluding that external factors were responsible. They do not allow themselves to consider their own contributions to their unhappy situation: poor planning, errors in judgment, lack of persistent effort, insufficient courage, limited talent or skill, alienating personality, or dearth of imagination. In treatment such individuals repeatedly ask the therapist for ideas and suggestions they can use in another attempt to reach those objectives, but they either reject such recommendations or, ostensibly accepting them, never carry them out. This may occur because they are afraid to try again and fail, or because success with the help of someone else will demonstrate that the source of previous difficulties was within themselves.

If the therapist continues to supply suggestions, he is caught in a trap. The way out is to help the client become strong enough to take full responsibility for his part in his underachievements. His previous efforts toward his goals are reviewed with him in detail and, gradually and sympathetically, the human shortcomings and mistakes which undermined his effectiveness are pointed out. The focus now is no longer on *what* the client might try in another attempt to achieve certain accomplishments. Instead, the therapeutic work concentrates on developing in the client accurate perceptions of strengths, weaknesses, and special talents and a realistic judgment as to which of his goals are within his capacity to reach. When inappropriate goals have been discarded and the client has started to think in terms of *how* best to use his particular combination of strengths and weaknesses to reach his objectives, deciding *what* to do may not present any major difficulty. If it does, the client is now ready to ask for suggestions from the therapist and accept them. He is no longer afraid to act because he has accepted responsibility for past mistakes and future ones. Having been faced with the ineffective ways in which he handled himself in the past, he is aware of pitfalls and has hopes of avoiding them.

Another trap for the therapist can be the one-dimensional presentation of the problem by the client. While he begins where the client is, the cognitive therapist always regards the client's description of his situation as the latter's unique, personal perception of events that is subject to distortion and limitation. Limitation sometimes takes the form of omission of certain facts that do not support the impression the client wishes to make. Although therapy must deal with the client's view of the world, the cognitive therapist is at all times actively engaged, with the client's permission, in assembling reports from other professionals and listening to other family members' versions of the problem. It is essential for the therapist to be able to measure the client's picture of his situation against objective, verifiable, or at least different material from other sources. Only in this way can the practitioner stay out of the trap that so many personal counselors on radio and in newspapers are falling into these days. It is quite alarming to observe these "experts" giving advice about problems on the basis of a statement phoned in or written in a letter by one person.

The final trap we shall discuss here has to do with the client's behavior during treatment sessions, which may be quite different from the way he conducts himself at home, school, work, or in the community. In Chapter 6 we mentioned the child who, while very troublesome outside the therapist's office, acts quite differently in the treatment sessions where his needs for attention and/or control are better met. The cognitive therapist looks upon most behavior as a psychosocial phenomenon, the reaction of an individual with a certain personality to his perception of a situation with certain characteristics. He is therefore careful not to judge the client's status or progress entirely by what he says or does in the office, although a change in attitude or behavior within the treatment setting can be significant. In the long run, what really counts is how the client deals with people, problems, and pressures in the real world, so the therapist guards against the trap of overestimating the client's gains on the basis of his behavior in a relatively safe, nonthreatening environment.

Incidentally, a client's display of less aggression, more honesty, more cooperation, or more self-control in the treatment session as compared to what he exhibits in his lifespace can have positive implications. Instead of indicating merely that his behavior in the therapist's office is atypical and not representative of his real-life conduct, it may also give evidence of an unsuspected potential for more constructive behavior under favorable circumstances. An example of this is the child who is hyperactive because of a physiological condition (Minimal Brain Dysfunction) and hard to manage in a very stimulating school setting. This same youngster in a subdued treatment setting may have greater self-control, and knowledge of this can be quite useful to educators and physicians in determining educational and medical strategies.

The fear of success

It is unfortunate that some teen-agers hold back on working to the best of their ability in school. They have a genuine fear of success. The well-recognized crucial importance of peer opinion at this age has a destructive effect on some young people whose immediate subculture devalues academic excellence. The leaders of that subculture, those who set the tone, may themselves be academically limited, hostile to authority in general, or driven by other motivations. Whatever the particular dynamics may be, the net result is the creation of an atmosphere in which doing well on school examinations, being prepared and participating in class, and receiving good report cards are regarded by the group as the mark of a teacher's pet, a sissy (in the case of boys), a square, or someone who has surrendered to the establishment.

The cognitive therapist seeking to help a bright adolescent who is doing poorly in school sets himself quite a task. In addition to academic underachievement, the young person may also have been influenced to exhibit acting-out behavior to prove that he or she is tough and one of the crowd. In essence, the problem is that of a person who has decided not to be all that he or she is capable of becoming. The client's perception is that the payoff for holding back is greater than it would be for working up to maximum ability. The therapist, by all the means at his disposal, tries to counterbalance the influence of the subculture and convince the client that one of the greatest satisfactions in life is the feeling that one is using all one's capacities. Making certain that the boy or girl realizes the practical advantages of a successful school career may be of some help, but more helpful than that is assisting the youngster to enter another circle of peers where scholastic and intellectual activity is valued. Otherwise the youngster is being asked to break away from his original group and to cope with the pressures it may exert on him without any sense of belonging anywhere and without emotional support from anyone his own age.

Fear of success is also found in individuals who do not wish to grow up, get promoted on the job, or admit recovery from a physical or emotional injury or illness. The common denominator here appears to be a reluctance to leave a situation where one is comfortable for a situation where additional demands will be made. The child (or adult) who does not wish to grow up is unwilling to take on more chores, tasks, and responsibilities either because he fears he will fail to accomplish them or because he wants to avoid a change that will make life less convenient and require more effort from him. Some individuals do not seek job promotions for similar reasons. Those who maneuver to remain at the hospital or at home in the role of a patient longer than their physical illness warrants, as well as those who find it hard to terminate psychotherapy, minimize the extent of their recovery because it is difficult for them to give up their "secondary gains": greatly increased concern, attention, or pampering from those close to them; a sense of security created by their regular contacts with health and mental health professionals; and/or the taking over by the family of their daily tasks and problems as long as they are considered to be incapacitated.

Again, what is at work in these cases is the client's perception that standing still pays off better than moving ahead.

His concept of success is not the same as that of the cognitive therapist, who defines a successful person as one who has found a way to function at his maximum potential. For these clients, success seems to mean the avoidance of pain, pressure, and inconvenience. The therapeutic task, by exposing the client to new ideas and experiences, is to help him redefine his concept of success. As we have stated before, the client's goals flow out of his definition of success, and his goals are one of the types of thinking that shape his behavior. Only when the client can begin to view success as involving risk will he set goals for himself that call for movement, reaching out, and taking on more responsibility.

A common reference in the literature has been the so-called "dependent personality," an individual presumed to have a deeply rooted pattern of depending too much on other people and consequently being unable to function in an independent fashion. We do not make use of this concept here in our discussion of people who fear success because it appears to this writer to be too static a notion. To us it does not seem helpful to ascribe overdependent behavior to a "dependent personality" because this is a tautological construction. While many of our clients do exhibit habitual, repetitive behavior of this sort, we do not think the label serves a useful purpose. Regardless of how we classify such clients, cognitive treatment in each case involves discovering those perceptions of the individual which have kept him from functioning as a person in his own right. As inaccurate perceptions of himself, others, and his world are examined and modified, and as more autonomous ways of dealing with realistic conclusions are explored, it is possible for a habitually nonindependent individual to change.

Fear of success often becomes evident in working with marital problems. A wife, previously dominated by a husband who restricted her to a mother-housekeeper-sex-object role, is beginning with professional help to assert herself and to insist on the freedom to take a job and get involved in community activities. She observes that, as she grows stronger and more independent, her spouse becomes more tense and unhappy. She expresses concern that her growth is straining the marital relationship. The therapist agrees that this may be true and points out that the former state of balance in any marriage is likely to be upset when one partner changes and the other does not. The client begins to question whether or not she wants to continue in psychotherapy, since her success may threaten her marriage.

In such cases, the husband's participation in the therapy may enable him to accept the changes in his wife and to grow with her. What happens very frequently, however, is that the man has been opposed to his wife's obtaining counseling in the first place, sees nothing wrong with the way the marriage used to function, and will not come anywhere near a "shrink." The client is then left with a very difficult decision: to grow or not to grow. The choice must be hers. If she is willing to accept the risks involved in moving ahead, the therapist supports her efforts, simultaneously letting the husband know of his availability should the husband wish to talk to him in person or via telephone. As can be seen, in this instance the fear of success (functioning at maximum potential) occurs in two variations: the husband fears his wife's success, and the wife fears her own.

Termination

The cognitive therapist brings up the matter of terminating treatment under one of the following circumstances:

1. A specific number of sessions, agreed upon in advance, will soon be completed;
2. Objectives, formulated jointly by client and therapist, have been attained;

3. Objectives have not been attained but are close enough for the client to reach on his own;
4. Objectives do not seem to be attainable in this agency or with this therapist;
5. Objectives are still not within reach, do seem to be attainable in this setting, but the client has been in treatment a long time and needs a "rest" from therapy to reduce the risk of "overdependency" and "addiction."

Twenty years ago a mental health center or a family service agency that stipulated in advance how many interviews a client would receive met with criticism or deep skepticism from most other professionals. Today this is a commonplace practice dictated by necessity: many agencies do not have enough staff to provide open-ended treatment for everyone accepted at intake. The general public has become very aware of the value of professional counseling and the demand for it has increased tremendously in the last two decades. While the provision of open-ended treatment may pose no problem for the private psychotherapist, a large number of agencies would soon find themselves with a long waiting list if they did not set some kind of time limit on their services as a matter of policy, with exceptions made when indicated. Other organizations, because of the characteristics of their clientele or of the help they provide, normally furnish a short-term service anyhow and have no need to promulgate a formal rule. There are some professionals who advocate preplanned short-term treatment as the therapy of choice without any reference to logistical problems involving waiting lists, staff shortages, or economics.

It has become clear that effectiveness of treatment has nothing to do with duration of treatment. This point was strongly confirmed by the well-known research study conducted by Reid and Shyne (1969), in which cases assigned to a service limited to eight interviews after intake showed consistently better outcomes at termination of service than cases assigned to an open-ended service. In this project, carried out jointly by caseworkers and researchers, the predetermined time limits seemed to motivate the clients and their workers to come to grips with specific essential problems more quickly, since both knew they had a deadline to meet. The workers were also prompted to use more direct methods to stimulate client change. This writer observed similar results during many years of seeing large numbers of clients for a maximum of ten sessions and supervising other therapists who did likewise.

For the cognitive therapist, when a predetermined number of sessions is not part of the treatment plan, the suggestion to terminate is based on the status of the client in relation to his original objectives. When both can agree that these objectives have been reached, there is little doubt as to the appropriateness of ending. When objectives have not been attained but, in the therapist's view, are close enough for the client to reach on his own, the client may resist termination if he lacks confidence or courage. The disagreement then needs to be negotiated and resolved, sometimes via a compromise whereby the therapist promises the client that he can return to treatment immediately if he tries to manage on his own and finds that he cannot. Another kind of compromise might be an offer by the therapist to extend treatment for a fixed number of additional interviews, after which termination is definite. In general, as we noted before, *every* client is told that the door is never closed to anyone and that he can always return in the future.

When objectives do not seem to be attainable in this agency or with this therapist, the therapist discusses his conclusion with the client in an open and frank manner. Even though the client or therapist or both may be uncomfortable, it is important to work out a mutually agreeable formulation of what contributed to the bottleneck. This is in keeping with the cognitive doctrine that every situation in the treatment process be perceived as realistically as possible by all participants. An accurate understanding of why objectives originally thought to be feasible turned out otherwise will help both client and therapist in the future. If either the client or the therapist or the agency did not fulfill their responsibilities, or if the client's history of himself or his situation was misleading or incomplete, or if either person found the other's personality irritating or unacceptable, such matters are brought up directly by one or the other. A mutually agreeable decision is made that may call for terminating completely at this agency or transferring to another staff member within the same organization. (See case vignette on p. 94.) If termination is the result, the therapist is obligated to refer the client to an appropriate resource and to check to be sure that contact is made, contingent of course upon the client's acceptance of the referral. The cognitive therapist in a private practice setting, with appropriate modifications, follows the same procedure.

Among circumstances that prompt the therapist to consider termination, the final one involves the client who, after a series of interviews, has not made much progress toward achieving the agreed upon objectives. The goals are still believed to be within the capability of the client to reach with the present therapist, but he or she has been in treatment for a considerable amount of time, has become comfortable, and perhaps is equating attendance at the weekly sessions as his or her full share of the treatment work. A vacation from therapy at this point can jolt such individuals out of their inactivity by delivering a message that treatment calls for active self-help and completing homework assignments between interviews, that interviews are not available just for a fee but also need to be earned by therapeutic effort, and that the client cannot expect to use the interviews merely for catharsis and ventilation. A prime purpose of the weekly session is to review what the client has *done* in the previous seven days and to plan for more things that the client can *do*. The vacation prescribed for such individuals is a temporary termination: treatment can resume when the client contacts the therapist with evidence of having confronted fears, tried new experiences, or attempted new ways of relating to others as previously discussed in therapy.

Some theorists and practitioners have written about the guilt that clients feel upon separating from their therapists at the end of treatment. This has not occurred in the writer's experience. As was previously described, the cognitive therapist and his client discuss what their roles will be in the treatment process at the very beginning of their relationship. Emphasis is placed on the two of them working as partners to reach mutually accepted goals in the shortest time possible. The cognitist advances the idea that the client's chief obligation is to become the best and fullest kind of person he can be, which includes the ability to be true to one's self and to function independently to achieve one's own goals. Any obligation the client may have toward the therapist is formulated in terms of meeting his responsibilities for dependability in attendance, openness in their discussions, and reliability in carrying out homework assignments.

When a client who has reached his treatment goals feels guilty about terminating the relationship with the therapist, we must presume that such guilt was instilled by the therapist. In cognitive therapy, the occasion when a client feels ready to move on and manage his life by himself is cause for celebration. It would seem unlikely that the humanistic type of relationship which the cognitist develops with his client would create any guilt at the time of leaving. The temporary regret or sadness that we all feel when saying goodbye to a friend would be the most probable emotion.

In cognitive treatment, termination of any type is accompanied by a final evaluation, which can be formal or informal. It may be written into the case record in addition to being conveyed orally to the client. The client's reactions to the therapist's statement, his comments and disagreements, are discussed fully and given serious consideration. In essence, the final evaluation consists of the practitioner's telling the client the following:

1. His judgment as to the extent to which treatment goals have been achieved;
2. His impression of changes in the client's perceptions, emotions, and behavior; and
3. His estimate as to how much progress toward his maximum potential the client has made.

More objective evaluations, suitable for research use or for a social agency studying outcome trends, are discussed in Chapter 10.

The final aspect of termination is planning for a follow-up. This is usually done in connection with a formal research project and is less likely to take place in a normal course of therapy. Most professionals and agencies are under too much pressure to undertake this additional chore. In principle, however, it can be fairly stated that a follow-up procedure (phone call, face-to-face interview, or mailed questionnaire) at a specified time following the last interview can yield important and perhaps surprising information about the more permanent results of therapeutic intervention.

Chapter 8

Cognitive Approaches in Group and Family Therapy

The last three chapters have described in detail how this writer applies cognitive theory to the practice of individual psychotherapy. That theory is equally applicable to group and family treatment, being not only compatible but useful in providing a point of view about the nature of those processes and the role of the practitioner.

Group and family treatment will be discussed separately in this chapter because their clients are so different that each of these two modalities has a distinct nature. The individuals who come together for a group therapy sequence are unrelated people whose admission to the group is by decision of the leader on the basis of predetermined criteria: diagnostic classification, a certain kind of problem, a particular age range, or whatever. Family therapy, as its name specifies, is conducted with a group of closely related individuals, usually parents and children but sometimes including additional relatives, for the purpose of improving the functioning of the family as a unit. In group therapy, the professional leader's intent is to help each individual member through the group. In family therapy, the focus of therapeutic effort is on those relationships and forces which are damaging to the family's stability and have impelled a spokesperson to seek help.

Group therapy

Since a therapy group, unlike a family, does not exist prior to the start of treatment but has to be formed on the basis of certain predetermined criteria, the cognitive therapist will evaluate each prospective group member in much the same way as he would an individual client (see Chapter 6). Before deciding whether or not to accept a person into a group, the therapist needs to formulate the nature of the candidate's problem, a specific diagnosis when necessary, his strengths and weaknesses, goals, reality perceptions, lifestyle, and mental status. Using the procedures outlined in Chapter 6, the therapist can gather the data needed to make tentative judgments about these aspects of the client's functioning, the extent to which he meets the criteria for admission, and his ability to benefit from this particular group experience.

The various applications of cognitive theory to individual treatment, as described in Chapters 5, 6, and 7, can with minor modifications be utilized in conducting a therapy group. It is our contention that cognitive theory is valid for all kinds of groups—recently divorced or separated adults, adolescents unhappy at home, phobic individuals, etc.—and our discussion will focus on general principles appropriate for any type. It is not the purpose of this chapter to examine the possible criteria and methods for setting up therapeutic groups: we shall assume that the group members have been selected and sessions are ready to start.

THE GROUP THERAPIST'S INTRODUCTION OF HIMSELF AND HIS TREATMENT APPROACH

The cognitive therapist discusses the main elements of the cognitive approach with the group in the same way as he would with an individual client. In addition, he indicates the special responsibility that each person has as a member of the group: to help the others. The therapist affirms his willingness to provide the assistance group members cannot give each other when this is possible because of his professional training, experience, or capacity to be more objective than they can be. He points out that although each group member has problems, the distribution of strengths and weaknesses varies from person to person, so that at least one group member is likely to have some strength in an area where others are weak. The therapist emphasizes that group therapy is a cooperative process in which each participant's problem is publicly defined so that the others all know his needs. The greatest contributions any group member can make to the progress of another are to challenge inaccurate perceptions and modify them in the direction of greater realism, give another the courage to face what is being destructively avoided, or by his own example of openness enable a fellow member to articulate unexpressed emotions that drain his energy and undermine his functioning.

Since accurate perception of one's self, one's world, and other people is the primary goal of cognitive treatment, together with the ability to take realistic action on one's own behalf, the therapist stresses the importance of the sharing of experiences by group members, honest appraisals of each other, and holding each other to promises of action that are made at group sessions. He recognizes the special values of the group situation and utilizes them in the interests of the members whenever possible: the fact that challenges to thinking or behavior are more effective when they emanate from several peers than from the therapist alone; the opportunity for a member to discover that he is not alone with his guilt or anger or fear or weaknesses; the potential of the group to restore a member's sense of worth by its acceptance of that individual; and the suitability of the group as a place to practice new behaviors and get feedback from both peers and therapist.

USING THE GROUP EXPERIENCE AS
A PREPARATION FOR LIFE

The cognitive therapist may assign his individual client "homework" to be carried out in the latter's home, place of work, or various social settings. In individual treatment, rehearsing for life (e.g., confronting one's boss) may also take place in the therapist's office in the form of role playing, practicing self-assertion, or visualizing positive imagery.

The group offers distinct advantages in connection with rehearsals for real-life situations. The simulated practice situations that one sets up for a single client are replaced in group therapy by much more natural experiences in which several other real people participate. The group process, in an uncontrived way, often brings its members to the point of trying out new behaviors in the group because of confrontations that develop or as a result of encouragement by peers. A client who tries out new behaviors in the group does so in the therapist's presence so that the therapist can observe directly and need not depend on the client's account of what transpired elsewhere.

Margaret was the most reserved member of her therapy group. Gradually she became more at ease and after a while appeared to be ready to speak up about her own problems and viewpoints. Bernard, however, a very controlling individual, was at this time making efforts to dominate the sessions by talking at great length. Most of the other members were able to break in and take the floor when they wished, but Margaret was unable to do this. She finally complained to the therapist that Bernard was making it hard for anyone else to get a word in. The therapist could easily have silenced Bernard and turned the floor over to Margaret, but such a tactic would have deprived Margaret of the opportunity to search inside herself for the courage and strength necessary to develop a new kind of behavior. Instead, the therapist encouraged Margaret to state her complaint directly to Bernard. With the encouragement of the group, Margaret was able to carry this off, and in subsequent sessions was increasingly more assertive and quite successful in dealing with Bernard's power drives.

Very often, group members can give each other insights, information, and understanding based on shared experiences which are simply not possible for the therapist to provide.

In a women's group conducted by a male therapist, Helen was quite depressed. She was pregnant with her fifth child, which was due in two months, and was very unhappy because she and her husband had not planned this pregnancy. Helen's four other children were now old enough for her to have been looking forward to increased freedom from household tasks and obligations. The unforeseen prospect of a new baby shattered these expectations and threw Helen off balance. Another group member, Rose, reached out to Helen and told her that, thirteen years ago, she had been upset and angry about her own fourth pregnancy. Today, her teenaged daughter is her closest friend and she rejoices every day that she had this child. Helen was very moved by the deep feelings that Rose shared with her.

FOSTERING SOCIAL INTEREST
THROUGH THE GROUP EXPERIENCE

As we stated in the previous chapter, the cognitist regards social interest, an attitude of cooperation with others for the common good, as a significant influence on human behavior. The degree to which a client possesses or does not possess social interest strongly shapes what he thinks and does. We pointed out further that this quality—a community feeling, a desire to live cooperatively with others, a sense of responsibility to society—cannot be directly inculcated in anyone but must grow out of a person's own experiences.

Group therapy can be one of the experiences that fosters or restores social interest, and the cognitive therapist bears this in mind. There are, for example, individuals who, thinking they have been hurt by others or rejected by society, become self-centered loners, hoping to avoid further pain by disengagement from the world around them. When such people find their way into a therapy group, they observe the friendship and support that the members give to each other and the resulting benefits. Such observations often can undermine the isolation of those who lack social interest.

Sam came into a therapy group at the insistence of a child protective agency. While not a child abuser in the strict sense of the term, he was very rough in the way he handled his three small children, and his wife had asked the agency to intervene. Sam was a physically strong individual, short in stature, who had a sharp mind, and was very knowledgeable about auto mechanics. Despite this, both society and he himself regarded him as a failure. He was a high school dropout, having found formal learning very difficult and lacked the self-discipline to persist. A quick temper contributed to problems both at school and in the world of work. His employment history was extremely uneven and fragmented. He had held many jobs in factories and auto service stations but did not stay long at most of them: he would either quit or be fired after arguments with his employers, usually precipitated by his tendency to be offended easily and by his conviction that everyone was trying to take advantage of him.

Sam's life experiences and short physical stature combined to make him a person who, at age thirty-five, was preoccupied with proving to the world and to himself that he was really a man and not someone to be trifled with. He had no patience with his young children and no ability to help them with their growth, since he had not solved his own problems in that areas. In addition, dominating them by harshness and intimidation perhaps counterbalanced part of the tremendous inadequacy he felt in the work situation. When he entered the group, Sam's primary focus was on himself. He had no close friends, his marital relationship was strained, and he was certain that society was dead set against him and not about to give him any breaks. Therefore, it was himself against the world. He used belligerence and aggressiveness to keep others from putting him down. On weekends, he went off to a track to drive a midget racing car, the only part of his life that gave him feelings of competence and manliness and some social contacts.

In his initial group sessions, Sam made it clear that he had not come voluntarily, had no intention of getting deeply involved, and did not believe the group could help him in any way. Gradually, however, he began to tell the others about himself. He revealed a surprisingly keen intelligence and wit, which delighted the group, and he responded to their appreciation. Additional bonds were created between him and others when he discussed his auto racing and members at each session asked whether he had won over the past weekend. Originally, Sam had declared that he had no suggestions to offer about problems brought up by various individuals, but as time went on he began to make some very practical, realistic comments based on his own encounters with life.

A few months later, Sam was fully involved with the group and feeling a sense of responsibility for helping others. He formed some strong friendships which continued outside the group, with people phoning him or meeting him to talk over problems. He in turn began to ask others for help in relating to his children more constructively, and listened to their ideas for more desirable ways of handling them. He was able to get a government grant to receive special technical training in a field with good employment opportunities. His application for these funds came about after several sessions of intense discussion with the group about the value of education, his attitude about the establishment, his doubts about himself, and his problems with interpersonal relationships in the work setting.

Shortly after, when Sam was about to move out of the area, he came for his final session. The man who had been a loner without social feeling, as he said goodbye, was embraced by all the women in the group and left with the respect of all the men.

Family therapy

Family therapy began around 1950 and is now considered a specialized field with its own spectrum of theories. An outstanding feature characterizing many of these theories is their departure from traditional concepts of human behavior that were originally developed to explain individual functioning. Some leading American family therapists have commented that traditional theories were unsatisfactory as a guide for understanding family dynamics and needed to be augmented or replaced by new conceptual frameworks. It is of special interest to the cognitist that these new theories are congruent to a considerable degree with cognitive principles and approaches.

Bell has stated the following:

> I tried applying psychoanalytic theory, but I found that its ideas and the interpretations to which they led lacked relevance for some of the behavior that was the special concern of family treatment. . . . In family group therapy the primary data to analyze relate to the interactions among the members of the family. In individual therapy one turns his attention more to the symbolic evidence of intrapsychic events. . . . But in family therapy we are not so much concerned with family members as individuals. By conscious intent we think of the family as an organic whole, individuals taking on their definition only as structural parts of the family field.
>
> . . . If we regard the family as a unit, it is as justifiable to consider what the child does to the parents as it is to consider what the parents do to the child. Because psychoanalysis has emphasized the importance of early childhood and its genetic processes in personality formation, there has grown up a tendency to ask about the nature of the parent in relation to the child, to single out the more significant influences of the parent on the child that occur at particular stages of child development. . . .
>
> In family group therapy it is not possible to empathize with a child to the extent of evaluating the parents only from his perspective. To do so would lead to thinking of the parent primarily in terms of his contribution to his child's pathology. It is not hard to see how parents would be of-

fended at being reminded that the sins of the fathers are visited upon the children. In family therapy we have to think, also, that the sins of the children are visited on the parents. [Bell, 1961, pp. 48-49]

Zuk (1972) discusses how the family as a system often resists the therapist's efforts to change it. In his view, change takes place as a result of negotiations between the therapist and family members, rather than as a result of working through individual unconscious transference distortions in family relationships. He does not engage in the exploration of unconscious processes or attempt to reconstruct the historical sequence of pathology. Instead, his approach calls for observing the sources of leverage and power in the present situation, regarding disturbance as a result of interaction with others, and studying the treatment process as a series of negotiations between family and therapist, with the focus on here and now.

Weakland, whose approach to family therapy is based on a communicational view of behavior, is another family theorist who found it necessary to reexamine traditional ideas about human functioning:

> Put bluntly, a sizable part of our work on communication now appears related to digging ourselves out of individual-centered, depth-psychological views of behavior, problems, and therapy in which we originally were imbedded, rather than to any elaborate creation of new views. . . .
>
> The two central ideas [of the communicational view] of equal importance and closely interrelated—from which all else logically flows are: 1) that specific behavior of all kinds is primarily an outcome or function of communicative interaction within a social system; and 2) that "problems" consist of persisting undesired behavior. [Weakland, 1976, p. 121]

Weakland has spelled out the implications of the communicational view of behavior. Many of these are an integral part of the cognitive orientation. We now summarize some of his basic assumptions (Weakland, 1976, pp. 122–123). Weakland points out that his view puts an emphasis on observable communication—statements and actions—in the here and now. The kinds of problems that people bring to therapists are seen as matters of difficult or deviant interpersonal behavior that is currently persisting or worsening. To ask what is wrong with a particular individual is not the appropriate question. The relevant question is what is going on in the system of interaction (family, school, work, etc.) that produces the behavior labeled as a problem by the client or others. The common concern of many treatment approaches over what the *underlying* problem is also is not considered relevant by Weakland. If behavior is seen as primary, the "tip of the iceberg" idea no longer makes sense; the main focus of treatment is the behavior that is being complained of or labeled as requiring change. Feelings or past traumatic experience are not neglected but are considered in relation to present behavior and dealt with by appropriate changes in that behavior.

The search for a root or original cause of any problem is foreign to the communicational view, as is the belief that the "cause" corresponds in magnitude to the presenting problem. From a cybernetic view, which is implicit in a communicational approach, attention is focused on the structure of the system of interaction, on the feedback that takes place, on the behaviors which are reinforcing the client's problem, and on how the system dealt with the precipitating event or difficulty to transform it into the problem brought to the therapist. From this approach, it can be understood how large effects can readily arise from initial events of minor importance through a process of snowballing and vicious circles, whereby difficulties of everyday life are repeatedly mishandled until a pattern of behavior develops which maintains and increases the original difficulty. For example, Weakland refers to a person who says "isolation" is a problem, and comments that it is highly pertinent to consider how he behaves to avoid other people and to keep them from making contact with him. The focus is not on any original precipitating event, which in the author's experience can be a relatively minor social rejection.

Weakland asserts that, for the therapist, the central question is not how problems originate but how they organize and persist. Problems consist of behavior; they exist only in continuous or repeated performance. Treatment centers on matters open to current inquiry, with a minimum of inference about unobservable past or intrapsychic events.

> The resolution of problems correspondingly appears as primarily requiring a change of the problem-maintaining behaviors so as to interrupt the vicious positive feedback circles, and the therapist's main task as promoting such changes. Such alternative behaviors are always potentially open to the patient and other members of the system, but ordinarily it is not possible for them to change their usual but unsuccessful problem-solving behaviors on their own; those who can, do so, and therefore do not reach our offices. The therapist's job, accordingly, is to find and apply means of intervention that will help them make such changes, and the test of both specific interventions and the general approach is highly pragmatic: Do beneficial changes occur? [Weakland, 1976, p. 123]

Finally, Weakland describes five procedures he uses in family treatment that completely coincide with cognitive methods. He asks direct questions of clients to get a clear statement of presenting complaints and their order of importance. He asks in a similarly concrete way what clients are doing to try to handle their problems, the assumption being that problems persist only if they are somehow maintained by other behavior—i.e., their efforts to deal with their troubles. Thirdly, all parties are asked to state their minimal goal of treatment, the premise being that a small but significant change can initiate a beneficient circle, while pursuing vague or global goals is apt to produce uncertainty and frustration. Next, it is important for the therapist to decide who is the main client, the person who most wants to see real change in the problem situation. Lastly, Weakland attempts as soon as possible to grasp each client's "language"—the ideas and values that appear to be central to him. He believes that the therapist must perceive and utilize existing motivations and beliefs. It is then the therapist's aim, based on the goals that have been formulated, to interdict the problem-maintaining behaviors he perceives and to promote the substitution of opposite behaviors (Weakland, 1976, pp. 125–126).

The following case illustrates the efforts of a cognitive therapist to bring about changes in a family on the basis of goals formulated by the parents. The therapist, in the family interviews described, tries to persuade its members to behave differently, stop protecting each other, and avoid deceiving themselves and each other.

Mr. and Mrs. Gerard have brought their sixteen-year-old son, Alex, to a cognitive therapist. Mrs. Gerard is the boy's stepmother. Until a year ago, Alex lived with his natural mother for several years following his parents' divorce. The natural mother never remarried but pursued a career instead, in the process leaving Alex mostly on his own without supervision. Alex became an undisciplined adolescent who was used to doing things his own way and to having a minimum of household responsibilities. Behavior problems developed and it was decided to have him live with his father and stepmother.

After a year, the Gerards sought family therapy because Alex, a bright young man, was making no effort in school, getting drunk on alcohol, and refusing to do a minimal amount of chores at home. During the treatment sessions, the parents stated their concerns and with the help of the therapist negotiated an agreement whereby Alex would apply himself in school, stay away from beer and wine, and do his share of household tasks. In return, the boy would receive certain privileges and freedoms that he wanted. Alex, however, did not carry out his part of the arrangement.

In a subsequent session, Alex transmitted nonverbal messages that he really had no intention of changing. The therapist perceived these messages but the father, because the boy did not state his true feelings outright, found it possible to convince himself that Alex might still come around to holding up his end of the contract. At this point, it appeared that the stepmother realized Alex's real attitude but was saying nothing to protect him from his father's anger. The therapist decided to bring everything out into the open, and stated that it seemed clear that Alex did not like the agreement he had previously accepted and was not going to carry it out. Alex did not deny this. Mr. Gerard became furious, grabbed Alex roughly by the arm, and pulled him out of the office. They argued violently in the street in front of the building. Later that day, Alex left home and hitch-hiked to another state where his natural mother was living. Subsequently, arrangements were made for Alex to return to the Gerards, but under very specific conditions which included the stipulations of the original agreements.

Cognitive treatment with another family illustrates the cognitive/humanist emphasis on openness, confrontation, and providing clients with opportunities to develop courage, take risks, and reexamine the patterns of their lives.

Bobby and Ann Henderson are ten-year-old twins, both bright and charming children, who are coming to family therapy with their parents because they lie to their mother about various incidents of minor misconduct in which they become involved. In this particular session, the children are first seen together without the parents. Bobby explains that he avoids admitting any mischief to his mother because her usual reaction is to yell and lecture him interminably. Ann agrees and adds that they will always tell the truth to their father. The therapist wonders about this. With great hesitation and tears in her eyes, Ann finally blurts out that she is physically afraid of her father, while her mother's behavior is merely unpleasant. The therapist suggests that they talk about their feelings to their parents later on in the session. Both children are very reluctant. The therapist says he can understand their hesitation but, as a parent himself, he knows that their father and mother are unhappy when they see how uneasy Bobby and Ann are. The therapist would want his own children to come to him with anything that bothered them, including complaints, because in the end everybody in the family would benefit. He himself has felt bad in the past when his children were worried and he did not know why.

The children agree to tell their parents how they really feel. Mr. and Mrs. Henderson join the group and the therapist sets the scene. Bobby talks about how he dreads his mother's nagging, and to his surprise she concedes the justice of his criticism and promises she will try to avoid this in the future, while still reserving the right to penalize him for any misconduct. Ann, with an intense effort, tells her father that she does not lie to him because she is terribly afraid of him, and then bursts into tears. Mr. Henderson, who is an athletic type devoted to all kinds of sports, is taken aback. He takes Ann into his arms and comforts her, assuring her that he loves her very much. He explains that he has always favored a tough approach with children to prepare them for the game of life and admits that he deliberately chose to inculcate in his children a "little" fear of him. He did not realize that he evidently went too far, to the point where he frightens his daughter. Very serious and thoughtful, Mr. Henderson says that he has a lot of thinking to do.

The therapist encourages the parents to examine how they are functioning as a team. What has emerged from this session is that the children were caught between a mother whose scolding made her unapproachable and a father with whom they could relate but only at considerable emotional cost.

To sum up, the application of a cognitive orientation to family therapy results in dealing with clients as integral parts of a structure. Relationships between parents and children are regarded as two-way streets. The cognitist focuses on the here and now and on observable interactions, with a minimum of inference or speculation about unobservable events. Disturbance is considered to be the result of interaction with others. Change takes place in response to negotiations between family members and the therapist, encouragement by the therapist to try new behaviors, and new perceptions that arise out of the family encounters.

Chapter 9

Case Illustrations of Cognitive Concepts

A humanistic approach to treatment is best clarified by human illustrations. Although case material has been included in the foregoing chapters, in this chapter we shall restate cognitive concepts and illustrate them with additional case examples.

Cognitive concepts may be divided into two categories: assumptions about why people behave as they do (personality theory) and actual psychotherapeutic techniques to be used in the individual or group interview (treatment theory). In this chapter, various assumptions and techniques will be listed, each one followed by brief supporting case material. There will also be more extensive and detailed accounts of therapy with clients which exemplify the application of several cognitive concepts to a single treatment case.

Assumptions

THE CLIENT LARGELY
DETERMINES HIS OWN LIFE

Twelve-year-old Augustus, whenever he is rude, loses his temper, lies, or shirks his chores, insists that he really wants to improve but cannot help himself. Spoiled by his father when his parents lived together, he now resides with his fifteen-year-old sister and his divorced mother. The father has remarried and moved to another part of the country and is virtually out of the picture.

The boy's mother does not indulge him the way his father did, and Augustus found it difficult to accept this change in his status. He became resistant and defiant to his mother. On the other hand, his sister, always cooperative and easy to manage, continued to be a source of great satisfaction for the mother, who understandably was more attentive and more kindly disposed toward her than she was to Augustus.

Currently, the boy is very jealous of his sister and is able to admit this. His mother deals firmly with his resistance to chores, dishonesty, and cruel behavior toward his sister. Despite loss of privileges and other inconveniences, Augustus persists in his self-defeating behavior, continuing to claim that he would like to do better but is overpowered by forces beyond his control.

The cognitive therapist assumes that the boy is behaving precisely as he wishes to, that in his anger toward both his mother and sister he has set himself the goal of punishing them. His behavior is shaped by his goal, and the satisfaction he derives from upsetting them is for him worth the penalties or inconveniences that result. Treatment in part will consist of disputing the client's contention that he wants to change, facing him with the fact that he wishes to act as he does, and insisting that Augustus has the power to change his behavior when he changes his goal.

THOUGHT SHAPES BEHAVIOR

Dorothy is a forty-year-old, married woman with children who is depressed. Her husband, because of his own needs, keeps her in a subordinate position, is continually critical, and opposes her becoming involved in any activities outside the home. The therapist is interested in why she continues to accept this state of affairs and takes the position that the way she thinks is maintaining the way she behaves. The client soon reveals that, a long time ago, she made a generalization from a traumatic incident in her distant past that is still operant. The conclusion she reached in her childhood was that she was unloved and of no value, and this perception has persisted up to the present, causing her to believe that such a worthless person as herself has no right to stand up to her husband or to make any demands.

Twenty-eight years ago, at age twelve, Dorothy was living with her widowed mother and several siblings. It was necessary for her mother, who had contracted tuberculosis, to spend some time at a sanitarium. The children were distributed among several relatives for temporary living arrangements, except for Dorothy. Having run out of available relatives, her mother placed her in an orphanage. Dorothy could never stop asking herself, from that day until the present, why her brothers and sisters were able to stay with family while she alone was sent to an institution. Her answer to herself was that for her mother to do such a thing, her mother must have regarded her as worthless and did not love her. In treatment twenty-eight years later, Dorothy tells the therapist she still views herself as having no value, unworthy of being loved, and therefore compelled to be satisfied with her current lot.

It should come as no surprise that the judgments made about us by significant others, both valid and invalid, exert a powerful influence on our lives. Equally powerful are our own interpretations, both valid and invalid, of the attitudes of significant others. In this case, Dorothy's own perception of her mother's motives has colored most of her life. To help Dorothy overcome the depression which has been triggered by her belief that she is trapped, the therapist will help her to reexamine the conclusions she drew about her mother's actions twenty-eight years ago. If she can see her mother's behavior in a different light, some of her negative self-image may be undermined. If not, the next therapeutic task is to reeducate Dorothy to understand that her value as a person is not determined by what her mother did nearly thirty years ago. In addition, the therapist should attempt to alter some of the husband's destructive behavior. All these approaches have the objective of changing Dorothy's view of herself as worthless and having no right to assert herself; if she can be freed to take action on her own behalf, she will simultaneously be on the way out of her depression.

AGGRESSION IS A POTENTIAL RESPONSE, NOT AN INSTINCTUAL DRIVE

Cognitists deny that aggression is an inborn urge that must be continually satisfied; instead, they view it as one kind of response that humans can make to their circumstances. The case against its being an instinct is that it is not universal, since there are nonviolent cultures. We subscribe rather to Alfred Adler's belief that people can be trained in either direction, that is, to be aggressive or nonaggressive. Individuals who have developed aggressive patterns of behavior can give them up when an important new goal or change in goal requires it, with psychic benefit rather than psychic harm to themselves.

Joe Carter, a married man with two active sons aged eight and ten, modeled himself after his father when it came to his role in the family. In relating to his wife and children, for whom he genuinely cared, he frequently displayed temper and impatience. When the boys got into mischief or neglected their chores, he tended to be harsh and to frighten them. He was shocked when his wife, who had feared to speak up for a long time, suddenly announced that she was thinking of separating from him.

Mr. Carter sought professional help immediately. After his initial discomfiture, he was glad that his wife had confronted him since he wanted very much to continue this marriage and now he knew what her dissatisfactions were. In a discussion with his therapist he quickly recognized that he had to get to work at once on the task of curtailing his belligerence toward the members of his family. Within a month he was reporting far fewer tensions with his sons, who were now seeking his companionship and help with school work instead of avoiding him. His wife, who joined him in therapy, conceded that he was really controlling his temper and impatience with both her and the children, but she was still skeptical about the permanence of this change and needed to see it continue for a substantial period of time. She was, however, no longer thinking about a separation. Mr. Carter, on the other hand, was quite optimistic, because he had proved to himself that he could control his aggressive behavior in order to attain his goal of preserving the marriage.

THE PROBLEMS OF CLIENTS ARE PROBLEMS OF CONSCIOUSNESS

Naomi, aged thirty-seven, is one of several sisters and brothers who were brought up in a closely knit family. Everyone was taught that parents were to be honored and children were to be loved. Naomi is married and the mother of a son and daughter, both teen-agers. She is being seen in treatment for feelings of guilt which she cannot overcome. The therapist approaches this as a problem of consciousness: in the cognitive framework, guilt and other emotions are conscious phenomena. It is not possible to feel guilty without knowing why, inasmuch as such a feeling is the result of making a judgment about oneself. In this instance, Naomi is feeling terribly guilty because she hates her son Buddy.

Buddy and his sister, Joanne, are completely different. Joanne has always been a cooperative child, eager to please, a bright student, and a joy to her parents. Since infancy Buddy has been troublesome, defiant, and demanding. Since he was two years old, Naomi has never been able to respond to him with the same warmth that she felt for Joanne, two years his senior. At the present time, Buddy is both an academic and behavior problem in school, concealing these difficulties from his parents, and forging their signatures on his report cards. In the home, he resists doing his share of the chores, disobeys Naomi's instructions, and ignores curfews that are set for him. He curses and throws tantrums when his mother tries to discipline him.

Naomi readily identifies the bases for her guilt. Raised in a family where all the children were given great affection, she faults herself for never having been able to respond warmly to her son. She is certain that part of Buddy's current antagonism against her stems from his sensing the distance she has put between them over the years. He surely compares his mother's treatment of him with her behavior toward his sister. In recent months, Buddy has become extremely difficult to handle, and Naomi has found herself hating the boy, then recoiling in horror from the vehemence of her emotion and what it implies about her as a mother. Naomi's husband works at two jobs and is seldom home when the confrontations between the boy and Naomi take place. When her husband is in the house, he either tries to avoid involvement or identifies with Buddy and minimizes the seriousness of his behavior. Nearly the entire burden of dealing with Buddy is carried by Naomi alone.

A cognitive approach assumes that Naomi's guilt can be relieved by expanding her consciousness in regard to her feelings about Buddy and his responsibility to her. The therapist will help her to understand that her anger toward Buddy makes sense and is shared by many parents in similar circumstances. The therapist will also suggest a concept that differs somewhat from the indoctrination Naomi received from her own parents: children are to be loved, but they have some responsibility to earn that love. When Naomi's emotional energy will no longer be drained by guilt over her negative feelings, she can engage more effectively in efforts to improve the relationship with her son and to secure more cooperation from her husband.

IT IS NOT NECESSARY TO KNOW THE CAUSE OF A PROBLEM IN ORDER TO SOLVE IT

The physician who treats a person lying in the street with a broken leg does not need to know if the victim was struck by an automobile, a bus, a trolley car, or a flying brick. What is necessary is that the doctor examine and diagnose the injury and arrange for the appropriate treatment. Similarly, it is a cognitive premise that, in dealing with an emotional problem, the therapist's primary focus should be on diagnosing limitations and distortions in the client's consciousness. Once the problem is formulated in these terms, treatment can proceed. It is not necessary to know what brought about these limitations and distortions, although very often their causes will become clear as the helping process goes on.

The reader may feel uneasy about this assumption, accustomed as we are to the image propounded in films and literature of the psychoanalyst who probes for the hidden cause of the patient's distress and cures him by discovering it. But things do not work that way in real life. Warren's problem (p. 103), a fear of heterosexual relationships, was not solved by his realization that the pattern was started in his childhood by his pathological mother. Viewing women in a highly distorted fashion, Warren could not change simply because he knew the "cause" of this distortion. He needed help to reach the point where he would risk trying out nonneurotic behavior with the opposite sex. The cognitive therapist would use this same treatment plan whether or not the origin of Warren's inaccurate thinking was known: a treatment plan is based not on the cause of the problem but on the problem itself. It is more important to know what is maintaining a problem than to know its cause.

Zachary is a successful businessman in his forties who in the past has traveled all over the world, handled difficult international financial negotiations, and spoken before large gatherings of important people. He carried out all these activities without fear and with great self-confidence. Now he is coming for therapy because recently and inexplicably he developed a phobia of the air travel in which he engaged for so many years without a second thought. Business conferences in Europe are coming up soon, and Zachary wants to overcome his problem as quickly as possible.

The therapist decides that investigating why this particular phobia developed at this particular time will be time-consuming and unnecessary for solving the problem. He chooses instead to concentrate on Zachary's thinking: what sentences he is saying to himself, what he specifically fears about sitting in an airplane. What the client tells him will enable the therapist to define the exact nature of the phobia and design a treatment plan appropriate for that phobia, a plan that would not be altered by knowing why Zachary developed a fear of flying at this time.

AN INDIVIDUAL'S BEHAVIOR IS MOTIVATED BY A DESIRE TO SOLVE PROBLEMS, COMPLETE TASKS, OR REACH GOALS

Cognitive theory regards motive as the basic reason underlying a certain kind of behavior. The motive is a wish to solve a certain problem, a wish to complete a certain task, or a wish to reach a certain goal. In every instance, the problem, task, or goal has been brought into being by an individual's personal perceptions of reality. Motive is considered to be a conscious entity.

The Hannigan family—mother, father, and eighteen-year-old Constance—are seen together to deal with some tensions in the home. Constance and her parents are presently embroiled in a struggle that characterizes so many American households: the struggle over the issue of how much freedom and how much control is appropriate for a teen-ager. Mr. and Mrs. Hannigan and their daughter have been fighting this battle for over a year. Constance has become very resentful of parental efforts to set a time for coming in at night, impose restrictions on her activities, and compel her to do her share of chores. Always a good student in high school, she is now failing all major subjects in her senior year.

In one of the family sessions, the focus is on Constance's failing academic grades. The cognitive therapist assumes no unconscious motivation: his premise is that virtually all behavior is directed at problems, tasks, or goals of which the client is aware. He suggests to Constance that her academic deterioration is no accident but has a conscious motive. The girl, surprised by the therapist's simple and direct approach, replies candidly that she is deliberately doing failing work to punish her parents for what she considers their unfair treatment of her. Thus we learn that Constance has set up for herself the goal of taking revenge on her mother and father; the motive behind her poor school performance is to accomplish this goal.

PERCEPTION, EMOTIONS, GOALS, AND BEHAVIOR EXERT RECIPROCAL INFLUENCE ON EACH OTHER

Irving, a sensitive young man in his twenties, perceives himself as unattractive and not too bright. A high school graduate, he was required by family circumstances to go to work and forget about even applying to colleges. Locked into a routine clerical job, he is a sad individual whose chief goal is to hold on to his present job in the face of uncertain economic conditions. His behavior tends to be reserved and self-effacing, a consequence of viewing himself as unworthy of anyone's attention. He feels inferior to the many college graduates who work in the same company.

When Irving finds his way into a therapy group, the reciprocal relationships among perception, emotions, goals, and behavior are activated. Encouraged by the therapist, he gradually becomes comfortable with participating in the group's discussions. Not dull at all, he earns the interest and attention of other group members, including Gloria, who is his own age. His successful behavior within the group begins to alter his low opinion of himself. This change in self-perception is given added momentum by a personal relationship that develops with Gloria, first in the therapy sessions and later outside the treatment setting. The fact that Gloria, whom he admires, can like him and that he can hold his own in conversations with other members of the group compels him to revise his evaluation of himself as not attractive and not intelligent. As we indicated previously, when there is a contradiction between what one thinks and what one experiences, this discrepancy—a cognitive dissonance—is eliminated by a modification of thought in the direction of reflecting reality more accurately.

Irving's changed view of himself, encouraged and reinforced by Gloria, leads to changes in his emotions and goals, contributes to his seeing his total situation in a new perspective, and results in behaviors he has never practiced before. At work, he becomes more outgoing and is no longer the sad, self-effacing person he used to be. Gloria is a part-time college student at night and with strong support from her he decides on a similar plan for himself. He begins to look at his employment situation in a different light and is no longer content simply to maintain the status quo. He asks for an interview with his personnel manager to explore the possibilities of moving upward in the organization, learns that they do exist and what he needs to qualify. He sets his vocational goal at a higher level, aiming eventually at a supervisory position, and chooses his college courses accordingly.

ANXIETY AND NEUROSIS ARE DEFINED IN CONSCIOUS TERMS AS RESPONSES TO ALL KINDS OF LIFE SITUATIONS

The cognitist does not regard anxiety as a signal of repressed material breaking out of the unconscious and does not regard neurosis as the defenses against anxiety thus defined. Rather, anxiety is viewed as a state of apprehension combined with involuntary physiological reactions which is triggered off by an actual or fancied failure, by the dread of a future event, or by the inability to evaluate a new phenomenon and place it in perspective. Neurosis is assumed to be a way of living based on unrealistic guilt, fear, or anger and accompanied by continuing anxiety.

Phyllis came to a mental health clinic with an intense fear of contracting cancer through infection by "cancer germs." Both her own physician and the clinic psychiatrist had explained that cancer is not contagious and is not transmitted by "germs," but to no avail. She remained extremely anxious, dreading the possibility of becoming ill with this disease, and the neurosis based on her unrealistic fear persisted.

The client's "private logic" dominated her thinking and consequently her feeling. Her reasoning processes were full of contradictions: she had been a licensed practical nurse for several years, working in a hospital with seriously ill people, including cancer patients, and was not ignorant of the true nature of cancer; her own mother had died of cancer and Phyllis herself had nursed her through the final months without ever worrying about "catching" the disease. Then, two years ago, Phyllis one day suddenly found herself unable to report for duty at the hospital, incapable of facing her patients, and resigned her position. She became increasingly preoccupied with her particular fear and began developing compulsive behavior patterns.

These compulsions centered in an elderly neighbor who lived several houses away on the same street and was suffering from cancer. If anyone who had recently visited this woman came into Phyllis' home, Phyllis would immediately scrub her foyer and living room with disinfectant as soon as the visitor had departed. She invented all kinds of excuses to keep her son from playing on the same baseball team as the grandson of the sick woman so that the cancer would not be transmitted through the boys into her house. When these manipulations failed to prevent her son's participation on the team, on two occasions she found a way to discard his "contaminated" sneakers and replace them with new ones. In addition, she used to intercept the mailman and get her letters from him before he got to the ill woman's mailbox; otherwise he would be delivering the mail to Phyllis' box after his hands had touched the neighbor's box. All of this created a severe strain on the client's marriage. Her husband became increasingly irritated by what he considered her crazy ideas and he absolutely refused to consider her plea that they move to another town.

Phyllis had strong incentives for seeking professional help: her marriage was in danger and her daily functioning seriously impaired. Nevertheless, she could not accept assurances from physicians that her cancer fears were unfounded. She stated that the medical profession did not know everything about the disease and that perhaps it was occasionally possible for it to be transmitted in the ways she feared. Also, maybe she was more susceptible to cancer than other people and needed to take extra precautions.

Treatment of this case was initiated on the assumption that Phyllis was presenting a problem of consciousness, a misconception of reality. Not only had she reached inaccurate conclusions about the nature of cancer, but she combined these with a dread that she herself was especially vulnerable. Her highly neurotic behavior was an impossible endeavor, an attempt to eliminate all risk. The treatment plan included continuing educational discussions to augment her information about cancer, arranging for "corrective experiences," paradoxical instructions, behavior modification techniques, and emphasis on accepting the necessity of taking risks as a part of life. In connection with this last approach, it was essential to help Phyllis overcome her tremendous feelings of insecurity and weakness; her husband needed to be involved in the treatment process so that he could put aside his anger in favor of a more supportive role. The clinic psychiatrist prescribed medication to lower Phyllis' anxiety level. The drug was not regarded as any kind of solution for her central problem; it was given on a temporary basis to make Phyllis more receptive to the various psychotherapeutic techniques and to enable her to function day by day with less distress.

EACH CLIENT IS EMBEDDED IN HIS OR HER CULTURE, ENVIRONMENT, AND SOCIETY

This is another way of stating a basic social work tenet, the psychosocial approach to human behavior as the interaction between what a person is and his social surroundings. Applied to psychotherapy, this assumption requires the therapist to refrain from labeling a client's behavior as "deviant," "pathological," "abnormal," "inappropriate," or "maladaptive" until the following have been unmistakably established:

1. The client is acting in a fashion that is not typical of, or encouraged by, his family, ethnic, cultural, religious, peer, or socioeconomic group;
2. The client is acting in a fashion that has no rational link to actual events or experiences in his life, including conditioning by the communication media.

If a client's behavior aims to preserve or improve acceptance by a group which is important to him, if it is modeled after the actions of people in his family or in other meaningful groups, if it is based on information he has received, or if it represents a realistic attempt to deal with the world around him, then the source of any difficulty is not judged to be a "sickness" within the client. The types of behaviors just described are appropriate to their contexts. If these behaviors create trouble for the client because they are, in the perception of those who control society, nonconforming, inconvenient, or dangerous, it is the therapist's obligation to help the client develop new conduct patterns that will satisfy both the client and the systems of authority. In so doing, the therapist bears in mind that social action on various levels will be needed to deal with those forces that fostered or condoned the "unacceptable" behavior.

We referred previously to the bright adolescent in school who deliberately holds back on working up to his or her full capacity so as not to alienate antiacademic peers. Other children engage in vandalism or rowdy behavior to maintain relationships with others who do such things and have status in their eyes. Culture is very much at work here. While we hold each child fully responsible for his or her self-defeating or antisocial actions, we recognize the perceptions that may be involved: both the individual child and the influencing group may be seeing the conduct in question as normal and expected. In such cases, our client is seeing his or her segment of reality quite accurately, perceiving what kind of behavior is necessary to remain in the group. It is the group or some other force in the environment that has the "pathology."

Among some groups in American society, teen-age sexual activity and pregnancy are commonplace and accepted without stigmatization, and the adolescent mother's own mother as a matter of course may take on much or most of the responsibility for raising the new baby. Contributing factors to this phenomenon include ignorance of birth control methods or failure to use them, a cultural or familial lifestyle that does not model or teach sexual restraint, group attitudes which confer status on the young mother, and a public assistance system that will support the infant. Adolescent parents, viewed in terms of all their connections to the world they occupy, are evaluated by the cognitist as he evaluates all other clients: on the basis of limitations and distortions of consciousness. If the teen-aged parent perceives his or her world accurately, correctly judging what kind of behavior that world expects, encourages, or accepts, such a client is not deviating from its norms and is in fact "socialized" when actions satisfy those criteria. Regardless of how this behavior conflicts with the therapist's own values, he has to regard it as rational within the client's cultural context. If, however, the way the client behaves disrupts his life, prevents him from reaching his goals, endangers his well-being, or keeps him from growing, the therapist can point this out and perhaps stimulate a desire for change. While the therapist cannot label the client's behavior as irrational, he feels free to insist that it is destructive.

Cultural factors can also be active within an interview. As we have urged before, the therapist should know as much as possible about where the client is coming from, so that misreading of the client's reactions can be kept to a minimum. A social worker in Hawaii once reported on her difficulties in talking to clients of Japanese ancestry, among whom it was forbidden to disagree with a person of higher rank. Since a therapist was considered to be of higher rank, the worker could never be certain of the true significance of confirmation or agreement on the part of the client: it would have been a gross violation of traditional etiquette to voice a dissenting opinion. Thus it was extremely difficult to get at the Japanese client's true feelings. A completely different kind of problem is presented by the kindergarten pupil who tells his teacher that he has a Superman costume and can jump out of the second-story window of his house, flying to the ground without getting hurt. Knowing the amount of time that many children spend in front of a television set, the

teacher does not assume that her student is psychotic. Setting
the child straight on the facts, she is equally concerned with
reaching one of the boy's parents to apprise that adult of the
potential danger and make a strong case for monitoring and
interpreting the youngster's future television watching.

Passing negative judgment on a particular behavior without consideration of its environmental context can be unfair
and may create unnecessary guilt.

Peter, a bright nine-year-old boy, was enrolled by his parents in
an American school after the family escaped from a country that
had no democratic liberties. The parents, who were highly educated, knew that Peter was ready for grade five, although his age
would place him in the grade below. Since the boy knew English,
the parents lied about his age and got him enrolled in the fifth
grade. Peter was informed of the strategem from the very beginning.

Peter did very well in his new school, but one day he became
greatly upset. During a class discussion, his teacher emphasized the
idea that honesty was a prime virtue and that lying was an immoral
act which was never excusable. Peter became confused and guilt-
stricken as he recalled to himself the recent lie about his age and
the numerous times that his parents had lied to the authorities in
his native country. In the culture of an absolute dictatorship, people had to lie to protect their welfare and their lives: one never expected fairness from those in power. Coming to this country, his
parents brought with them their strongly conditioned distrust of
authority and built-in readiness to lie.

Peter subsequently continued to be unhappy and preoccupied in
class but did not feel free to tell his teacher why when she expressed
concern. Referred to the child study team, he was finally able to
blurt out the truth to the school social worker. A special conference was set up, attended by Peter, his parents, his teacher, the
principal, and the social worker. The whole matter was aired in an
atmosphere of sympathy and understanding. The teacher publicly
modified her rigid moral stance about honesty to accommodate
extenuating circumstances and environmental factors, Peter was
allowed to remain in the fifth grade because he was clearly capable

of doing the work, and his parents began to learn that not all authority is malevolent.

Techniques

HELPING THE CLIENT TO FACE A FEARED SITUATION

Generally speaking, anxiety (a state of apprehension with somatic discomfort) tends to abate when an individual experiences a feared situation and discovers that he or she can survive, that the situation is not as devastating as imagined. The therapeutic plan for Zachary, whose problem was described earlier in this chapter, consists precisely of a program based on this phenomenon.

Zachary and his therapist agree on a strategy for overcoming his fear of flying that involves his taking a plane flight. He is not, however, being asked to fly alone, as he usually did in the past. The plan calls for his brother, who knows about the phobia, to fly with him. In addition, Zachary is instructed to carry out certain activities that may lessen his anxiety level. Since he jogs daily because he finds it relaxing, he is told to create positive images of a pleasant air trip and successful business transactions afterward whenever he is running. The purpose of these exercises in mental imagery is to develop bonds of association between air travel and anything pleasant in the client's life. Furthermore, as Zachary each day practices imagining a happy ending to his imminent one-hour flight, he weakens the expectation of anxiety which plays a large part in triggering the very thing that is dreaded.

The therapeutic plan is also influenced by Wolpe's concept of "reciprocal inhibition," which holds that anxiety is not likely to occur in the presence of something which is incompatible with anxiety. The presence of Zachary's brother will be one such force operating against anxiety. Along the same lines, Zachary is advised to talk to a stewardess when he boards the plane, inform her of his phobia, and ask her to stop by at his seat at intervals for a brief supportive chat.

Zachary carries out his pre-flight assignments, arranges a business trip with his brother to a city one hour away, and talks to a stewardess upon entering the plane as instructed. After the trip is completed, he reports to the therapist that he was somewhat nervous and tense on the way to his destination, but at the same time pleased that he had faced his fear and was able to go on the plane. Coming back, he was more relaxed but still not fully at ease. Zachary concludes, however, that he is on the way to conquering his fear and expects to be able to handle the long European air trips he has to take in a couple of months. It is agreed that he will continue meanwhile to take other short flights, following procedures worked out with the therapist.

When Zachary is asked what sentences he is saying to himself when he feels anxious about flying and what he specifically fears about sitting in an airplane, his reply is similar to that of many phobic individuals. He is not afraid of the object or situation itself but of how he himself will behave. He imagines himself having difficulty breathing, feeling closed in, throwing up, or about to faint, followed by screaming or agitated behavior in public that would humiliate him. He does *not* fear that the plane will crash or catch on fire.

Zachary's negative imagery has no basis in real life, since he has never experienced any of the things he fears. His thinking (images of what might happen) is shaping his emotions and behavior, so the therapist counterattacks simply by having him replace anxiety-provoking imagery with mental scenes that have happy endings. He teaches Zachary the necessity of facing what he dreads, but under conditions that contain forces which inhibit anxiety. Medication, not used in Zachary's case, is of course one of the factors that can lessen subjective feelings of apprehension.

HOMEWORK TASKS

Mrs. Talmadge is a divorced woman who is raising three sons alone. She had hoped that Jack, the oldest, would be a source of assistance and support to her but things have not worked out that way. She comes for professional help because her family is often tense, the boys fight constantly among themselves, and Jack is belligerent and resentful. He often hits his brothers.

In family therapy sessions it is revealed that Jack is angry at his mother for two reasons: he blames her for the parents' separation and divorce, and he resents her failure to protect his privacy against the other two boys, who annoy him when he is in his room and handle his possessions when he is away. Furious over his mother's failure to control his brothers, he takes matters into his own hands and hits the youngsters, all the while blaming his mother for his not having his father in the home.

Frank discussions with the entire group about events leading up to the parent's separation give Jack a less simplistic understanding of his father's departure and a beginning awareness that no one person was the villain. Meanwhile, Mrs. Talmadge continues to hold back on dealing firmly with the younger brothers' provocations against Jack, explaining that she feels sorry for them because they do not have a father with them all the time. At this point the therapist indicates the necessity for Mrs. Talmadge to assert her authority and her proper parental role. Her homework assignment is now to practice setting limits on the younger boys' behavior that will be fair to them and satisfactory to Jack. Jack volunteers the comment that he would feel more relaxed in general and have no reason to strike his brothers if his mother could take this burden away from him.

It is understood that Mrs. Talmadge's assignment is to be carried out every day at home, but the therapist wants her to start immediately in the interviewing room. He wishes to observe for himself if she is on the right track and to help her build up some momentum before they all leave for home. Successfully completed homework assignments of new ways of behaving can alter the balance of forces in a client's or a family's life; the opportunity to practice in the treatment session itself may increase the chances of such success. Therefore, when the two younger boys become disruptive and defiant in the second half of the treatment hour, the therapist openly asks Mrs. Talmadge to bring them under control. With some difficulty she succeeds, and the pattern for her to follow at home has been demonstrated.

USING THE CLIENT'S STRENGTH

Family therapist Marianne Walters makes the point that people under stress forget what they formerly knew about being competent. A basic cognitive technique is to remind the client of previous competencies by labeling any past successes or accomplishments that he may mention as areas of strength. The cognitist also insists that nearly everyone has strength and courage within himself, although it may be extremely difficult to mobilize these qualities at certain times. That, however, is part of the therapeutic task: to help the client reach into himself and make use of these powerful forces.

As we have already suggested, one of the great advantages of group therapy is that it makes available the strengths of several people for helping individual members of the group as needed. In a group setting, the therapist will call this outside strength into play to help a particular member; in individual treatment, the therapist evokes the inner strength of the client.

Eleanor has survived the breakup of her marriage to a man whom she trusted and thought she knew. Without warning, he left her for another woman. For a while she was thrown off balance and became extremely depressed but she gradually worked her way back to a productive level of existence. The chief motivating force in this mobilization of strength was her wish to give her young son and daughter the best possible parenting.

Years have passed since the separation and subsequent divorce, the children are now fairly self-sufficient, and Eleanor has met a man with whom she has developed a serious relationship. He has asked her to marry him but she is afraid. She tells the therapist that she does not know if she could cope with another disappointment in her personal life. She trusted her ex-husband completely and he deserted her without warning; isn't it possible for this new man to do the same? Client and therapist have a candid discussion of this dilemma. The therapist agrees that it is within the realm of possibility that the same thing could happen again; it is also possible that remarrying could bring the client great happiness. Since her future cannot be predicted or guaranteed, the focus of attention should be elsewhere, specifically on whether her decision about remarriage is going to be made from a position of strength or from a position of weakness.

The therapist expounds the idea that the most important question is not whether this man will fulfill Eleanor's hopes but whether she wishes to live a full life or a limited one. Living a full life entails the risk of being hurt; if she limits her relationships to avoid pain, she may not be hurt but she will not be fully alive. If she accepts the humanist principle that each person is obliged to strive for the fullest, richest existence possible, then her decision will be made not on the basis of minimizing the risk of pain but on the basis of accepting opportunities to grow and once again experience intimacy with another.

Eleanor herself has already recognized that backing away from this new relationship is tantamount to leading an antiseptic existence. She will not be hurt but neither will she be alive; she will be safe but she will be empty. But she fears that she will "fall apart" and not survive if the second marriage does not work out. It is at this point that the therapist makes an all-out effort to put Eleanor in touch with her own strength. He reminds her of all the incidents she has recounted in which, struggling to bring up two young children by herself, she stood strong, she was a rock against the world, and she survived. On the basis of her history, the therapist expresses his confidence in Eleanor as a survivor. He cannot decide for her about marrying again, he can only encourage her to decide for herself from a position of strength: from such a position, the question Eleanor needs to answer is not how much pain a course of action might bring but how much more human it will enable her to become.

EXPECTING MORE FROM THE CLIENT THAN HE OR SHE DOES

In the next chapter, we shall cite an article which affirms that the therapist's expectations of the client can significantly influence the course of treatment. The essence of this technique is that the therapist *genuinely* believes the client can accomplish more than the client thinks is possible, and says so. The fact that the therapist estimates the client's potential to be greater than the client imagines can alter the client's perception of him- or herself and can result in setting and attaining higher treatment goals.

The author recalls two female clients, both of whom had unhappy marriages and extremely poor self-images.

Both Beatrice and Cara had been made to feel inferior and incompetent, first by their parents and then by their husbands. Since both women had children and were planning to end their marriages, they shared a major concern about how to go about preparing to be as financially self-sufficient as possible.

Beatrice had dropped out of nursing school fifteen years earlier to get married. Becoming a registered nurse would solve her economic problem but she dismissed this notion as nothing more than a fantasy. She had recently contacted her old nursing school for general information and had been informed that the amount of elapsed time and her present age (thirty-five) precluded her readmission with credit for work previously accomplished; nor was she eligible to enter as a new student. Beatrice was greatly discouraged by this information; she also doubted her ability to keep up with younger students and endure the rigors of training if she were accepted.

From discussions with Beatrice, it became apparent to the therapist that she had been an excellent student in nursing school, was a "natural" for this profession, and would be a completely dedicated student if given the opportunity. The therapist then took the position that a return to nursing school was not an impossible expectation: while technicalities were being put in her way, it was also true that professional nurses were in great demand. Beatrice was encouraged to keep trying, the therapist emphasizing that he had no doubts about her ability to succeed in her training.

With this support from the therapist, Beatrice persisted in her contacts with her former nursing school. After a year, she managed to get a special hearing before the program administrator, who remembered her from before, and she was finally readmitted by a decision to waive some of the rules on her behalf. Two difficult years of study followed, complicated by the need to make all kinds of arrangements for the care of her children, but finally culminating in Beatrice's graduation as an R.N. The therapist was present at the commencement exercises.

Cara was a high school graduate who after ten years of marriage was now faced with the task of choosing a vocation and preparing herself for the world of work. Her parents' rejecting attitudes during her adolescence were so severe that despite an excellent intelligence and sharp powers of observation she did poorly in high school and came to regard herself as "retarded." She came into therapy as a confused, depressed young woman who felt trapped. As the therapist came to know Cara through their weekly treatment sessions, he observed an extremely bright mind, an original sense of humor that had been bottled up in the past, and an underlying strength.

Cara's fantasy was to become a teacher of young children, but she brushed this aside as impossible in any discussion about job planning. The therapist, on the basis of his perception of the client, insisted that she pursue this dream. For a long time Cara reiterated that this was an unreasonable expectation but finally yielded to the therapist's estimate of her potential. She was able to enroll in a local college and was in attendance there for six years during which she saw the therapist from time to time. With a different perception of herself as compared to her high school days, Cara from the very beginning took to college academic work, enjoyed the process of learning and expanding her consciousness, and became an excellent student majoring in early childhood education. Six years later, the therapist again, as in the case of Beatrice, was very happy to be present at the graduation exercises.

THE THERAPIST'S USE OF HIS OR HER OWN EXPERIENCES (TRANSPARENCY)

We have previously discussed how the humanistic approach favors transparency on the part of the therapist whenever such a technique is in the service of the client. Used appropriately, such reference by the therapist to his or her own experiences can be instructive or supportive to a client involved in a similar situation and can strengthen the human bonds between them.

A female therapist finds that she increases her rapport with some of her clients by using this technique. In sessions with adolescent girls she observes that they respond to her anecdotes about herself as a teen-ager and about her daughter. With mothers or fathers who are struggling with disciplinary problems involving their children, she admits to having had comparable problems with her own offspring and tells of some of the solutions she has tried. The therapist does not try to project herself as an all-knowing guru but as a fellow human who knows where the client is coming from, having been there herself. Her ability to help derives not from superior wisdom but from a professional training which fosters objectivity and provides a broader view of human problems than the client may have. The benefits of her training are made available to the client when the therapist, calling on her own humanness, translates them into practical terms relevant to the problem at hand.

HELPING THE CLIENT TO MAKE HIS OR HER OWN DECISIONS

The cognitist, out of respect for the client, does not take over the responsibility for making the client's decisions. At the same time, he does not retreat into an unproductive neutrality by declining any aid when the client asks for suggestions or guidance. The middle road between taking over from the client and deserting him is for the therapist to assume the obligation of making the client aware of all possible choices, viewpoints, and solutions. The client makes the final decision himself, but he makes it on the basis of knowing all the alternatives. In addition, the cognitive therapist will be sure to supply any factual information necessary to give the client the best chance of making a sound judgment.

Mrs. Tarkington is worried about her eighteen-year-old daughter Sandra, a high school senior with a superior I.Q., who is planning to go to a prestigious university to pursue a career in science. Sandra's older brother has dropped out of a college located in another state. Mrs. Tarkington interpreted this turn of events as a direct consequence of lack of parental supervision to make him apply himself to his books. She believes that Sandra is developing the same pattern: the girl's grades are falling, she is not completing academic assignments, and she has missed out on participating in coveted extracurricular activities because of her own negligence. For example, she was chosen to represent her high school in a statewide oratory contest but was unable to take part because she failed to submit registration papers by a certain deadline.

Mrs. Tarkington's pattern has been to nag and check up on Sandra's school activities relentlessly, frequently reminding her of what happened to her brother. The result is great tension between mother and daughter without any improvement in school performance or attitude. Mrs. Tarkington comes for counseling sessions to work out her dilemma. She examines the problem from all sides with the therapist.

Client and therapist consider all the possibilities. Sandra, now viewing herself as an adult, may resent her mother's attempts to control her life, even though such efforts are intended to protect the girl from the consequences of her seeming lack of self-discipline. Perhaps Sandra failed to file papers for the oratory competition because she doubted her ability to do well and feared she would not meet her parents' very high standards of performance. Sandra's poor school performance may be an attempt to punish her mother for what the girl perceives as unbearable pressure. The therapist points out that the client has been reminding Sandra of how her brother has disappointed the family; Sandra may feel hurt at being identified with her brother and not treated as an individual in her own right. The therapist recognizes that Mrs. Tarkington is torn between understanding that Sandra needs to be free to make her own choices and fearing what will happen if her daughter is left to her own devices.

Possible outcomes are frankly discussed. Sandra may fail some of her major subjects and not be able to go on to college on schedule. Because of laziness, lack of confidence, or disorganization, she may lose out on special honors and opportunities. The therapist, however, asks the client to consider whether constant hovering over her daughter will really prevent such negative outcomes. He informs Mrs. Tarkington that many parents report closer relationships with children of this age when they let go: when the parent stops pushing, the child does not have to push back in self-defense.

Finally it is Mrs. Tarkington who makes the decision as to how she will relate to Sandra in the immediate future. She chooses to let go after giving the girl a candid statement of her concerns and affirming her belief in Sandra's great potential. Six months later, she reports that Sandra has regained her former high academic standing in school, seems much happier, and has abandoned the hostility which originally prompted the client to seek professional help.

INTERPRETING DREAMS AS CLUES TO UNMASTERED PROBLEMS OF LIVING

The cognitive approach to dreams is not as "the royal road to the unconscious" but as reflections of problems that the client has not yet mastered in his waking life. In the treatment interview, discussion of a dream can help to identify or clarify the client's central concern. The premise is that problems or situations not worked out in the daytime impinge during sleep on those parts of the brain that are still active, producing "moving pictures" characterized by varying degrees of reality. The technique is to have the client describe a dream and follow this with a joint effort by client and therapist to relate the content to the client's real life.

Sue Ann, a single woman in her late twenties, has been living with her parents while maintaining an intimate relationship with Herb over a period of several years. Until recently Herb avoided the subject of marriage although Sue Ann wanted this very much. Sue Ann has stayed in the relationship despite the little emotional support she receives from Herb, who has frequently been destructively critical and has followed a deliberate pattern of making her feel inferior. Over the years, he has seldom been interested in problems she had at work or at home, has rarely taken her out to a show or restaurant or place of interest, and in general has placed her at the bottom of his priority list: seeing her is something he does only after taking care of all other activities, especially college courses he is taking to advance his business career.

Partly as a result of discussions in her treatment sessions, not long ago Sue Ann finally voiced her dissatisfaction with Herb's attitudes toward her and said she was considering ending their relationship. Herb responded to this by making an effort to be more sensitive to her needs and suggesting marriage. Confronted with the actual marriage proposal that she had wanted so much in the past, Sue Ann suddenly found herself reluctant to accept it. Contemplating her future as Herb's wife, she saw life with him as boring, unexciting, and unimaginative.

As therapy proceeds, Sue Ann and her therapist examine why she stayed in this relationship for so many years and why she has now declined Herb's offer of marriage and yet continues to see him. Sue Ann is highly ambivalent, feels confused about her motives, and does not perceive her situation clearly. She describes a recurrent dream she has been having, and the therapist's interpretation of it seems to bring the essential problem into sharper focus for her.

In her dream, a house is on fire. Sue Ann, choking on the smoke and unable to breathe, rushes out of the building to safety. Once outside, however, she discovers she is not safe. A group of men come running toward her and the dream ends with her fleeing as they pursue her. The therapist suggests that the house in the dream is her own home where there has been tension between Sue Ann and her parents and where she has felt smothered by them. Living with her parents is in a way a direct result of her relationship with

Herb, because she would not be there if they had married. Leaving the house is equivalent to changing the entire status of her life, but such a change brings danger. Out in the world on her own, Sue Ann has to deal with other men. Although she is still seeing Herb, she is thinking seriously of dating others and has already told the therapist of this intention. She has not been out with another man in many years, so she will be entering the current singles scene as a novice and has admitted to the therapist that she is very frightened.

Putting the dream together with what Sue Ann has been telling him of her present perceptions and feelings, the therapist comments that the dream appears to reflect Sue Ann's wish to get out of a suffocating situation (both the parental home and the relationship with Herb) and her fear of what will happen if she carries it out. In this context, perhaps she has held on to Herb so long in the hope that through marrying him she could move out of her parents' home and avoid reentry into the frightening world of the single adult. Continuing to see Herb without any permanent commitment seems to be her way of effecting a compromise between recognizing that marriage to him no longer has any appeal and still having him to fall back on should her excursions into a new social existence become too threatening.

ENCOURAGING BEING TRUE TO ONESELF

Evelyn is a divorced woman with a teen-age son. She took her child and left her ex-husband many years before because he was cruel and irresponsible, but for a long time she felt guilty for "depriving" the boy of a father. Now she has met a man whom she is planning to marry, but intermittently she backs away from that plan, giving two reasons for her vacillation. She does not want to upset her mother, who is opposed to the marriage. Her son likes his prospective stepfather, but she does not know if she has the right to uproot him to marry this man: they would have to live in a different part of the state and the boy would have to leave his present school and friends.

Therapeutic sessions first concentrate on Evelyn's unfounded feelings of guilt, which are systematically explored and undermined. Her perceptions of what she "owes" her mother and her son are critically examined. Since her guilt has distorted her concepts of filial and maternal obligation, the reduction of guilt decreases Evelyn's need to atone by excessive sacrifice. The therapist then focuses on the importance of being true to oneself, using all opportunities to enrich one's life, and not feeling responsible always to please others.

Evelyn is asked to consider the alternative to not being true to herself: giving up this man to avoid her mother's disapproval and inconvenience to her son's social life. Do pleasing her mother and shielding her child from change have the same value as making a new life for herself? Evelyn finally concludes that if she calls off this marriage, she will be a bitter and angry person who is not likely to make either her mother or son very happy. She begins to understand that making choices that fulfill her needs is not necessarily a self-centered act: the strength and security that come from pursuing her own goals can be transmitted to others in her family.

TEACHING THE CLIENT TO BE AN INDIVIDUAL

Nora cannot separate herself from her teen-aged son Matt. The client and the boy's father broke up when Matt was very young. Nora did not feel equal to the task of raising the boy alone, so she permitted him to be brought up by his paternal grandmother in the ghetto area of a large city while she lived in the suburbs with her own parents, who did not want the boy in their home.

After some years had passed, Nora moved to her own small apartment in the city; Matt came to live with her at age 15, after his father had been killed during an attempted burglary. But, by this time, Matt was already a street-wise product of the urban slums. His father had been his hero. Matt gravitated back to the inner city—a few miles but a world away—whenever he possibly could. His friends were school dropouts, his preoccupation was to come across as tough and cool, and his true belief was that anything he did to survive was justified.

In the past year, Matt, now 18, has returned to the ghetto, rooming there with another family, working at odd jobs, and apparently intoxicated with his freedom to do anything he pleases and stay out at night as late as he wishes. He left Nora after three years because of increasing tensions created by his dropping out of high school, chronic lying, staying out all hours of the night, and losing a good job when he stole a large sum of money from his company.

In treatment, Nora presents problems of guilt and inability to separate herself from Matt. She tortures herself with the notion that Matt would have turned out differently if she had raised him. To ease her guilt, she has tried to protect Matt from the consequences of his poor judgment. A case in point is Matt's current involvement with the court. The judge has agreed not to send him to jail if he pays back the money he stole in small weekly amounts, returns to complete his final year of high school, and comes back to live with his mother under her supervision. Matt promised to do so but followed through on none of these conditions. Nora intervened with the authorities to get him one more chance and additional time, and held off on reporting that he was staying out at night in defiance of her curfew.

At the present time, Matt is back in the inner city, drifting from day to day, not attending school, and making no effort to pay back the stolen money. Nora is upset over the waste of a life: Matt has above average intelligence and an appealing manner that charms everyone. An important element in the total situation, one that has been present for a long time, is Matt's continuing cruelty to his mother: he makes no effort to help her when she is ill, promises to visit and fails to show up or communicate with her, and is often hostile. Yet he will act pleasant if he needs money or assistance. A court hearing is imminent and he faces the possibility of a jail sentence.

The therapist's work with Nora is now focused on helping her to separate herself from Matt. He tries to give her facts to use in her emotionally charged dilemma, and reminds her that regardless of past events Matt's present troubles are the result of self-defeating decisions that he is making now under circumstances where he can easily make constructive choices and find help in carrying them out. The therapist points out that Nora has offered Matt her love and her practical assistance, and he has deliberately chosen not to accept them. It is time for her to allow Matt to take responsibility for what he does, just as the therapist holds her responsible for her behavior. When Nora declares that she is crushed by the thought that her son may go to jail, the therapist helps her see the distinction between situations for which sadness rather than guilt is the appropriate reaction. In this instance, it is fitting to feel sad about Matt but self-destructive to feel guilty. She will survive if she can grieve for him without guilt, bearing in mind that a brief jail sentence now may possibly deter Matt from more serious deviant behavior in the future. Whether or not it does, she needs to go on with her own life, just as Matt has asserted his right to exist on his own terms.

Nora continues to struggle with the task of individuation and the forces that bind her to Matt. It is a difficult and painful struggle. She slowly gathers strength. While Matt awaits his trial, she manages to separate herself from him and takes a two-week vacation in another part of the country.

PARADOXICAL INTENTION: PRESCRIBING THE SYMPTOM

In earlier chapters, we have made passing reference to this technique without describing or illustrating it. We shall conclude our review of some of the techniques used by cognitive therapists by presenting concepts and examples of paradoxical intervention from the writings of Viktor Frankl and Jay Haley. The paradoxical approach is not derived from any part of cognitive theory and may appear directly to contradict it, but in actual practice the two are compatible. The paradoxical approach is recommended to cognitists for study and use.

Viktor Frankl identifies paradoxical intention as a logotherapeutic technique, a procedure developed by the school of psychotherapy founded by him known as logotherapy. Logotherapy is considered to be one of the existential therapies. It aims to help people transcend suffering by finding positive meaning in life, even in its cruel aspects.

Frankl gives the example of a young man who had a phobia of sweating. Whenever he was introduced to someone he would perspire excessively, and the next time he was in a similar situation he expected to perspire again. Each succeeding time, the anticipatory anxiety precipitated the profuse perspiring that he feared. His therapist advised, should his anticipatory anxiety reoccur, that he show anyone he met just how much he could really sweat. A week later, the subject reported that whenever he met anyone who triggered his anticipatory anxiety, he said to himself that he was now going to pour out ten times as much sweat as he did previously. He discovered that, after suffering from this phobia for four years, he was able after one therapeutic session to free himself of it permanently. He no longer perspired even when he tried.

The treatment, Frankl explains, consists of various elements: (1) reversing the subject's attitude toward his phobia so that trying to avoid sweating is replaced by an intentional effort to do so; (2) the approach is to be carried out with a sense of humor, which makes it possible for the individual to place himself at a distance from the symptom and separate himself from his neurosis; (3) since a phobia is reinforced by the anxiety arising out of efforts to avoid it, paradoxical intention decreases the symptoms by bringing the sufferer to the point where he ceases to flee from them but exaggerates them instead. Frankl rates humor as an important and basic human capacity, noting that no animal is able to laugh: "As a matter of fact, when paradoxical intention is used, the purpose, to put it simply, is to enable the patient to develop a sense of detachment toward his neurosis by laughing at it" (Frankl, 1967, p. 147).

Frankl offers some additional examples of paradoxical intention:

1. A medical student who feared she would tremble whenever her professor of anatomy entered the room overcame this phobia by deciding she would show him how much she could really shake. Once she had made up her mind to tremble deliberately in his presence, she was unable to do so.

2. A junior high school student, who had a stuttering

problem, was given the role in his class play of a character who was a stutterer, but had to withdraw from the part because onstage he was completely unable to stutter.

3. One woman suffered greatly for twenty years because of a compulsion to go back and check the lock on her front door several times whenever she went out. A paradoxical approach was used much as it is used with phobias: the woman's fear of being robbed if the door were not locked was reversed by having her tell herself that it did not matter if the door was open and everything in her apartment was stolen. She began to say this to herself every time she left her home and was able to ignore her impulse to check and to go calmly on her way. Three months later she reported that her compulsion was gone.

4. A man was obsessed with the thought that he might break a store window. Frankl told him to go right up to the window with the intention of smashing it. When he did this, the fear disappeared; he knew he wouldn't go through with it and subsequently all fears and impulses to do this vanished.

5. Fear of insomnia increases sleep disturbance because anticipating anxiety completes and perpetuates the vicious circle. As Frankl (1967, pp. 158–159) puts it, "we advise the patient not to try to force sleep, since the necessary amount of sleep will be automatically secured by the organism. Therefore, he can safely try to do just the opposite, to stay awake as long as possible. In other words, the forced intention to fall asleep, arising from the anticipatory anxiety of not being able to fall asleep, should be replaced by the paradoxical intention of not falling asleep at all! (Which in turn will be followed very rapidly by sleep.)"

In summing up the mechanism of paradoxical intention, Frankl states that it mobilizes the basic human potential for psychonoëtic antagonism, the capacity for self-detachment.

Jay Haley has worked a great deal with paradoxical intervention. His interpretation of why it succeeds differs from that of Frankl. For example, in treating a family with a child who will not go to school, Haley might suggest that it would be better if the boy just stayed home, and he might offer various reasons for saying this. According to Haley, this approach is based on the idea that some families who come for help are resistant to the help offered and tend to oppose the therapist, so they may change if told not to change. The therapist might also comment that perhaps the family would get upset if the boy went to school like a normal child, in which case the parents might change their handling of the situation in order to prove the therapist wrong. In the same vein, Haley contends that the therapist can contribute to the continuation of a positive change either by telling the family that the change is probably only temporary and they will soon revert to their old ways, or by announcing that the change has happened too fast and he would like the family to "relapse" and go back to the way they were before.

In another illustration Haley describes an overprotective mother who hovers over her child to such an extreme that he has no freedom to make his own decisions or be responsible for his actions:

> If the therapist tries to persuade her to do less for the child, she may respond by doing more, often saying that the therapist really does not understand how handicapped the child really is. One can take a paradoxical approach by asking the mother to spend a week hovering over the child. She is to watch over him, protect him, and do everything for him. . . . To use this approach well, the therapist should ask for more extreme behavior than the mother has been showing. . . . If this approach is done well, the mother will react by rebelling against the therapist and hovering over the child less. [Haley, 1978b, pp. 70–71]

Haley explains that the mother will hover less because she will not like doing what someone has told her to do (i.e., hover more). In addition, she will not enjoy hovering even more than before because she may believe the child is already making too many demands upon her. Haley adds that the same approach can be used with couples who are always fighting in an unproductive way. If the therapist wants them to fight less, he can ask them to go home and fight at a certain hour of the day for a specified length of time. People do not like to fight on orders from someone else. "To use the paradoxical approach, a therapist must develop skill and must practice. He also needs to be able to think about problems in a gamelike or playful way even though he realizes that he is dealing with grim problems and real distress" (Haley, 1978b, p. 71).

When a therapist helps an individual or family to make a positive change, Haley cautions that the therapist should avoid taking credit for it. One way to avoid credit is to be puzzled by the improvement. Once the therapist reveals that the improvement achieved is what he was really hoping for, he risks a relapse by his client(s). To maintain a recently achieved improvement, in some cases the therapist may need for a while to characterize the client as not cooperating.

Both paradoxical intervention and the cognitive orientation as a whole recognize that behavior and emotion are shaped by thought. Frankl uses the paradoxical approach to detach the client from his neurosis so that he can perceive his relationship to it in a new light, that is, so that it no longer controls him. When this happens, self-defeating behavior and anxiety can be overcome. Haley, in employing paradoxical tasks to help the client reach therapeutic goals, counts on the tendency of some clients to perceive opposition to the therapist's orders as necessary and justified.

Longer Case Reports

JODY

When Jody's parents were divorced and his mother remarried, he went to live with his mother, stepfather, and four other children. He was born abnormally small and received a diagnosis of congenital dwarfism from the pediatric endocrine clinic of one of the nation's leading hospitals where the parents have taken him for comprehensive examinations. They have been told that the condition is permanent and he will always be abnormally small. Jody is nine years old.

The boy is hyperactive at home and is often in conflict with his siblings. At school he has a competent and understanding teacher in the special class he attends for children with "health" problems. She reports aggressive, destructive behavior, extreme need for attention, temper outbursts, and a chronic chip on the shoulder. He obviously resents his small size, is desperately anxious about the future, and anticipates derision and teasing from everyone. He is very thin and fragile appearing, with a long, thin face reminiscent of a fairy tale dwarf or elf. His appealing but odd face is probably as much a reason for the teasing as his small stature.

The mother and stepfather believe that they have a good marriage which is slowly being ruined by Jody's difficult behavior. The stepfather tends to be rigid in regard to the standards of conduct he sets for Jody, recalling that a doctor at the hospital asserted that the boy should "toe the mark like any other child." The mother is more indulgent and less demanding. The parents try not to disagree in front of any of the children but find there is a sharp difference between them as to the way Jody should be handled. This conflict has irritated them both and spills over into the mother's dealings with the other children. She becomes irritable and tense with them. There is some feeling that Jody gets favored treatment, which is perhaps one of the underlying reasons for the clashes among the siblings.

Between parental inconsistency and the anxiety he feels about his size, Jody is not in a good position to cope with the pressures at hand. His mother has told him to defend himself against those who tease or bother him; Jody has learned to fight back and has gone one step further to the point where he now starts fights before he is actually provoked. He is so worried and angry about being abnormally small that he continually fights the whole world, craves inordinate attention to allay his fears, and greedily grabs everything in sight to be sure he gets his share and is not slighted because of his insignificance.

The mother and stepfather are seen without the boy during the first interview and both frankly admit the problem. They agree their marriage is a good one and worth saving but worry that it may break apart because of the tension created by their disagreement over how to handle Jody. It has reached the point where they are both willing to change their approach if someone will help them and show them how. With this in mind, it is arranged that the therapist now interviewing them will see Jody while another staff member of the agency will work with them.

In December Jody is seen in the play room for four sessions. He reveals his profound preoccupation with his size in his play and conversation. He makes a chalk mark on the blackboard to indicate his present size, then climbs up to show how high he would like to grow. He says he will settle for any amount of growth as long as he becomes taller than he is now. He talks about being a thousand times smaller than other children and how it is bad to be little. The therapist reflects back his feelings of wanting to strike out at others because he is so angry about being small. Although Jody admits the general pattern, he feels compelled to deny belligerency in specific incidents that the therapist brings up for discussion.

Jody can express himself more deeply in his play than he can with words. He uses sand and sandbox toys for mildly aggressive play such as bombing and burying, which are carried on without great vehemence. He likes opportunities to display physical strength, and gets recognition for carrying heavy objects and boxing vigorously. The therapist tells him stories in which the small, clever hero wins out, and explains how in aircraft factories the work could not be completed without the use of small people to assemble certain parts.

Jody has a favorite puppet with whom he performs a play at each session. Jody has named the puppet "Mr. Sad Face," and he is sad because nobody likes him. The boy likes to sing so the therapist brings a guitar to one session and they have fun singing together. Jody turns out to be an intelligent child who can do well at his school work when he concentrates. His speech is spontaneous and fluent but has an infantile intonation. This, however, is not too startling to an observer because of his very small size.

It becomes apparent that Jody needs the opportunity to express his fears about himself, get them out in the open where they can be faced and coped with, and find sources of security and self-esteem that do not depend on his being the same size as his peers. The therapist hopes that the boy's aggressiveness will peter out as it becomes less needed for defense.

Jody is seen for three play therapy sessions in January. He continues to act out little plays with the puppet, Mr. Sad Face, who acquires a tiny dinosaur for his friend. Prior to one session, Jody expresses to his stepfather a resistance to coming for treatment, saying that he does not know how to explain to his friends where he goes on Saturday mornings. The stepfather finds this puzzling because Jody does not have any friends who care that much about his activities. The therapist sees the incident as indicative of the child's feelings of being different from his peers.

During January there is less preoccupation with size than there had been the previous month. Jody shows overt signs of affection toward the therapist, bringing him a lollipop and putting his arm around the therapist's shoulder. He volunteers to talk about school and how he enjoys learning what he calls "mathematics." He takes great pleasure in figuring out simple money problems that the therapist puts on the blackboard concerning the price of a car and a house and how much money one needs to become a millionaire.

In the third January session, Jody draws a picture of a house and his own family. His stepbrother Carl, who is slightly older but almost twice his size and is the one with whom Jody clashes the most at home, is described as "bad": "He's sick, but he's bad." He then goes on to play with his puppet, Mr. Sad Face, "who is bad—nobody likes him." The therapist takes part in a game where Mr. Sad Face hides and the dog puppet that the therapist is manipulating has to find him. The dog finds Mr. Sad Face by following the scent. Jody gets excited. He complains that it is not fair to find Mr. Sad Face by smelling his trail, and a vigorous fight develops between his puppet and the dog, with Jody manipulating both. This is the strongest expression to which the boy has given vent thus far. Mr. Sad Face and the dog have a fierce battle, certain phases being repeated over and over, until the dog is the victor and "Mr. Sad Face is really hurt."

Aside from this forceful outburst, Jody's play is only mildly aggressive most of the time. When asked about behavior at home or school, he casually says there is no trouble and changes the subject. He seems to look forward to his weekly sessions.

With the parents' permission, the therapist telephones Jody's teacher near the end of January. She reports that his biggest recent improvement is in regard to appetite. Jody has always eaten poorly at lunch when he brings food from home. He has recently been switched to hot lunch in school and eats much better now. Jody's reading level is between 1.9 and 2.4, two grades below normal expectations. He can reach his potential in any subject if he applies himself. His educational problem is that he refuses to work in small study groups with others and will try to learn something new only if the teacher gives him her undivided, individual attention. As a result he ends up with much less coaching than any other pupil in the class.

Jody is popular in his special class, has lots of clever ideas, and displays creative talents. He antagonizes other children only when he gets into one of his aggressive moods and does things like putting tacks on their cots. The ten children in the class range in age from six to eleven. The school atmosphere is pleasant: none of the children in the class has an obvious physical disability, there are children Jody's size so that his stature does not make him conspicuous, and physically he can do as well as anyone else. In classic mold, despite his own suffering because of difference, he has been making fun of two cerebral-palsied children with speech defects. The teacher is convinced that the key issue is Jody's lack of confidence in studying with others, and hopes that the therapist can help with this. His aggressiveness is not the main thing, although he does have a bad temper when all does not go his way. His mother has been very helpful with his homework, sitting down with him regularly.

Three more play interviews take place during February. Jody puts much less emphasis on his size. At the same time, his play becomes more aggressive and vigorous, less inhibited. He looks forward to his sessions; his prevailing mood is largely a happy one. The most important developments, however, take place outside the interview.

The therapist talks to Jody about making an effort to participate in study groups in school rather than wait for the rare occasions when the teacher can give him time alone. He agrees to try and reports a week later that he is now working with other children and it is "great" (his teacher later confirms this).

Jody's therapist communicates with the parents' therapist. In a phone discussion, she describes how the mother and stepfather do not focus in their interviews with her on Jody as the chief cause of conflict in their marriage. They tell her they are having difficulty with raising all the children. The parents' therapist believes the mother is finding raising five children overwhelming—she had only two before her remarriage. Jody's mother appears to want to avoid facing the job and tries to escape by concerning herself with her own appearance and clothes.

Jody tells his therapist that he thinks his mother loves the little baby best (the only child of her second marriage). He does not know whom his stepfather likes best.

In March, there are again important outside events, while four more play sessions continue rather uneventfully. Feelings of difference crop up once in a while but not with the desperate quality they possessed a couple of months ago. Jody brings up the subject of rocket trips, and how nice it would be if he could go on a trip to the moon because he is small and light and will not take up much room.

Jody's natural father, without the mother's permission, arranges a birthday party for him in school. Jody is upset for several days after, beginning with anxiety over the possibility that his classmates will find out who the donor is (someone different from his stepfather). He starts again to talk about being small and resenting the fact that he takes a special bus to school which sets him apart from the students in regular classes. Two days after the birthday party he comes home from school hysterical and his mother has a hard time calming him down. This particular upset centers on his now not wanting to attend this school, even though he likes his teacher. It seems as if anxiety triggers a reaction in which feelings about size and difference predominate.

The mother tells the therapist in March that Jody's behavior at home is no longer a special problem. It is not perfect, there is some fighting, but in general it is fairly good and she can handle any difficulties that arise. This is decidedly in contrast with her earlier attitude that Jody's conduct would break up her marriage. She now shifts her emphasis away from Jody and states that her chief concern is the aggravating behavior of her ex-husband.

Jody's father sees him and his natural brother, Leo, once or twice a month. This man is obsessed with the idea that his two sons should continue to use his last name rather than that of their stepfather. Such insistence is upsetting Leo greatly; Leo, in junior high school, would like to be known by his stepfather's name and not have to explain anything to his peers. The stepfather is very unhappy over the tensions that the father of his stepsons is creating for them.

Jody avoids discussion with the therapist of the birthday party that his father arranged in school. He blocks, sucks his finger, acts like an infant, and curls up on a table. Afterwards, he plays with toy automobiles in a violent, disorganized fashion.

Toward the end of March, the therapist again speaks to Jody's teacher on the phone. She reports a great improvement. He is now working with others three-quarters of the time, occasionally straying off by himself or walking out of the group. Temper tantrums are much less frequent, and when he does have them, he directs them at himself instead of striking out at others.

During the last session in March, Jody and his therapist play ball outside the office. Jody makes a point of demonstrating his self-reliance and his agility in climbing up rocks. He is given full recognition for his progress in school and is encouraged to maintain it. An all-around improvement seems to be taking place. The therapist is hopeful that Jody will make further progress, but this will depend in part on the parents' receiving help to deal with problems of total family management and on finding a way to modify the upsetting influence of the natural father. In April, Jody's mother reports that he has been in very happy spirits for a month and that she sees a basic change in him.

The case of Jody illustrates some basic cognitive assumptions. His aggressive behavior is not viewed as an instinctual drive demanding continual satisfaction, but as a response to particular situations. Sometimes this kind of behavior is an expression of his anger over being different; sometimes he attacks others in order to head off an anticipated attack from them; sometimes he is aggressive to ensure that he will get his share of what he believes he is entitled to; sometimes he strikes out at others to avenge perceived rejection or threatening competition; and sometimes he plays mean tricks (e.g., putting tacks on the classroom cots) to achieve a fleeting sense of power. Second, the therapist regards Jody's anxiety reactions not as intrapsychic phenomena but as related directly to actual happenings in his life. In this context, anxiety is defined as the dread of a future event: the birthday party in school arranged by the boy's natural father activates Jody's fears that the other children will discover he is living with a stepfather; the prospect of participating in small study groups with some of his classmates triggers fears that he will be neglected by the teacher and / or be unable to keep up with the others. Third, this case exemplifies the proposition that the problem a client brings to us is a problem in living which is firmly embedded in that person's culture. Jody's disordered behavior and emotions are generated by a physical characteristic. The link is not created by internal psychic forces but by the world in which Jody lives. His culture has made his size a problem; there is nothing intrinsically "bad" about being very small.

The therapist works with Jody on the premise that his turmoil arises out of his perception that "it is bad to be little." One of the treatment techniques employed throughout the case is continuous effort to alter this perception. Another principal technique is to get Jody involved in new experiences which modify prior perceptions and lead to more productive behaviors. In this category can be included the teacher's arranging for him to get hot lunches from the school, which results in a change in his eating patterns, and the therapist's encouraging him to take part in classroom study groups, which enables Jody to receive much more academic help and feel more competent.

Cognitive therapy, a humanistic approach, seems particularly appropriate for Jody. The reader will recall the incident with the puppets in which the boy is highly indignant because when Mr. Sad Face (himself) tries to hide, the dog finds him by smelling his trail. Through his own private logic Jody somehow perceives this as an offense to his dignity as a person. More than anything, Jody wants to be accepted as part of the human race.

THE WATERBURY FAMILY

January 24. For the first interview, Mrs. Waterbury is seen alone. She comes to discuss her son Tom, her only child, who is

twelve years old. She is a former teacher, an intelligent and percep-
tive person who can see the problem as a whole with considerable
astuteness.

Tom was adopted shortly after birth. He was found to have
double vision which impaired his reading ability. With special
remedial help, he learned to read two years earlier when he was in
the fifth grade and is now an excellent reader. His I.Q. is unusually
high. In the sixth grade, through a series of unfortunate events, his
regular teacher was ill most of the year and Tom had more than
twelve different teachers. As a result, according to his mother, he
learned very little and had to repeat the sixth grade. This has upset
him, together with the other children teasing him during the last
year because he is an adopted child. His parents have never con-
cealed from Tom that he was adopted.

This year Tom is repeating his sixth grade in a different school
where he is no longer teased about his adoption. His current academic work, however, is poor and he may fail again despite
superior intelligence, primarily because he fell behind the previous
year with all the substitute teachers, lost confidence in himself, and
has not been trying this year. The tutor who helped him with his
reading has the mother's confidence, and is available for helping
Tom with math and other subjects if the therapist recommends it.
Mrs. Waterbury wonders whether Tom's prime need at this point
is psychotherapy and whether, by itself, it will be sufficient to re-
lease his bottled-up potentialities. She will go along with the therapist's decision as to whether therapy alone is called for at present,
or whether it should be combined with remedial academic tutoring.

Tom's problems are complicated by his parents' marital situation. As Tom grew up, basic differences developed between
mother and father over how to handle him. In Mrs. Waterbury's
opinion, her husband has always indulged the boy and granted his
every request and whim, never setting any standards for Tom to
meet. As a result, the boy always expects to have his own way.
When she recently denied one of his requests, he hit her and ran
away to his father's office. Lately she thinks her husband has begun to recognize how he overindulges the boy and is realizing that
Tom does not necessarily like his catering father better than his
disciplining mother. Mrs. Waterbury explains that she has carried
the role of disciplinarian in this family. Mr. Waterbury's awareness of his overindulging ways has improved the marital situation a

bit but she thinks she will eventually separate from her husband. But she will not do this until Tom has become emotionally stable and able to tolerate such a shock.

Mrs. Waterbury also states that her husband does not have a strongly masculine personality. He has never been able to teach and encourage Tom to take part in baseball games and other such activities. He works as an office manager but is a frustrated musician. She herself plays the piano for a hobby. Tom has balked at learning music and she thinks it is because he regards her as very good and does not want to be unfavorably compared to her. Tom wants friends but has none. She is not sure why this is so; she mentions "bad breaks" which have interfered with occasional friendships that did develop in the past. The boy once wanted to be a scientist, but has now given up this ambition in the face of school difficulties and presently has no faith in his ability to achieve this. At the same time, he is very self-sufficient, travels all over by himself, and likes building model airplanes.

Mrs. Waterbury hopes that treatment will relieve Tom's anxieties and help him to overcome his currently low self-esteem. She is convinced that the key problem is his feeling of worthlessness (he says, "I'm just an orphan") and his inability to mobilize his talents. She would like him to develop stronger male identifications in therapy. The therapist, in turn, is thinking to himself that additional therapeutic goals may include the promotion of Tom to junior high school (seventh grade) in June, and resolving the open clashes of the parents at home over how to deal with his behavior.

January 31. The therapist sees Tom alone. The youngster is cagey and careful at first. He tries to keep the conversation on a very intellectual level and avoids revealing any emotions. Tom is a good-looking, neat, clean, red-headed child with excellent speech and refined manners. He states that ballistics is his favorite subject, but it turns out that he has not read much about it. He surprises the therapist with his naiveté, claiming that of course he can hit a target two miles away.

In a discussion about his previous reading difficulties, Tom denies that they had anything to do with defective vision. He thinks he is coming to the therapist for help with his problem of having no friends. He says that he has no friends because school is far from home. He is vague about his reason for not wanting to change to a school nearer to where he lives. The therapist suggests that passing in school will also be a problem this year and Tom reluctantly agrees. The therapist tells the boy that he would like to talk to his teacher. Tom becomes frightened and refuses to give his permission, claiming he has the right to say no. He is afraid his teacher will tell other people and that word will get around that he is seeing a therapist, which means that he is "different."

The therapist assures Tom that he will not contact the teacher without the boy's consent. Tom then begins to discuss his feelings of being "different." These come from the fact that he is adopted, has red hair, and is "much less than average." He comes close to tears as he brings out these matters. He is sure that his peers are rejecting him for these reasons. The therapist tells him that he is constitutionally the same as everyone else—very much average—and that it must be something in his behavior that alienates others. Tom offers the idea that others consider him a sissy. The boy and the therapist discuss this at length; the latter makes the point that rougher kids often tease gentler ones with this label. Tom adds that sometimes a person is teased because the teasers are envious of his speech or manners and need a scapegoat.

The therapist observes that Tom has lost confidence in himself. Tom asks the therapist to elaborate on this statement, because he does not understand the meaning: there are all kinds of confidence. The therapist spells out that he has lost faith in his ability to do things such as school work of which he is easily capable.

In reply to the therapist's question later on, Tom states that he likes his father better than his mother. But he and his father are not pals and do not do many things together.

February 7. Before the interview, Mrs. Waterbury calls the therapist on the telephone to report Tom's recent attitudes. The boy has commented at home that his parents are married legally but not mentally. He has announced that he has solved his problem of making friends through the therapist's help and does not have to return to see him, since he followed the advice the therapist gave him last week in their first session.

Nevertheless, Tom does appear for today's appointment. He says: "I followed your advice and examined what I was doing to antagonize others. I was acting silly, so I stopped it, and I'm making friends. I like playing the part of the weaker, smaller person. In this way, I'm not expected to compete or fight. There is a disadvantage—I'm not picked to play on ball teams until the very last—but it's worth it. I choose kids to be friends with who aren't in any fights, because their enemies will pick on me too."

Asked to describe himself in a couple of sentences, Tom replies, "Physically weak, trouble with schoolwork but I think I'll pass, hobbies are ballistics and rifles." He informs the therapist that he will not be going to camp this coming summer because the cost of his therapy is a financial burden on his family and they will not be able to afford camp. The therapist probes further and Tom admits that he is not going to camp partly because he wants to avoid facing a new group of children and having to make decisions about relationships.

The therapist suggests that Tom talk to his teacher about his chances of passing. Tom says he has never thought of this and will do it in the coming week. At the end of the session, Tom asks the therapist if he can change Tom's handwriting to right-handed. The boy is left-handed and his penmanship is very poor. In summing up this interview for himself, the therapist concludes that Tom is still acting, still putting on a performance most of the time.

February 14. Mrs. Waterbury telephones before today's session to bring the therapist up to date on events of the past week. Tom touched or hit a girl in school and the principal wants to see the parents in a few days' time. The principal called Mrs. Waterbury in the boy's presence and told her that his behavior is immature and his work is better but still inferior. The day after the incident with the girl, Tom, afraid of trouble, wanted things to "cool down" and did not go to school. His attendance this year in general has been poor because of high susceptibility to bronchial infections and equally owing to "emotional" pains in the stomach and head. Yesterday Tom went back to school exceedingly upset, having been made very anxious by an outburst from his father. Mr. Waterbury lost his temper and accused Tom of being no better than those delinquents who are suspended from school. Tom was honest in telling his mother about the incident in school, but in other respects he is not honest: he pretends to do his homework and lies to his mother about having finished it.

When Tom is seen today, he tells the therapist that nothing has happened all week. The therapist brings up some of the events reported by his mother. Tom does not want to discuss any of them, and especially refuses to describe what he did to the girl in school. He insists that it is none of the therapist's business. The therapist does not press him further and turns to a review of Tom's previous facile optimism. The boy agrees that his problems cannot be solved so easily when he is confronted with last week's superficial assertions that he had worked out his difficulties. The therapist observes that Tom will not reach down for feelings—he keeps the therapist at a distance. The therapist tries to persuade him to share some of those feelings. The interview ends on this note.

The therapist subsequently learns that Tom was furious when he came home from his treatment session. He was very angry at his mother for telling the therapist about what had transpired in school and vowed he "would never trust her again." During the week before the boy's next appointment with the therapist, Mrs. Waterbury has a conference with the school principal and asks about Tom's chances for being promoted at the end of the year, the subjects that require the most attention, and whether the principal thinks he needs a tutor. The principal's opinion is that Tom can pass if he works on his spelling and writing. Mrs. Waterbury is ready to begin at once to sit down with Tom every night and help him with his homework. The boy refuses. His father complicates the situation even more by telling him that he does not have to work on these subjects. Mrs. Waterbury becomes very angry with her husband.

February 21. Tom is seen alone. Again he is evasive. He says the conference with the principal is none of the therapist's business. He does not need the therapist's help. The therapist senses what is necessary to overcome Tom's negative attitude and proposes an agreement: the therapist will have no further communication with his mother on the condition that Tom will communicate fully with the therapist from now on. Tom accepts.

The boy then opens up. He talks about how he does not love his mother. She is mean, always nags, cares nothing for his father, only married him for his money, and thinks only of herself. Tom claims she neglects the home, sleeps all day, and is always out with friends. If only she would leave for good, he and his father could manage nicely. He explains that his father understands him, and says with deep emotion that the therapist will never know how much his father's love means to him. The therapist can contact his father anytime about anything.

After the session, the therapist telephones Mrs. Waterbury to advise her of his new agreement with Tom. She is willing to co-operate and will refrain from communicating about Tom with the therapist, who now plans to work through Mr. Waterbury. A few days later, Tom gets angry with his mother for criticizing him and hits her from behind with a thermos bottle. She becomes frightened and leaves home, staying away with friends for several days. Tom's next appointment with the therapist is supposed to take place while she is still out of the house.

February 28. Tom comes for his appointment, waits three minutes, and leaves before the therapist can see him. Mr. Waterbury excuses the boy on the ground that he just received a new gun and was impatient to look it over. The therapist believes that Tom was afraid to face him today. On the phone Tom insists he really wanted to talk to the therapist.

Meanwhile both parents keep in touch with the therapist, who effects Mrs. Waterbury's return home on March 2. During her absence Tom has been openly delighted over her departure and has had his father all to himself. With his mother's return to the household, Tom proceeds to badger her continually, trying to punish her and drive her out, striking her and acting quite aggressive. Mrs. Waterbury is very bitter because her husband is immobilized by all the tension and freezes up. He stops giving her money for household expenses, does not speak to her, and feels unable to use force to stop Tom's aggressive behavior toward her. He does not believe in physical methods of discipline.

March 5. Mr. Waterbury asks for an appointment with the therapist and is seen today. He seems to be a sensitive and sincere individual. He finds the present home situation intolerable and wants help. The therapist recommends that he tell Tom in Mrs. Waterbury's presence that he will no longer permit any physical aggression against her. He also thinks that Mr. Waterbury should resume giving his wife money to run the house. Finally, he emphasizes that every possible effort should be made to help Tom get promoted and to break his pattern of failure.

Mr. Waterbury talks about himself. He holds a supervisory position and has been with the same company for a long time, so that he has some status and security at his work. He reveals that he gets psychological, not organic, heart palpitations under strain and usually goes to bed at 9 P.M. because he is so tired. He has no energy for physical activities like baseball or other sports with Tom, although he would certainly like to be able to participate in such things.

In regard to the therapist's recommendations, Mr. Waterbury says that he appreciates the therapist's approach of dealing only in general principles and allowing him to decide on the details of carrying them out. He admits that he has done nothing to stop Tom from replicating his own bitterness toward Mrs. Waterbury.

March 6. The therapist receives a phone call from Mrs. Waterbury, who expresses pleasure at the turn of events since her husband came to see the therapist yesterday. He has resumed giving her money for household expenses and took a stand with Tom in regard to his behavior. They have begun to discuss their mutual problems and her attitude toward Mr. Waterbury is already more positive in response to his attempt to set standards for their son. She believes that Mr. Waterbury's session with the therapist enabled him to realize that he does not help Tom by condoning violence and that he has to break out of his "frozen" state.

March 7. Tom is seen. He expresses strong hostility toward his mother and insists that he and his father can manage well without her. He himself did the shopping and cooking while she was away and everything worked out fine. He goes on at length about her constant nagging, carelessness, and neglect of household chores. Tom's contention is that the house is a mess when his mother is around, but without her he and his father put things in order. According to Tom, she is always running off to visit people or go places. He complains that she does sewing to earn money and then puts these earnings into her own bank account, which is not fair. The therapist points out that she may want to save for a future emergency, but the boy is not in the least sympathetic.

The therapist and Tom discuss how to improve the immediate situation and his relationship with his mother. He replies that his mother should love his father. If this cannot happen, they should go for marriage counseling. The therapist comments that the latter course of action is being considered and he can ask his father about it. Tom says with great interest that he will. The therapist then suggests that Tom, for his part, should give up aggression against his mother as a way of handling problems since his unremitting hostility is futile. Tom responds that he could manage better if his mother were not always criticizing and finding fault. He also notes another problem: he and his father want to live in the country (where Tom can do rifle shooting) while his mother prefers city living.

March 14. Tom is seen. The therapist explores further the boy's hostility against his mother, his affection for his father, and his perception that Mrs. Waterbury is neglecting the home and does not care for him. The therapist begins to form the impression that she may be demanding too much from her husband and son and, not getting it, has retaliated by neglecting her household responsibilities.

The therapist gets Tom's permission to write to the school principal for a progress report.

March 21. Tom is seen. The therapist observes that it is becoming easier for the boy to express feelings and face his problems. Today he raises the question of what the therapist thinks of his maturity and self-control. It turns out that he wants to use the therapist as a lever in dealing with his mother, who does not think he is ready to do rifle shooting when his father takes him and his friend to the country for a weekend two weeks from now. The therapist declines to discuss the issue of maturity in connection with rifle shooting, but instead gives Tom his evaluation of the boy's maturity in more general terms. He points out that Tom's surprisingly poor work and attitude in school, together with his constant striving to split up his father and mother, are not indicative of maturity. The therapist confronts Tom with his deliberate efforts to make his mother miserable. The boy answers that he is trying to teach her to be different and to protect his father. The therapist demonstrates that his belligerent actions have not accomplished this purpose and are now upsetting his father, who is capable of protecting himself. Tom insists that his father does not know how.

The therapist urges Tom to respect his mother as a human being and to bear in mind the possibility that those characteristics of hers which he dislikes may have been in part created by her exclusion from family affection. Tom states firmly that if his mother ever offers him love, he will not accept it. He cannot, after all she has done. He becomes very emotional and chokes up as he again speaks of his love for his father. He says he cannot describe what this means to him.

March 28. Tom comes for his appointment. The therapist is five minutes late and Tom does not wait. Later, on the phone, he is hostile: "I've given you my quota for this week." Another appointment is scheduled for tomorrow.

March 29. As Mr. Waterbury is bringing Tom to the office for his rescheduled session, the boy runs away by bolting out of the bus in which they are traveling. He tells his father that the therapist probes and gets him to talk and that he has to lie to the therapist. He does not want to see him any more. Mr. Waterbury keeps the appointment in Tom's place.

Mr. Waterbury is planning to take Tom and a friend of his to the country for the upcoming weekend. The boys will be shooting their rifles. Tom, of course, has been eagerly looking forward to this occasion, but is willing to give it up if it is conditional upon seeing the therapist. Mr. Waterbury has threatened to cancel the weekend unless Tom continues to come for treatment. The therapist advises Mr. Waterbury to disassociate the weekend from the therapy: the former should not be contingent upon the latter. The therapist thinks that father and son should go ahead and enjoy their country weekend. Mr. Waterbury is not to mention the idea of another appointment to Tom, but should simply tell the boy that the therapist understands why he did not come today. The therapist then discusses with Mr. Waterbury why he thinks the boy is now refusing to come after showing signs of resistance for a month: the therapist has not always told him what he wanted to hear; in addition, Tom may be blaming the therapist for the parents' improving relationship, which threatens his exclusive possession of his father.

Also on this date, a report is received from the school which describes Tom as defiant, disruptive, disorganized, and discouraged, alienating his peers with deliberately offensive mannerisms. Mrs. Waterbury telephones to convey how delighted she is with the way her husband is trying to set limits for Tom, prohibit violence, and maintain consistent communication with her for the first time in a long while.

April. The therapist has no contact with Tom but does have one treatment session with Mr. Waterbury in which the school report is discussed. Tom tells his father that he has no intention of seeing the therapist again. Mr. Waterbury and the boy really enjoyed their country weekend. Also during this month, the therapist and Mr. Waterbury go to Tom's school together to meet his sixth-grade teacher, who appears to understand what he needs and is willing to deal with him on an individual basis. She gives a surprisingly favorable report: in the last month he has begun to improve noticeably so that now, at the end of April, he is showing marked gains in writing and spelling and is coming out of his shell. The peculiar antagonizing behavior described in the school report a month before is disappearing and Tom is starting to participate in class discussions instead of withdrawing. He displays great interest in exhibiting a project at the science fair. A decision has been made to promote him in June to junior high school. He and his present classmates will go to the same school in September. The teacher will inform Tom of the good news.

The therapist and Mr. Waterbury agree that there will continue to be no pressure on Tom to resume therapy. The boy had been notified in advance by his father of the arrangement for the therapist and Mr. Waterbury to visit the teacher together.

May. Tom, very upset, telephones the therapist to inform him of a new decision by the school authorities. Because of a technicality, Tom will not be going in September to the same junior high school as his present classmates. The therapist assures the boy that he will contact a high official in an effort to reinstate the original decison; he sends a letter which reads, in part:

> Tom is a boy of superior intelligence who, nevertheless, has deep-rooted feelings of inferiority. This has been a factor in his poor relationships with other children, and in his feelings of being isolated, worthless and not accepted by his peers. Recently, in his present sixth grade class, he has begun to come out of his shell, to make friends, and to feel once again that he can be accepted by others. Conduct problems have disappeared, and Tom now goes to school with enthusiasm and ambition. He was looking forward eagerly to moving on with his classmates in the fall.

Suddenly, he learned that he was going to be returned instead to a different school, the one he had attended prior to being transferred to the building where he is now. There had been unpleasant situations which made the transfer necessary, and the prospect of a return to that same school has been very crushing and upsetting to Tom.

It is our considered opinion that Tom should go to the same junior high school as the rest of his current class in September. To send him to any other school would definitely interfere with the treatment process and would set this boy back immeasurably. What he needs more than ever is to continue the positive experience which he has succeeded in finding with his present class. Not to go on together with his present class would be a serious blow to the feelings of self-respect that he is just beginning to develop. Please be assured that this agency will stand by and will be available for any situation which may arise concerning Tom.

Shortly afterward, the change in promotion plan is rescinded and Tom is officially notified that he will be going on to the same junior high school as the other students in his class.

June. As in May, there is no face-to-face contact between Tom and the therapist. Mr. Waterbury keeps the therapist informed of what is going on. This is done through telephone calls. The therapist learns that Tom continues to be enthusiastic and happy about attending school. Clashes with his mother decrease sharply, and at the moment there are no serious crises in the home. Tom is looking forward to junior high school in September. Prior to that, his mother will be spending the summer months with him in the country. Mr. Waterbury will join them for weekends.

Work with the Waterbury family is based on various cognitive assumptions. Primarily, as has been indicated throughout this book, the therapist regards the behaviors of each of the three clients as products of their respective perceptions of the school, the family, and themselves.

Because Tom was adopted, held back in school, and possesses certain physical traits, he feels "different" and incompetent, and has suffered a loss of belief in himself. At the start of treatment he is not trying to do his work in school. This may be out of a fear of

failing again: doing poorly because he does not try may be less devastating for him than making a genuine effort and still doing
poorly. When the therapist first meets Tom, the boy is exceedingly
hostile to his mother, a former teacher, so that serious academic
and behavior problems in school may also serve the purpose of em-
barrassing or disappointing her. His extreme resentment against
her may have resulted from the inconsistent handling of the parents. Mr. Waterbury, not physically vigorous himself, has possibly
overidentified with Tom's physical problems (vision and susceptibility to respiratory infection) and concluded that he "owes"
the boy compliance with all his wishes to make up for past unhappiness. Mrs. Waterbury, on the other hand, recognizes the boy's
potential for overcoming his problems and the value of holding
him to limits. From her efforts to deal firmly with Tom, who is
used to his father's indulgence, the boy comes to perceive her as his
enemy.

Mr. Waterbury does not cope well with pressure and is sometimes overwhelmed by it, especially when it is associated with demands from his wife for Tom to apply himself in school and for
him to control the boy when he is defiant or violent at home. Mr.
Waterbury, at the onset of therapy, is retaliating against his wife
by undermining her authority with the boy and by not communicating with her. She, in turn, disappointed by her husband's lack
of strength and support and frustrated on all sides, seeks satisfaction in outside activities and neglects household duties. Tom uses
this complicated state of affairs to justify his animosity toward his
mother. He also may sense that as long as he causes difficulties, his
parents will disagree over how to handle him and he may be able to
drive his mother out of the home.

Another assumption upon which the therapist proceeds is that
treatment takes place outside as well as inside the office. When
Tom refuses to continue his weekly interviews but begins to show
substantial progress in his real world, the therapist shifts gears,
keeps in touch with the father, and monitors the therapeutic process from a distance. Later, when Tom needs him to intervene regarding the change in promotion plan, the boy asks for help and
the therapist serves as his advocate.

The therapist also acts on the premise that the purpose of behavior is the advancement of an individual's interests as he sees them. When a given behavior no longer achieves what the person thinks he wants, the maximum possibility for change exists. When the therapist is able to help Mr. Waterbury set limits for Tom in the home and support his wife's authority, defiance and belligerency toward her will now displease Mr. Waterbury and be punished, so that Tom has to give them up.

The therapist uses his belief that human beings have a basic tendency to strive for competence and a sense of completion. Knowing of Tom's superior intelligence, he believes that the boy will put it to work when he can no longer play one parent against the other and is faced with demands from his father to work in school and cooperate at home.

Another principle applied in the Waterbury case is that it is essential for the therapist to perceive his clients as accurately as possible. Therefore, although Tom is the index client, all three members of the family are seen in treatment so that each one's version of the situation is available. Further objectivity is sought by a visit to the teacher in school.

The assumption is made that psychotherapy plus concrete services is the highest level of professional help, likely to be more effective than psychotherapy alone. In addition to the informative school visit, the therapist meets the parents in a restaurant to bring about the mother's return home, and writes to a school official to protect Tom's promotion.

The cognitist in this case, as in the case of Jody, operates on the premise that perception is strongly influenced by the surrounding culture. Both boys fear being regarded as "different." Again, being adopted, red-haired, and left-handed are seen as deviant by Tom only because society tolerates prejudice against those who vary from the general average. For the same reason, he wants to conceal that he is seeing a therapist or that he has a visual problem.

Finally, cognitive theory assumes the possibility of rapid change after a long period of unchanging behavior. This can happen because behavior changes quickly in response to a basic shift in perception. Once perception is altered, even longstanding behavior patterns break up and assume new forms to be consistent with a person's new way of looking at his world. For quite a while, Tom shows no change in his difficult school and home behavior. Then, as various forces, insights, and experiences make themselves felt, improvement in many areas is reported in a short space of time.

A few of the treatment techniques used in working with the Waterburys include advocacy, goal focus, confrontation, and paradoxical intention.

Taking the role of advocate on behalf of Tom becomes mandatory for the therapist when the boy's improvement is jeopardized by a bureaucratic technicality. Reversing the destructive school board decision not only preserves the conditions needed for Tom's continued progress but also cements his relationship with the therapist. Even though he has stopped seeing the therapist face to face, he now has further evidence that the therapist cares about him and is ready to help if future emergencies arise.

A fundamental technique of the cognitist is to deal with the client's goals, which strongly influence behavior. Antisocial goals produce antisocial conduct and unrealistic goals lead to frustration, while healthy goals can evoke constructive behavior. Because one of Tom's main goals is to keep his father's love and approval, the therapist focuses his efforts on this goal and uses it as a lever. By persuading Mr. Waterbury to disapprove of Tom's defiance at home and poor performance in school, the therapist creates a new situation in which the boy must change his behavior or fail to achieve his goal.

We have previously defined confrontation as the act of bringing a client face to face with factual truth by means of some direct action on the part of the therapist. This often requires considerable courage from the therapist, a willingness to endure tension in order to help the client grow. When Tom asks for an evaluation of his maturity, the therapist uses the opportunity to confront the boy with his shortcomings. This is a kind of calculated risk that a professional helper frequently must take. In this case the therapist weighs the chance to modify some of Tom's perceptions against the possibility of straining the therapeutic relationship, and decides in favor of the former.

Lastly, the therapist uses a paradoxical approach when Tom refuses further treatment sessions. This results from the therapist's conclusion that having Mr. Waterbury compel the boy to come will produce a situation in which Tom will continually sabotage the therapy. Tom can be expected to engage in subtle and not so subtle opposition to the person who, in his perception, has teamed up with the enemy (his mother), and who by the very nature of his therapeutic role makes him feel "different." The paradox consists of telling a client who needs change that he does not have to work with a change agent. Actually, however, the therapist sets Tom free to change himself.

Chapter 10

Research in Cognitive Therapy

Research to measure the outcome of specific types of intervention has always been a challenge and a source of frustration to all the helping professions, including social work. When a research study is being designed, serious difficulties can arise in answering questions such as these:

How do we define improvement in client functioning?
How do we measure the extent of this improvement?
How much importance do we assign to the client's own judgment about his improvement?
How much importance do we assign to the therapist's judgment about the client's improvement?
How can we know if improvement was primarily a result of the treatment being studied?
How can we know if the population studied was truly representative?

Fischer has called for the incorporation of research into social work practice, in line with his conviction that we should move on a large scale beyond merely understanding clients to build various techniques for helping them change. His belief is that the use of objective research procedures to accompany the delivery of a particular treatment technique will give us a scientific tool for validating its usefulness. We will then be able to decide on a rational basis whether to continue or discontinue this technique.

Turner, who believes that the social work profession should commit itself fully to the principle of continuing research, addresses the issue of what kind of research is to be done:

> It appears that in the late 1970s we finally reached a clear awareness that efforts to engage in the vast, all-encompassing research questions are in vain. Without retelling an oft-told tale, it has now been sufficiently demonstrated that research projects that deal with such questions as "is casework effective" or "does psychotherapy help" or "is marriage counseling useful" are in vain. By now we have aptly demonstrated that such efforts to deal with these large questions will usually be inconclusive or at best give some minor supporting evidence. The risk of these kinds of projects is that findings are quickly politicized and used to bolster or weaken various arguments engaged in for other than disinterested motives.
>
> We seem now to have learned something that our colleagues in other disciplines have long known; knowledge is advanced by very minute steps. The payoffs from research on a study-by-study basis are very minuscule. What does succeed is the accumulated interconnected knowledge that comes from a number of small, well-developed, and implemented programs of research. [Turner, 1978, pp. 199–200]

Fischer agrees that "the huge investment of time, money, and energy in gross evaluation efforts, such as studies using group experimental designs, is unlikely to have any real payoff in the near future" (Fischer, 1978, p. 88). These controlled group experimental studies represent the "extensive" research model. Fischer proposes that we focus on the "intensive" model in the immediate future:

> The intensive or practice-oriented design (also called $N = 1$ or single-organism design) is used for research that pertains

to single-case studies, more or less formalized to the extent that conclusions about effectiveness in individual cases can be established by varying certain conditions over a period of time. . . . This differs significantly from the extensive model where conclusions can be generated only about group effects and where, as a result, the possible variations in effects between individuals, except in the grossest sense, may be lost. [Fischer, 1978, p. 89]

. . . Several replications of intensive, individualized case studies can form the basis for an informed, properly conceived study based on the extensive model. Thus, the two models of research can work hand in hand. The intensive case study, which tends to be limited in generalization potentials beyond a specific client and a specific worker, can provide the basic data for generating hypotheses for more elaborate group experimental designs following the extensive model. And conclusions from research using such extensive designs can, in turn, form the empirically validated basis for effective practice. [Fischer, 1978, p. 92]

Fischer discusses five general models for evaluating practice with individuals. Their prototype is the time-series design, which consists of measuring the extent of a given problem on a repeated basis over a period of time to see if a specific intervention produces any changes. Alterations are measured by such procedures as actually counting the problematic behaviors, repeated administration of a questionnaire, outside data such as school attendance records, or continuous reports by the client himself about his behavior. Not only is the client's performance compared for various time periods after therapeutic intervention has begun; differences in performance between the baseline and various intervention periods can also be measured, the baseline being the measurements taken before the start of any treatment process.

Fischer suggests that for most social workers who have minimal experience with, interest in, or time for conducting complicated statistical procedures with their clients, the best method of dealing with the data obtained during a treatment process is to record them on a simple chart. Then discontinuities (major changes) in the level or slope will be visually discernible. Level refers to the amount, frequency, intensity, or duration of behavior. Slope refers to the trend of the target behavior, the rate at which some aspect is increasing or decreasing during a given period of time (Fischer, 1978, pp. 89-90).

Experimental investigation of single cases

The first of the five approaches to evaluating techniques of individual treatment is the experimental investigation of single cases. This type of clinical outcome study requires that each technique be objectively identifiable so that it is clear when it is being applied and when it is not; that the behaviors for which change is deemed desirable be objectively identifiable; and that there be a method of observing, preferably in the natural environment, the occurrence or nonoccurrence of these target behaviors. A target behavior that one wishes to change is measured as to how many times it occurs in a given period of time, its duration each time it occurs, the number of time periods during which the behavior occurs at least once, and/or the intensity of each occurrence. The first measurements are made before treatment starts and these baseline data are later compared with those obtained during time periods when a particular treatment technique is being applied. In this experimental design, the criterion for success, behavior change in the desired direction, is built in and it is possible in each case to tell whether a technique works without sophisticated statistical procedures. In order to be sure, however, that the behavior change is directly related to the therapeutic technique under study, a procedure known as reversal is employed, whereby there is a return in alternate time periods to baseline conditions by not using the technique. If the new, desirable behavior markedly decreases during these reversal periods and returns during periods of therapeutic intervention, it is reasonable to conclude that client improvement was directly related to the technique.

Fischer discusses the limitations and weaknesses of this experimental design, as well as some variations that can also be used by the practitioner to evaluate the effectiveness of treatment techniques with individual clients (Fischer, 1978, pp. 93–100). For an example of the investigation by social workers of a single case using a time-series design, the reader is referred to the experiment reported by Bloom and Block (1977, pp. 130–136).

The objectified case study

The second in Fischer's list of experimental approaches is the objectified case study, in which the intervention technique is systematically varied and results are carefully recorded. The purpose is to determine what particular technique, what variation of a technique, or what combination of techniques produces maximum desirable change in specific kinds of clients. As with other types of intensive design, measurements are made before, during, and after periods of intervention by noting the actual occurrence of problem behavior, by eliciting client and worker evaluations, and by employing psychological and personality tests, inventories, and checklists. If a certain technique or combination of techniques applied to one client appears to be successful, the practitioner can then apply it in exactly the same way to other clients who are either matched with the first in regard to presumably significant characteristics (nature of problem, age, sex, socioeconomic status, ethnic background, etc.) or who present a different problem or different personal characteristics. As in the experimental investigation of single cases, it is presumed that the technique applied and the behavior to be modified are objectively identifiable, and that there is a reliable way to measure the target behavior.

The measurement model

Another intensive design, the measurement model, uses short questionnaires that are filled in by the client at periodic intervals during treatment. These scales consist of a small number of questions that can be answered in a very brief time. The same questionnaire is used on each occasion. It attempts to tap the client's feelings in a problem area and to come up with a score which can be compared at each repetition with those that preceded it. Thus, a regular, ongoing feedback is provided to client and worker regarding changes in the client's perceptions about a particular aspect of his life while being treated with a particular technique.

Fischer refers specifically to seven short instruments recently developed by Hudson and his associates (Fischer, 1978, pp. 108–109) to discover the presence and extent of marital conflict, depression, poor self-esteem, sexual dissatisfaction, and parent-child problems. Hudson, a social worker, chose these problem areas because they were important and common in casework practice. There are many other instruments available, developed mainly by psychologists. The use of such scales as repeated measures gives the therapist a means of assessing and modifying the course of treatment on a continuous basis.

The *a priori* model

Another systematic process for evaluating the effectiveness of treatment of individual clients is the *a priori* model. This involves the determination *in advance* of the stages through which a therapeutic technique will pass, the premise being that the worker and client cannot move on to one stage from another until specific criteria are met. Meeting these criteria implies a successful outcome at the lower level. According to Fischer (1978, p. 117), in 1978 this model was still largely theoretical, awaiting the development and validation of actual experiments.

Systematized recording

The final method discussed by Fischer for building research into practice calls for introducing more systematic ways of keeping records in social agencies. In essence, this would require that all case records in a given agency follow a precise structure in which various data are listed in a uniform manner, quantified and coded when possible, so that most of this information can be recorded in simple numerical form. Fischer furnishes an example of systematized recording in which all the data about a terminated case fit on one sheet of paper. Included is the following information: client characteristics; target problems; specific goals and indicators for determining success; time limits; worker roles; tasks assigned to the client; specific techniques of the worker in regard to specific goals; client activities and accomplishments; periodic evaluation of problem solving and attainment of objectives; evaluation of the extent of attainment of specific objectives by means of a five-point numerical scale; overall evaluation of the extent of problem resolution by the same type of numerical scale; amount of contact; and follow-up plans (Fischer, 1978, pp. 120–124).

The present writer has had first-hand experience for over fifteen years with another system of uniform and coded recording in which data are written on five preprinted IBM cards. This system has the advantage that it can be used in two ways. The data are written by hand within boxes and spaces on the various cards, preceded by a code number when possible or sometimes consisting only of a code number. (See figure 10.1 for the first of these cards, the "opening card.") In reviewing the case or doing research, the information can be read right off the cards. A key-punch operator can also punch the cards for selected data directly over the written words or numbers, thus facilitating more complex research efforts such as determining correlations between large numbers of variables. Having a key-punch machine and a sorter available, an agency could quickly process thousands of cases to determine if there were any correlation, for example, between treatment outcome and the total number of interviews given to a client.

At the psychiatric clinic where the writer participated in the use of this system, another benefit was that the compilation of monthly statistics for government agencies was speeded up greatly. This result was accomplished by punching these data cards, as well as another IBM card used for a brief narrative account of each interview, for the required statistical items. At the end of each month, with the use of a sorter it was relatively easy to compile the total number of interviews (including which members of the family saw which therapist), the total number of patients seen, the total amount of time devoted to various categories of direct treatment, and whatever patient characteristics were requested, as well as to make comparisons with the same month in previous years.

In the recording system under discussion, which was devised by Robert P. Kemble, M.D., everything about a case is put on preprinted IBM cards. When service is completed, a case will consist of five data cards and a number of interview cards, one card or more for each unit of staff activity: treatment session, phone call, letter sent, psychological or psychiatric examination, or outside visit. The activity is briefly

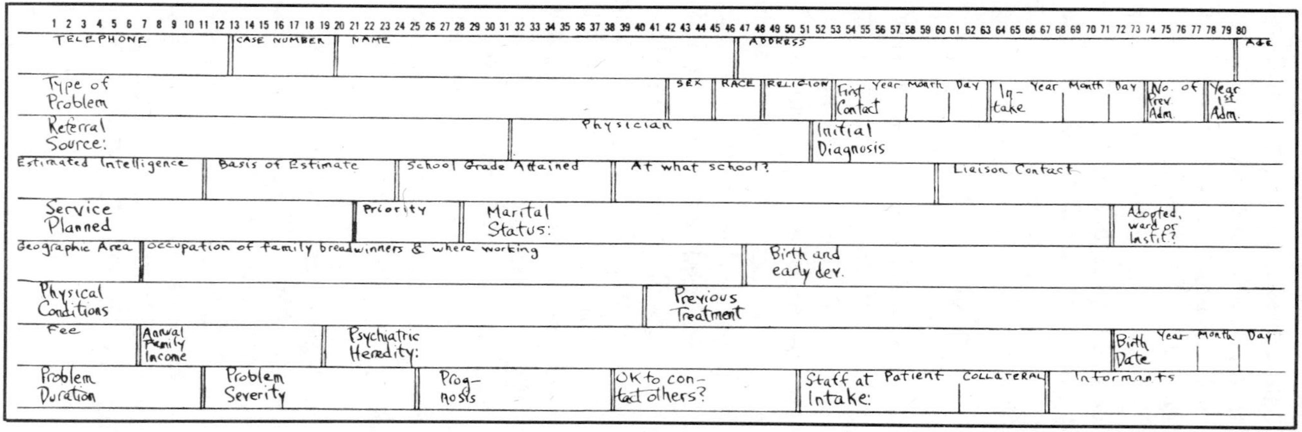

FIGURE 10.1 First of a series of five preprinted IBM cards for uniform data recording, designed by Robert P. Kemble, M.D.

summarized on the interview card in narrative form. The text of any letters sent out is put down verbatim. These interview cards are mostly blank, with just a few small boxes across the top for the index patient's name, file number, type of service rendered, member(s) of the family actually seen, the staff person involved, date, and duration of the session or length of time to make a phone call, write a letter, or complete an outside visit (e.g., .3 hour, 1.2 hours). All the IBM cards—$3\frac{1}{4}"\times 7\frac{1}{4}"$—pertaining to a case fit into a small folder of slightly larger dimensions and occupy very little space. The cards are not fastened to the folder or to each other and can be removed individually at any time for perusal by a therapist, supervisor, or coworker.

The information collected on the five data cards about the index patient includes: name, address, and telephone number; date of birth; description and history of problem and chief complaints; personal characteristics such as age, sex, ethnic background, and place of birth; referral source; name of family physician; estimated intelligence; amount of education to date; family composition; marital status; geographic area of residence; occupations of family breadwinners; anything noteworthy in birth, developmental, or health history; previous treatment; annual income; psychiatric heredity; problem duration; problem severity; initial and final diagnosis with DSM code number; services supplied and whether or not they were completed; date of intake and date of termination; principal worker(s); total number of interviews with each family member by each professional discipline; number of group sessions if applicable; weeks case was active; degree of improvement; and brief summary of the case (presenting problems, services supplied, and outcome) (Kemble, 1959, pp. 52–54).

The potential that systematized recording procedures have for facilitating future research on treatment outcome is very great, but it cannot be fully realized until processes of measuring the degree of goal achievement, and through it treatment success, are maximally objectified. Meanwhile uniform and concise codified recording systems within and among agencies provide opportunities now for studying, comparing, and improving many aspects of the way practitioners and agencies deliver services to clients. Furthermore, as Fischer points out, such recording systems allow us to identify goals and the specific techniques employed to attain them if we include these items in our particular setup as distinct entities which we want to track. In this connection, therefore, it would seem important in the recording of services supplied always to enter them as specific techniques ("assertiveness training," "confrontation") rather than as "individual counseling" or "insight therapy." All this is consistent with Fischer's conviction that the great immediate need is for technique building and for the kind of research that will validate the effectiveness of a specific technique for a specific problem or type of client. As Fischer indicates, the goals of treatment in each case should be one of the items uniformly recorded, thus making it possible to evaluate the effectiveness of the techniques applied on the objective basis of goal attainment. The Kemble system does not include treatment goals among its data, a shortcoming which should be rectified.

The accessibility of cognitive practice to research

If it is agreed that single case studies, mostly using a time-series design, and revisions of recording procedures to make them more usable in research are worth doing, cognitive therapy easily lends itself to these purposes. The philosophy, theory, and practice of the cognitive/humanistic approach place no obstacles in the way of a therapist who wishes to study its effectiveness with his clients. Actually, of course, he will be studying the outcome of the way he personally has applied one or some of the techniques in the cognitive repertoire to a particular client in a particular setting. Techniques are the structure within which the therapist's personal influence is applied; therefore, in addition to our principal focus heretofore on the evaluation of outcome, we do need to build into our research provision for measuring personal factors that may be influencing the results of treatment. It is essential to improve our ability to sort out the respective contributions of the specific techniques and the therapist's personal style to the progress of the client.

Single case studies and systematic recording procedures will work well with clients receiving cognitive therapy because of its basic characteristics: the techniques are objectively identifiable; the therapy focuses on behaviors of people (thinking, feeling, and acting) that are also objectively identifiable; it makes no attempt to postulate unverifiable, unconscious dynamics; it works with the client's own reports about himself as valid data subject to perceptual limitations and distortions; and it is committed to the method of setting up treatment goals and evaluating outcome in terms of extent of goal attainment.

Categories of cognitive procedures

Cognitive therapy, as the reader has seen, is not a monolithic entity but is composed of many different treatment techniques which can be employed singly or in combination. Therefore, in outcome studies based on either single-organism designs or controlled group experiments, what is usually being measured is not the effectiveness of cognitive therapy as a whole but the effectiveness of a single cognitive procedure or cluster of procedures.

Fischer divides cognitive procedures into the four following categories:

1. Cognitive restructuring: changing misconceptions and unrealistic expectations;
2. Changing irrational self-statements;
3. Enhancing problem-solving and decision-making abilities;
4. Enhancing client self-control and management. [Fischer, 1978, pp. 176–177]

Evidence on the effectiveness of cognitive procedures

Fischer (1978) summed up the findings to date of controlled group studies on the effectiveness of cognitive procedures. He noted that there were several controlled studies of one or another form of cognitive restructuring that reported positive results. Rigorous research dealing with the three other categories either could not be located or concentrated on individual components of a category. Fischer suggested that future studies must focus on an entire category—that is, the combination of all the specific techniques that are employed, for example, in enhancing problem solving. He concluded that the evidence for the effectiveness of cognitive procedures as a whole was best described in 1978 as "promising" but not "proved." This was because most of the controlled research had been conducted only in the very recent past. Nevertheless, the bulk of what had been done up to that point showed positive results, so that evidence on the effectiveness of cognitive procedures was growing. Fischer also pointed out that research on cognitive procedures was increasing dramatically (Fischer, 1978, pp. 187–188).

Controlled group studies of all the specific techniques that are used in a particular category of cognitive procedures are needed to validate the effectiveness of the category as a whole. The amount of research done thus far (1980) still seems to be relatively small as regards group studies of cognitive techniques applied to the whole range of important common problems. These problems include depression, anxiety, paranoid states, phobias, compulsions, feelings of inferiority, confusion about goals, unwarranted guilt, marital conflict, strained parent-child relations, delinquent behavior, family violence, lack of confidence, inability to make decisions, feelings of being trapped or overwhelmed, grief over a loss, difficulties in adjusting to changed life situations, over-aggressiveness, and psychophysiological ailments.

Mahoney took a similar position when he wrote in 1977:

> Our daily clinical responsibilities go far beyond the snake-phobic or unassertive college sophomore. . . . we have spent too much time researching procedures and target problems which have little *demonstrated* relevance for the majority of clinical problems. . . .
> The demonstration of an unequivocal success is rare in psychotherapy research. The demonstration of a success which can be logically attributed to the therapy in question is extremely rare. The demonstration of a successful intervention and an identified therapeutic source plus long-term maintenance of improvement has been about as common as a mute politician. If cognitive therapy researchers want to really show their stuff, long-term follow-ups with clinical populations will offer a fitting arena. [Mahoney, 1977, pp. 8–9]

Mahoney also stressed the importance of communicating negative results and failures to replicate. If we do not do this, cognitive therapists will have a distorted view of their strength and will lose out on opportunities to gain valuable information from these failures which can be used to improve cognitive procedures (Mahoney, 1977, p. 15).

Admittedly, we shall have to wait until all four categories, studied as integrated entities, yield positive results in a large number of group experiments before we are justified in claiming that cognitive therapy as a whole is an effective treatment orientation for specified problems. Built into the research designs should be means of assessing how much relative influence on successful or unsuccessful outcome was exerted by each of the specific techniques in the category under study, and by the setting in which treatment took place.

Colby, Faught, and Parkison appear to be optimistic about the results of research on cognitive therapy:

> For a system of psychotherapy to be taken as a serious candidate for a rational technology, it must demonstrate its effectiveness in systematic therapeutic trials using independent judges, control groups, quantitative measures, and long-term follow-ups. Among the current therapeutic schools, only four qualify by these criteria—cognitive therapy, psychoanalytic psychotherapy, behavior therapy, and client-centered therapy. . . . Cognitive therapy is the most promising of these approaches since (1) it contains the most useful ingredients of the others . . . (2) it has a basic science foundation in cognitive psychology using its concepts and vocabulary . . . , and (3) it subjects itself to evaluations of well-designed clinical trials. [Colby, Faught, and Parkison, 1979, pp. 55–56]

Clinical outcome studies of groups

We turn now to four recent group studies of cognitive treatment that appeared in *Cognitive Therapy and Research*. This journal devotes a part of each issue to precisely the kind of experimental studies in which we are interested and probably publishes more research of this type than any other periodical. The brief sampling that follows is intended to give the reader a sense of how cognitive therapy is currently being studied and how some experimenters are finding that cognitive methods are effective.

TREATMENT OF DEPRESSION

Rush, Beck, Kovacs, and Hollon compared the effectiveness of cognitive therapy and an antidepressant medication in the treatment of outpatients with unipolar neurotic depression. The subjects were randomly assigned to individual treatment with either cognitive therapy or imipramine. For the cognitive therapy patients, the treatment protocol specified a maximum of twenty interviews over a period of twelve weeks. The pharmacotherapy patients received up to 250 mg of imipramine daily for a maximum of twelve weeks. While both treatment groups showed statistically significant decreases in depressive symptomatology, the cognitive therapy group showed significantly greater improvement on a self-administered measure of depression and various clinical ratings. Follow-up contacts at three and six months indicated that the observed treatment gains were being maintained: 68 percent of the pharmacotherapy group reentered treatment for depression while only 16 percent of the psychotherapy patients did so.

Cognitive therapy was used on the premise that the depressed patient systematically misconstrues his experiences and tends to regard himself, his world, and his future in an unrealistically negative way. The treatment applied contained the following elements: therapist and patient worked together to identify the patient's distorted cognitions; behavioral tasks were assigned which enabled the patient to master problems he formerly thought insuperable and to realign his thinking with reality; verbal techniques were used by the therapist to teach the connections between thought, feeling, and behavior and how the patient could replace his distorted negative cognitions with more accurate perceptions. The authors concluded that the study results indicated that cognitive therapy may hold great promise as a short-term treatment for depressed outpatients: it is economically feasible for a wide range of patients because it is a short-term modality; it can be used with people for whom pharmacotherapy is medically contraindicated; and it can be taught to relatively inexperienced therapists in a brief training period (Rush, Beck, Kovacs, and Hollon, 1977, pp. 17–37).

Becker and Schuckit subsequently commented on this study, rating it as a good initial investigation. They stated that it was not their intention to diminish the import of the findings, which were highly encouraging, but to question whether the medication type, dosage level, and duration used by the experimenters provided an optimal medication regimen. They pointed out that the type of medication used—the tricyclic antidepressant imipramine—was considered by many studies to be relatively ineffective in comparison with other drugs with chronic and recurrent depressed patients; that blood plasma levels in the subjects were not assayed to determine whether or not therapeutic dosage levels had been achieved; and that "only 3 weeks at a maximum dosage of 250 mg was permitted, whereas 3 to 6 months of high dosage maintenance is recommended by some clinical investigators." Their implication was clear: while cognitive therapy may be effective in treating depressions, its relative efficacy compared with pharmacotherapy may have been overstated because the drugs were not given a fair trial (Becker and Schuckit, 1978, pp. 193–197).

TREATMENT OF ANXIETY

Hussian and Lawrence applied cognitive restructuring techniques to the treatment of a group of highly test-anxious undergraduate students. The subjects were randomly assigned to one of four treatment conditions. Two experimental conditions, a test-specific stress inoculation training and a generalized stress inoculation training condition, were compared with two control conditions, a discussion control and a waiting-list control. Those in the experimental conditions were taught positive coping statements to repeat to themselves during actual future tests to counteract self-defeating statements they had told themselves in the past. The first experimental group was taught coping statements relating specifically to text anxiety; the second received coping statements dealing with anxiety in general.

The subjects were given various psychological examinations before and after the series of three treatment sessions and actual academic test scores before and after treatment were recorded. Treatment did not result in an improvement in test performance, but those receiving test-specific stress inoculation training indicated significant reductions in subjective feelings of anxiety compared to all the controls. Those experimental subjects trained with non-situation-specific coping statements showed some anxiety reduction, but less than those in the first experimental group. The authors concluded that the treatment of choice for a situation-specific anxiety should use situation-specific coping statements (Hussian and Lawrence, 1978, pp. 25–37).

TREATMENT OF COMMUNICATION APPREHENSION

Glogower, Fremouw, and McCroskey conducted a group study to assess the contribution to successful outcome of the following specific techniques within the category of cognitive restructuring: extinction (exposure to anxiety-provoking stimuli); identifying and monitoring negative self-statements; knowledge and rehearsal of coping statements; and the combination of exposure, identification of negative self-statements, and rehearsal of coping statements. A component analysis was made of the cognitive restructuring procedure developed by Meichenbaum as applied to treating a group of subjects who had communication apprehension. Communication apprehension (CA) was defined as the fear associated with either real or anticipated communication with other persons. Communication-apprehensive subjects were divided among four treatment groups (each receiving one of the specific procedures listed above) and a waiting-list control group. A low-anxious group was also included.

The group treated by extinction was exposed in its sessions to the very communication it feared by participating in discussions with each other. Those in the group that aimed at insight into negative self-statements learned how to identify such statements and practiced picking them out whenever they occurred between sessions or during discussions that took place within the weekly sessions. The group concerned with coping statements learned specific ones to use during communication situations (e.g., "Speak slowly, I can handle this"), and practiced saying them aloud frequently during and outside of their training sessions. Members of the group receiving the combination procedure learned the role of negative self-statements in anxiety and how coping statements can reduce anxiety; they identified their negative self-statements; and they learned and rehearsed coping statements.

Using self-report and behavioral measures, the experimenters concluded:

> The *comb* (combination) training procedure was consistently more effective than any single component on every dependent measure. Although the *comb* group was more effective than the *cs* (coping statement) component group on every dependent measure, this difference did not reach significance. The results suggest that while extinction and identification of negative self-statements produce some improvement, the coping statement component is the primary factor in the cognitive restructuring procedure. . . . However, the consistent superiority of the *comb* group over the *cs* group suggests that identification of negative self-statements should continue to be included in the training pro-

gram. [Glogower, Fremouw, and McCroskey, 1978, pp. 220-221]

DEVELOPMENT OF SELF-CONTROL IN YOUNG CHILDREN

Carter, Patterson, and Quasebarth set up an experiment to study the effectiveness of a particular kind of cognitive intervention in increasing the self-control of preschool, kindergarten, and second-grade children. A plan to facilitate self-control was presented to these youngsters in different variations. The experimenters operated on the premise that a plan invariably consists of at least two structural components: a *cue* indicating *when* the plan is to be executed, and a *command* dictating the *action* to be performed when the plan is executed. At each age, the experimental groups consisted of a full plan (cue plus command) condition, a cue-only condition, a command-only condition, a control (no plan instructions) condition, and an additional control group (fully elaborated but irrelevant plan).

In the experimental situation, the children were required to persist at a lengthy task in order to win attractive rewards. The task was to feed marbles into a jar painted and decorated to resemble a "Baby Bird." The marbles were to be carried in a scoop from a large container across the room to a small cup and then fed one by one to Baby Bird. A certificate called a "Good Player Award" was given to each child for participating in the game. A child could win up to six gold stars to put on the certificate if he or she persevered and fed Baby Bird a certain amount of marbles. Six stars would be awarded for the maximum amount of marbles fed to Baby Bird (300 or more) as indicated by the top line marked on the front of the jar. A lesser number of stars would be given for putting enough marbles in the apparatus to reach lower lines.

Subjects were escorted individually to the experimental room and the experimenter demonstrated in detail how to perform the required operations. This was done for all children. In addition, children in the cue-only condition were told that they could think of something to say when they had fed Baby Bird all the marbles in the cup. In the command-only condition, the experimenter suggested that the child, whenever he or she wished, could tell the Baby Bird that it was going to be fed more marbles. In the full plan condition, subjects were told that when they had fed Baby Bird all the marbles in the cup they could tell it that it was going to be fed more marbles. Children in the irrelevant plan condition were told that when they had fed Baby Bird all the marbles in the cup they could say: "Baby Bird, hickory, dickory, dock." Children in the no plan control condition were given no instructions about a plan. The adult then left each child alone in the room, explaining that he or she could stop playing at any time and receive the number of stars already won.

The two main dependent measures, amount of time spent working and number of marbles fed to Baby Bird, were recorded by an observer seated behind a one-way mirror. The results revealed that at the preschool level, only children in the full plan condition spent more time working than those in the control conditions. Among kindergartners, the time spent working by those in the cue-component-only condition did not differ from that spent by control subjects, but in the full plan and command-component-only conditions, a greater amount of time was spent. At the second-grade level, all subjects persisted for approximately the same length of time regardless of condition.

In general, there was a strong relationship between verbalization of the plan (to keep feeding Baby Bird) and finishing the entire task, except among the second-graders. The experimenters concluded:

> In summary, this study investigated the development of children's ability to use plans that are presented at different

levels of generality. Kindergarten children were more successful than preschool children in using generalized plans, but only if it was the cue component that had been left unelaborated. Second-graders' self-control performances were unaffected by the presentation of plans. These results indicate that both the structural level at which a plan is presented and the age of the individuals who are to use it can be important determinants of a plan's ability to facilitate self-control. [Carter, Patterson, and Quasebarth, 1979, p. 413]

Other research issues

We have discussed five models of the intensive or practice-oriented design and the current status of research on the effectiveness of cognitive procedures. Some recent clinical outcome studies of groups have been described. We turn now to a consideration of setting as a variable in cognitive treatment, the measurement of goal attainment, the distinction between effectiveness and efficiency, and the relationship of the therapist's personality to treatment outcome. Each of these research issues has a special importance for the cognitive practitioner.

SETTING AS A VARIABLE IN COGNITIVE TREATMENT

Turner, in a recent book, devotes a chapter to the significance of the setting as a component of practice. This material is recommended as important reading. Turner reminds us of the various ways that the setting influences the psychotherapeutic process: it affects how the client perceives the therapist; it affects how the therapist perceives the client; and it determines to a considerable degree the characteristics of the clients who ask for service (Turner, 1978, Chapter 8).

The cognitist, with his emphasis on the achievement of realistic perceptions of reality by both the client and himself, is always on the alert for distortions and limitations in the client's consciousness and in his own. He attempts to minimize the possibility of misperceptions on the part of the client by revealing his own human qualities and by explaining at the start of treatment exactly what will take place. If the client nevertheless does not perceive the therapist accurately, the therapist will as a matter of course turn to a discussion of the setting with the client in an effort to ascertain if some aspect of the setting has put the client off the track. Children in the outpatient mental health clinic of a hospital may have to be reassured that they are not going to remain in the hospital; the social worker in a family agency may have to clarify for a mother referred by the welfare department that the worker has neither the power nor the intention of removing her child from the home; and a probation officer may have to explain to a new probationer that, despite the fact that his office is in the same building as the juvenile court, his function is to help the young person avoid further appearances before the judge.

The reverse kind of distortion can exist when the setting influences the therapist to misperceive the client, usually because an erroneous assumption is made that any client present in a particular office, agency, or division of an agency must of necessity, just by being there, possess certain characteristics. Such a mistake by a therapist sabotages the entire process of cognitive treatment, which depends on an accurate, individualized assessment of each client at the very beginning of therapy. A cognitive practitioner cannot possibly help a client to achieve more realistic perceptions of himself and his world when the therapist has no understanding of that person or where he is coming from.

A social work supervisor in a county welfare department reported the following impressions:

As a supervisor of a social service unit in a county welfare agency, I have found that the workers have a tendency to regard the clients as outside the class of normal human beings, simply by virtue of being clients, or because they are asking for help. There is an assumption that they lack the normal self-help mechanisms that most people have. Therefore, they must be told what to do and must be rescued without question, because they are weak; they have tried everything and have failed, or else they have been discarded by the system.

On the contrary, many people do have strengths and resources of which they are unaware, and they can be helped to develop them, and they will be happier when they do so. Sometimes a worker will actually destroy the client's coping mechanisms rather than help them to be enhanced. . . .

The assumptions behind a welfare setting are perhaps outmoded and are left over from a different time. In addition, individual workers might be threatened by the thought that recipients and givers are each human beings with strengths and weaknesses.

Since social services and income maintenance have become separate, we in the social service section have tended to deal mainly with those people who have an identified problem. This has tended to reinforce the notion that clients are somehow not normal and cannot be expected to act like people we know in our own lives.

This is, in my opinion, a grave mistake, as it leads to loss of dignity in the client, with a greater inclination to dependency. This is exactly counter to the goal which we wish for people—to help them back into society, not to keep them subservient to the worker. [Paust, 1980]

The classic study of a setting in which the perceptions of intelligent and dedicated professionals were controlled by the situation is by Rosenhan (1973, pp. 250–258). He arranged for volunteer subjects who had never suffered symptoms of serious psychiatric disorders to be admitted to psychiatric hospitals. The experimental task was then to determine if they were subsequently discovered to be sane and, if so, how. In his well-known report of this study, he investigated the question of whether "the salient characteristics that lead to diagnoses reside in the patients themselves or in the environments and contexts in which observers find them."

Eight sane people, including Rosenhan himself, gained secret admission to twelve different hospitals. These pseudopatients included a graduate psychology student, three psychologists, a pediatrician, a psychiatrist, a painter, and a housewife. The presence of pseudopatients and the nature of the research program were not known to the hospital staffs. The identity of each subject (name and occupation) was disguised. Pseudopatients would call a hospital for an appointment and arrive at the admissions office complaining of hearing voices. Immediately after admission to the psychiatric ward the pseudopatients ceased simulating *any* symptoms of abnormality. They behaved on the ward as they "normally" behaved, attempted to engage others in conversation, told the staff they were feeling fine and were no longer experiencing any symptoms, and obeyed all instructions from attendants and others in a friendly, cooperative manner. They tried to convince the staff that they were sane.

Despite their public show of sanity, the pseudopatients were never detected and, except in one case, each was admitted with a diagnosis of schizophrenia and discharged with a diagnosis of "schizophrenia in remission."

> The evidence is strong that, once labeled schizophrenic, the pseudopatient was stuck with that label. If the pseudopatient was to be discharged, he must naturally be "in remission"; but he was not sane, nor, in the institution's view, had he ever been sane. [Rosenhan, 1973, p. 252]

Interestingly, it was quite common for other patients to recognize the sanity of the experimental subjects. In Rosenhan's view, the fact that the patients could do this while the staff could not raised important questions. He concluded:

It could be a mistake, and a very unfortunate one, to consider that what happened to us derived from malice or stupidity on the part of the staff. Quite the contrary, our overwhelming impression of them was of people who really cared, who were committed and who were uncommonly intelligent. . . . Their perceptions and behavior were controlled by the situation, rather than being motivated by a malicious disposition. [Rosenhan, 1973, p. 257]

Another aspect of the setting, its physical characteristics and geographical location, is also significant. How the outside and the interior of a social agency or mental health center look and on what street and in which neighborhood it is located will influence the nature of its clientele. It is now well established that some groups of people will not request needed services delivered from formal offices or imposing buildings but would come for the same kind of help from a storefront agency in their own part of town. Inside the agency, the mood set by the furniture, color, lighting, and privacy of the interviewing rooms can affect the receptivity of the client to treatment.

The physical setting can help to reinforce a sense of self-worth in the client. Where the surroundings are pleasant, and privacy and amenities are provided, client and worker can collaborate and solve the problem in dignity. [Paust, 1980]

In addition, the way an agency is administered can influence the course of treatment. A cognitive practitioner individualizes each client and directs his efforts to helping the client attain goals of his own choosing. To do so, the cognitist must be free to respond fully, using his own treatment style, to whatever he believes the client needs. If administrative policy and atmosphere or supervisors dogmatically committed to certain treatment ideologies and techniques restrict or predetermine the repertoire of interventions that may be employed, the essential flexibility of the cognitive approach will be lost and its effectiveness impaired.

To sum up, the setting has a direct relevance to research on the clinical outcome of cognitive therapy. It may prevent the client, out of fear, uncertainty, or uneasiness, from fully involving himself in the treatment process. It may influence the therapist to misperceive the client and his problem. Its appearance and location may keep various groups of potential clients from seeking help, thus preventing the determination of how successful cognitive techniques might be when applied to those individuals. It may limit the cognitist's opportunities to use his approach to its fullest extent. All this, of course, has to do with the possible negative effects of the setting on cognitive treatment, as well as with the resultant distortions of research findings.

The other side of the coin is that the setting may help the client to feel comfortable, understood, and respected. Helping to create this positive condition may be the auspices of the agency, a sponsoring group whose religious, ethnic, philosophical, treatment, economic, or political orientation may be a source of reassurance or security to the client. The client may find that the agency staff have no interest in labeling him. Professionals may be completely free to work in their own way. The physical surroundings, reinforced by friendliness and attention on the part of receptionists and secretaries, may put the client at ease immediately. Finally, positive treatment results can be influenced by the fact that the client is coming to an agency that is new to him or using a new treatment technique (the Hawthorne Effect), or by the fact that the agency has a prestigious reputation and is famous for its success with a certain category of problem (the Lourdes Effect).

THE MEASUREMENT OF GOAL ATTAINMENT

The measurement of goal attainment is a research issue that is central to the entire process of cognitive therapy.

Because the cognitive treatment of each client is built around the goal(s) he chooses for himself, it is considered valid to judge the success of outcome by the extent to which each goal is achieved. Since it is relatively easy to objectify and quantify goal attainment, cognitive therapy stands as one of the most readily measurable approaches.

We shall discuss the concept of goal attainment scaling as originally developed by Kiresuk and Sherman, and then describe how one particular mental health clinic applied it in daily practice.

Kiresuk and Sherman were seeking a means of setting up, before treatment, a measurable scale for each patient-therapist goal, one suited to each individual treatment situation. They decided that the goals must be described in concrete terms and should be directly related to the treatment effort. The purpose of the scale would be to determine the extent to which goals were attained, and to compare the relative effectiveness of the treatments used to attain them.

Kiresuk and Sherman proposed rating possible treatment outcomes on a scale from -2 to $+2$, as follows:

- -2 The most unfavorable treatment outcome thought likely;
- -1 Less than the expected success with treatment;
- 0 The expected level of treatment success;
- $+1$ More than the expected success with treatment;
- $+2$ The best anticipated treatment success.

In testing out these scales, rating was done after a specified period of time following assignment or start of treatment. As an example, a scale was set up for the treatment goal of reducing a client's dependency on his/her mother:

- -2 Lives at home, does nothing without mother's approval;
- 0 Chooses own friends and activities without checking with mother, returns to college;

+ 2   Establishes own way of life, chooses when to consult mother;

− 1 and + 1   Outcomes midway between 0 and 2 in each direction.

The experimenters recommended that two different people or committees should select goals and scale points so that any biases can be examined and questioned by colleagues. Too many easy successes or failures will soon become apparent and call for modifications. Numerical values can be assigned to goals to indicate their relative importance, preventing success or failure in relatively trivial areas from being equated with the same change in highly critical goal areas. Kiresuk and Sherman grant that this is a very subjective procedure. In regard to goal attainment scaling as a whole, however, they believe that the system has value: it can be adjusted for each case, and the results have a very direct interpretation (Kiresuk and Sherman, 1968, pp. 443–453).

José R. Lombillo put goal attainment scaling to use at the Collier County Mental Health Clinic in Florida. After a visit to that center in 1973, the author of this book reported as follows:

> Every patient who now comes into treatment makes a written contract with his therapist stating the goal of treatment. The goal could be to get over depression or to resume working. Whatever the goal, it is formulated in such a way as to indicate how varying degrees of success will be scored. The expected level of success is scored as 3, a maximum level of success is rated 5, while a minimum level of success is graded 1. Success levels between those listed above receive scores of 4 or 2. In regard to a goal of resuming work, a patient might get a score of 5 for returning to the professional field in which he previously worked; working for income at a non-professional job but with concrete plans and efforts to return to his profession might be score 3; working sporadically at menial labor would be scored as 1.
>
> A staff member who is not a therapist does a follow-up

interview with each patient at a specified point in time subsequent to the first clinic appointment. Two assessments are made. The extent of success in reaching the contracted goal is graded from 1 to 5. In addition, a questionnaire is filled out which attempts to arrive at a Consumer Satisfaction Index, that is, the extent to which the patient feels satisfied with the service he received from the clinic. All these data are fed into a computer to help in future planning.

The concept of reaching a formal agreement as to a goal has recently been extended by Collier County Mental Health Clinic to apply not only to treatment of individual patients, but also to the consultation services which the center provides to other social agencies. The center and the social agency agree on the goal or goals of consultation, and define different levels of success and the score that will be assigned to each level. [Werner, 1973, pp. 8–9]

THE DISTINCTION BETWEEN EFFECTIVENESS AND EFFICIENCY

Bloom and Block call attention to the distinction between effectiveness and efficiency:

Measures of effectiveness involve the question of whether the desired results have been produced; measures of efficiency relate to whether the desired results have been produced with the minimum of time and effort. [Bloom and Block, 1977, p. 130]

They indicate that efficiency grows out of effectiveness. Although these two factors are different, they are interdependent, and an ineffective treatment technique can never be efficient. What we are concerned with here is how to determine whether or not a technique objectively rated as successful with a particular client is also efficient in terms of its money, time, and energy costs to all concerned. According to Bloom and Block, much progress remains to be made in the use of efficiency measures based on objective data. If this is true, then future research should give an important place on its agenda to the development of simple, easily usable methods to measure treatment efficiency.

Therapists need these methods to help them decide whether it is worth the extra investment in everybody's time, energy, and money to continue working with a client who, after receiving a certain amount of a certain type of treatment, has made gains but not yet reached his specified goal. Such methods would make it possible to compare the relative efficiency of different treatment techniques applied to the same type of client and problem. Then there is the crucial question of how much therapeutic effort to devote to a client whose problem results in antisocial behavior which is hazardous to his community: if he shows little or no improvement after a period of treatment, we need a rational basis to estimate whether or not the various costs expended to continue "outpatient" therapy are likely to prevent future hospitalization or imprisonment and to be more economical in the long run than institutionalization.

In Chapter 7 we described how the cognitive practitioner approaches the termination phase of treatment. A decision to terminate includes not only the *fact* of stopping but the *time* of stopping. The cognitive orientation has a built-in commitment to efficiency by virtue of its humanistic outlook: it seeks to help people make changes and solve problems as quickly as possible so that their period of anxiety or suffering will be of minimum duration and the economic cost manageable. The aim in cognitive therapy is therefore to be both effective and efficient, and the timing of termination is geared to the earliest possible moment consistent with goal attainment or other professional considerations. Thus, a cognitive therapy sequence will terminate when a mutually agreed upon goal has been reached, a prearranged number of sessions has been completed, or the goal has not been reached but is close enough for the client to try going the rest of the way on his own.

The cognitist is mindful that efficient practice prevents the waste of both the therapist's and the agency's resources. Therefore, as discussed earlier, he is ready to terminate any case in which the client's goal does not appear attainable through work with this therapist in this agency. He will also give a "vacation" to a client whose goal seems to be attainable but is not yet within reach because of the client's lack of effort. In each of these circumstances, the cognitive practitioner is making a decision on the side of efficiency calculated to benefit all concerned. The therapist's judgment, however, is largely impressionistic. Cognitists will welcome the construction by researchers of efficiency measures that they can use to make more scientific and precise their already existing commitment to produce desired results with a minimum of time and effort.

RELATIONSHIP OF THE THERAPIST'S PERSONALITY TO TREATMENT OUTCOME

For this discussion, the therapist's personality is defined to be a particular combination of appearance, mannerisms, speech, attitude, and treatment style *as perceived by the client*. Cognitive practitioners view their theory and practice as a transmittable body of knowledge that can be readily taught to others. They have a real stake in finding out whether or not successful clinical outcome is primarily a consequence of the specific cognitive techniques that are used, or has more to do with the perceived personality of the therapist. Like those of other theoretical persuasions, cognitists would like to believe that their successful outcomes can be replicated, so that many therapists, employing a particular technique with clients having a particular set of characteristics, produce similarly effective results despite their individual personality differences.

Consequently, cognitists look forward to research findings

that will sort out the respective and relative contributions to treatment effectiveness of specific cognitive techniques, the setting, and the personality of the therapist. This will not be an easy research task: many questions will arise. In an experiment where several cognitive therapists separately apply the same technique to individual clients, each of whose characteristics presumably matches those of the other clients, how close can such match-ups really be in view of the uniqueness of each human being? Because cognitists are willing to reveal their own feelings and experiences in the service of the client, has the cognitive orientation built into itself a considerable emphasis on the therapist's use of his own personality? If there is validity in the widely held notion that any kind of psychotherapy is still half science and half art (i.e., half learned technique and half personal style), can we possibly hypothesize that the perceived personality of the therapist does or should exert minimal influence on treatment outcome? Finally, how can researchers measure how the client perceives the therapist's personality and treatment style?

Treatment style is the way the therapist, in the client's perception, uses himself to deliver a particular technique. An example of this can be found in the way the therapist works out an agreement with the client about a treatment goal. In utilizing the technique of goal setting, the therapist may try to motivate the client by letting him know he expects the client to accomplish more than he thought himself capable of achieving. According to Oxley (1966, pp. 432–437), the client may end up agreeing to a higher goal than he originally intended as a result of the increased confidence generated by the worker's thinking more of him than he himself did. Oxley maintains that expecting a little more than the client expects of himself can be a very important motivator.

Now the question for the researcher to answer is how all this can be measured for its influence on treatment outcome. Is the client aware of the therapist's treatment style, which is an aspect of the therapist's personality, and can he describe it or recognize its effect? This question and the questions previously raised, plus many more, await answers from cognitive experimenters.

EXPANDING THE CONCEPTION OF RESEARCH

A fitting conclusion to this chapter is the following statement by Eda Goldstein, who believes that social work practitioners need to move beyond a narrow conception of research:

> Research efforts involve more than the use of large-scale experimental designs and computerized information retrieval systems. They involve making explicit the questions workers have as practitioners as well as collecting data on the problems or stresses faced by one client, how this client copes, and what workers have done that is effective or ineffective in alleviating the client's stress or improving his or her functioning. Research can also involve the sharing among groups of practitioners of their observations about the difficult problems they face in their work and the interventions that have been effective and ineffective in their practice. It can mean keeping track of interventions in the helping process and noting where and how change occurs. It can involve documenting the stresses, problems, coping patterns, and available resources of clients living alternative lifestyles and can thereby enrich social work knowledge and extend it beyond the stereotypical. Finally, it can simply mean sitting down and talking with clients and documenting their needs. In short, workers must value what they know and positively and creatively exploit for the purpose of knowledge building the hours that they as "people helpers" spend with human beings. [Goldstein, 1980, p. 177]

Chapter 11

Completing the Picture

In this book we have outlined a picture of cognitive therapy as a process of evaluating clients in terms of their consciousness and helping them perceive reality as accurately as possible. The core concept of cognitive theory is that thinking shapes behavior and emotions. Achieving a true understanding of himself, others, and the surrounding world brings the client only to the halfway mark. Treatment is not finished until the individual puts his new understanding to use by taking action on his own behalf.

Locke expressed it this way:

> As a practicing (part-time) "cognitive" therapist, I am of the opinion that to get maximum benefit from therapy, a patient must (a) with the help of the therapist, correct errors of knowledge, resolve value conflicts, and modify faulty methods of thinking; and (b) put his new knowledge into action as soon as possible. [Locke, 1979, p. 124]

Cognitive therapy has been examined in these pages as a separate therapeutic entity but its overlap with behavior modification is recognized. We have shown how cognitists make use of training techniques to alter thinking in the same way that classical behaviorists used them to effect changes in behavior. Conversely, in the second half of the 1970s, classical behavior modification theory, which in the past paid little or no attention to the role of cognition in human functioning, began to rectify this view by giving increasing recognition to the way in which cognition mediates behavior. The two approaches are separate currents in American psychotherapy but they do converge at certain points. The emphasis of cognitive therapy on the client's translating new understanding into action illustrates this convergence and reveals its large behavioral component.

This final chapter is devoted to a brief elaboration of some of the points made in earlier chapters, clarification of others, and confirmation of still others by colleagues in the field. It will also contain afterthoughts and present additional issues pertaining to the cognitive/humanistic approach as a whole. It is hoped that this chapter will complete the picture by filling in some gaps and providing further details.

Criteria for a theory of therapy

Jay Haley has compiled a list of what he considers to be the most basic criteria for a desirable theory of therapy:

a. First of all, the theory should provide an orientation that leads a therapist to success in the outcome of his or her therapy. Not only should the therapist avoid a theory which leads to doing harm, but the theory should make possible results better than no therapy at all.

b. Secondly, the theory should be simple enough for the average therapist to understand it. A simple theory also keeps the therapist clear on important issues so as not to be distracted by clients who are experts in complexity.

c. The theory should be reasonably comprehensive. It need not explain all eventualities that arise, but it should guide the therapist by preparing him for most of them.

d. The theory should guide the therapist to action, rather than to reflection, if he is to cause change. It should suggest what to do.

e. The theory should generate hope in therapist, client and family so that everyone anticipates recovery and normality.
f. The theory should define failure and explain why a failure occurred when it did.

If these are elementary criteria for a theory of therapy, the opposite is what a sensible therapist should avoid. A therapist should not accept a theory that prevents therapy goals from being defined and leads to poor therapy outcome. He should avoid a theory so complex it is incapacitating, one that attempts to explain everything, one that leads to thought and philosophical speculation rather than action, one that does not generate hope, and one that causes everyone to be uncertain whether they have failed or succeeded. [Haley, 1978a, pp. 67–68]

These basic requirements for a useful theory of therapy were presented here because of our conviction that cognitive theory meets these criteria.

Confusion with the work of Piaget

Jean Piaget, the renowned Swiss psychologist, made monumental contributions to the study of human growth through his various theories about the cognitive development of children. He focused on the origins of intelligence in children, their perception of the world, how the quality of their thinking changes from one life stage to another, and their acquisition of judgment, reasoning, and the concept of number.

Piaget's ideas are sometimes categorized as cognitive theory; technically this is appropriate because he was concerned with understanding the process of thinking. As should be apparent, however, the term "cognitive theory" has an entirely different meaning as employed in this volume to describe a particular psychotherapeutic orientation that is practiced in social agencies and mental health settings. Cognitive theory as associated with Piaget refers to the study of the development of intelligence and intellect. Cognitive theory in the present context is a theory of personality (why people behave as they do, why they become upset) and a theory of therapy (what to do to help people).

Comparing various therapies

As social work and the other helping professions have experienced increasing pressure to demonstrate the effectiveness of their treatment services, there has been a corresponding growth of interest in finding out which therapeutic approaches work best with which clients. A recent example of such interest has been the establishment in 1980 by the American Psychiatric Association of a Commission on Psychiatric Therapies. This commission plans to describe dozens of therapies: psychotherapies (including cognitive therapy), somatic therapies, and social and milieu therapies. It will evaluate outcome results, collect other data, and produce a final report that will recommend which specific treatment is preferred for an individual with specific characteristics suffering from a given disorder. The report will also indicate which therapies are acceptable alternative or adjunct treatments, for experimental use only, or contraindicated.

Kettner has proposed a framework that social workers can use to compare practice models (Kettner, 1975, pp. 629–642). It is an outline for presenting and analyzing a practice model in a uniform manner. If social work theoreticians, researchers, educators, and practitioners would widely adopt this or some other format for presenting a specific treatment approach, the profession could bring some degree of uniformity into model building and comparison.

By using Kettner's framework, the cognitive approach can be outlined very easily. Kettner's ten points will not all be answered fully here but enough material will be sketched in to give some sense of how his framework can standardize the presentation of a practice model.

1. *A statement of the author's view of social work practice.* Social work is the systematic provision of help to individuals, families, and groups by a professional under an agency's auspices. The help may be in the form of money, material goods, concrete services, psychotherapy, advice, referral, opportunities for growth, or cooperation in challenging any system.

2. *Theoretical underpinnings of the model.* Human behavior and emotion are shaped by thought; aggression is not inborn but a learned situational response; drives can be deactivated when incongruent with important goals; people create their own destinies by their thinking and willing and choice of goals; people have an innate tendency to grow and seek competency and completion; the sex drive is not the primary source of emotional problems, but just one of several possible factors; the problems that people bring to social workers are problems of consciousness; growth is the expansion of consciousness, an increase in one's accurate perception of self, others, relationships, and surrounding environment.

3. *Level of intervention for which the model is appropriate.* Because the model does not make use of the concept of the unconscious, considerations of level or depth are viewed as irrelevant. Since the difficulties of clients are seen as problems of consciousness, problems of living, one is not on a deeper level than another. The ways in which problems do vary are in regard to intensity, chronicity, pervasiveness, dangerousness, anxiety level, and legal implications. The model is seen as an appropriate intervention regardless of the degree to which any of these variables are present.

4. *Target group.* Most people can benefit from cognitive therapy. The exceptions are those with psychoses, severe mental retardation, phobias, and substance addictions that markedly interfere with reality contact. The model requires

that clients be able to verbalize their perceptions, emotions, and goals and report about their behaviors and experiences outside the treatment setting. Thus, additional exceptions may include young children and individuals of all ages who (literally or figuratively) do not speak the same language as the therapist or cannot communicate for other reasons.

5. *Nature of the roles and responsibilities assumed by worker and client: (a) degree to which rules and regulations are spelled out in detail*—the therapist takes pains to spell these out fully at the beginning of treatment; *(b) relative activity or passivity of worker and client*—treatment is considered a partnership in which both have well-defined responsibilities requiring active effort to fulfill; *(c) relative importance of relationship*—relationship is of key importance, because positive rapport facilitates the client's development of security, courage, optimism, self-respect, and a model for action.

6. *Worker and client input into the decision-making process.* Continuous, cooperative and on an equal basis.

7. *Degree of specificity in setting objectives, delineating procedures, and stating outcome expectations.* The model stresses being open and precise about all these matters to remove any sense of anxiety or mystery about what is going to happen. Such specificity also provides the client, after mutual agreement, with a clear goal and helps prevent unrealistic expectations.

8. *Description of process, including, as a minimum, statements about (a) content of initial phase, (b) methods of assessment, (c) strategies and techniques of intervention, (d) evaluation of effectiveness, (e) termination.* These points have all been discussed at length in Chapters 5, 6, 7, and 10 and a process description could be formulated from that material.

9. *Value premises.* The value premises of the cognitive model are humanistic. Human beings are considered, as Ellis stated, "important in their own right, just because they are

alive." People should be completely accepted despite any limitations. The worth of an individual does not depend on the extent of his material success or conformity to the status quo but rather on the degree of humanness that characterizes his relationships with others: concern, consideration, and cooperation for the common good. The greatest value that a professional can have for a client is to help him become everything he is capable of becoming and choose goals on the "useful side of life" (Adler). Because human beings create their own lives by the choices they make, it is important that they be held responsible for their behavior.

10. *Research findings.* The experiments described in Chapter 10 could be summarized.

Cognitive therapy and the trend toward an eclectic approach

Eclecticism in theoretical orientation refers to the combination in one's practice of different ideological frameworks, either in part or as a whole. Some practitioners who call themselves "eclectic" use the term as a euphemism for not having any theoretical underpinning at all and "playing it by ear." In our view, practice must be guided by theory or it is in danger of being disorganized, haphazard, serendipitous, and not subject to replication when successful.

Another kind of eclecticism consists of combining what seem to be incompatible approaches. In Chapter 2 we referred to Jayaratne's national survey of clinical social workers to determine their choices of theoretical orientation, and noted that respondents frequently combined "psychoanalytic" and "humanistic," or "psychoanalytic" and "reality" approaches.

Fischer (1978) believes that effective casework practice needs to be based on an eclectic approach. He presents his own model of such an approach, not claiming that this is the final, definitive model, but offering it as one example of the new form that casework must take. He calls for the integration of four components to create an eclectic orientation: greater use of goal setting, planning and structure in the casework process; behavior modification; cognitive procedures; and the core conditions of empathy, warmth, and genuineness (based on the formulations of Carl Rogers).

Fischer proposes this model as a way for social workers to overcome the limitations and one-sidedness of past approaches. Its eclecticism is based on combining harmonious components and is a far cry from a nontheory or a hodge podge of contradictory elements. The cognitive orientation presented in this book is similar to Fischer's model.

Cognitive therapy, advocacy, and social change

Emotional problems are the result of limitations and distortions in the consciousness of clients or of those with whom clients are involved. Survival problems are the result of limitations and distortions in surrounding environments and systems which prevent them from providing clients with sufficient material needs, health care, or opportunities to learn. Survival problems can trigger emotional problems; emotional problems can undermine the strength, will, or effort necessary to survive.

The cognitist makes use of those resources in the environment and those systems which can expand the consciousness of the client and the significant others in his life. But when a system or environmental element warps the perceptions of clients or those interacting with them or fails to provide the requisites for survival, the therapist has a moral obligation to join the client in an endeavor to challenge or change the way things are. Such an effort can take various forms. The therapist can encourage the client to handle the problem on his own, he can accompany the client to a confrontation, or through professional channels he can use whatever status or clout he possesses to question or modify the offending entity. If a therapist—of any persuasion—is convinced that the total social structure is at fault, he has a further obligation as helping person and citizen to engage in appropriate political action.

Cognitive practitioners give full support to Glassman's call to social workers to function as forceful advocates for their clients. She referred specifically to work with older people who may be deprived of adequate medical care because of an erroneous diagnosis of senile dementia. Elderly individuals can become confused, disorganized, and delusional because of reversible conditions: depression, reactions to medication, anemia, malnutrition, and various other physical disorders. When such people are inaccurately diagnosed as senile, with its implication of untreatable, irreversible brain damage, a minimum of medical attention is given them and the underlying treatable condition can become chronic and irreversible. This kind of misdiagnosis results from a lack of interest or knowledge, failure to do routine testing, incomplete history taking, inadequate diagnostic procedures, and stereotyped attitudes on the part of physicians. Glassman described how, in one agency, social workers who were geriatric specialists challenged the status quo and developed teamwork between doctors and social workers to facilitate accurate diagnosis:

> The social workers in these cases recognized the importance of psychosocial factors in the differential diagnosis of senile dementia. They took complete psychosocial histories, evaluated the clients' current social functioning, and looked for factors in the clients' life that could cause symptoms of mental failure. Sharing this vital information with physicians and hospital staff was insufficient in many cases to obtain adequate medical care for the client. The workers' clinical assessments frequently had to be combined with ad-

vocacy, including filing complaints with hospitals and helping the clients find other sources of medical care. The social workers had to function as independent professionals rather than follow medical orders. [Glassman, 1980, p. 288]

Nord raises the question of whether humanistic goals can be achieved without major changes in a society's economic organization and distribution of power. He claims that with some notable exceptions, humanistic psychologists have focused their suggestions for change almost exclusively at the level of individuals and small social units:

I have been critical of many humanistic psychologists who have omitted attention to macrolevel social forces. In particular I have suggested that this lacuna is a major barrier to realizing humanistic aims because it leads the humanistic psychologist to underestimate the strength of a number of forces which influence human development. Such underestimation can be a factor associated with the production of radical sounding change strategies which are in essence quite conservative. [Nord, 1977, p. 81]

Nord concludes with the thought that "much of humanistic psychology may be too psychological to be effectively humanistic" (p. 82).

Cognitive therapy and the assigned task

Blizinsky and Reid (1980) recently gave experimental validation to the cognitive technique of holding a client to his goals and to completing the "homework" necessary to achieve them.

They tested out the assumption that, in task-centered social work, the degree of concentration on a problem is positively related to change. In an intensive study of eleven task-centered cases, the findings revealed that the amount of focus on target problems, measured by the cumulative amount of such attention, was related to the degree of change in those problems. In this study, the practitioners took major responsibility for maintaining the focus and for discouraging wandering off on tangents or focusing on non-problematic subjects. The clients' tendencies were in the opposite direction (Blizinsky and Reid, 1980, pp. 89–92).

Factors contributing to the process of perception

In Chapter 1, we defined perception as the sensing of an event combined with the evaluation made of that event. Figure 1.1 (Chap. 1) was presented to indicate that the process of evaluating is colored or distorted by an individual's own personality (the sum total of his thinking, feeling, and acting) and by the prism of his life's experiences. These were not examined in any detail in the first chapter, so it might be useful to do so now in brief fashion.

How people interpret the input from their senses depends, then, on what they are and what has happened in their lives. What they are is made up, in part, of their intelligence, height, weight, physical and facial appearance, cultural and ethnic background, general state of health, relative speed of body movements and reflexes, special talents, strength of will and courage, and vulnerability.

Vulnerability has been depicted by one writer in the following manner:

1   2   3

#1 characterizes the person of great vulnerability, easily upset when his thin protective armor is pierced. #2 portrays the individual of average vulnerability, who possesses more than one layer of protection. #3 refers to those who have an extra layer of protection and are not easily disturbed or hurt emotionally. The extent of one's vulnerability is both inherited and influenced by experience. The congenital component of vulnerability, in our view, is related to inborn disposition or temperament and would seem to depend a great deal on the kind of nervous system with which one comes into the world. Significant experiences which affect the process of evaluating include parental upbringing, interactions with others (peers, lovers, teachers, authorities, employers, etc.), involvements in organized groups or causes, and successes and failures.

Interpenetrating with personality characteristics and significant experiences at all times is the developmental stage of the individual (early school age, later adolescence, middle adulthood, etc.), which the therapist must always take into account in his efforts to understand the client's perceptions.

Personality and experience affect perception in either direction, contributing both to realism and error. We remind the reader again of some experiential influences that can generate perceptual errors: ignorance owing to inadequate education; traditional superstitions; stereotyping reinforced by the media; internalization of family misperceptions and myths; acceptance of invalid judgments by significant others; need to conform to majority or special interest group thinking; making unfounded generalizations from traumatic atypical events.

The growing internalization of the cognitive viewpoint

We have given numerous examples of practitioners who incorporate cognitive principles in their work without identifying them as such. Internalization of the cognitive viewpoint seems to be continuing, as evidenced by these excerpts from a daily newspaper and from an article by a leading social work theorist:

> Our thought determines and controls our activities and molds our characters. Tennyson's expression that we are "part of all we have thought and felt and seen" is more and more confirmed by human experience.
>
> If you know what people are thinking about, what constitutes their thought life, what makes up their meditations and reflections, the kind of sentiments they cherish, you know the kind of people they are. [*Sarasota Herald-Tribune*, 1980]

Florence Hollis recently reviewed the changes that have taken place in social work over the years. In describing some of the profession's contemporary outlooks, she in effect restated cognitive principles without naming them as such.

> Each individual client needs to understand things more accurately and fully, to think of how to bring change about and to gain skill in dealing with other systems. Sometimes clients must gain greater courage and greater belief in their own worth and abilities; sometimes they need a greater appreciation for the feelings of other people, especially those with whom they are closely involved, and a greater awareness of the nature of the transactions taking place between themselves and other members of the family systems of which they are a part. The worker's helpfulness will depend not only on an accurate perception of the family's transactions, but also on an understanding of the individual family members, their readiness to change, and the obstacles and resistance to change that they face. . . .
>
> There is added emphasis on the need for openness and frankness with the client. An open agreement on goals and problems to be worked on, sometimes called a contract, is now in wide use. Some think it a must; others believe tacit agreement is sufficient under some circumstances. Much more informality or "mutuality" in the relationship is now

thought to be helpful in many cases where formerly a more formal relationship was thought best. [Hollis, 1980, pp. 6, 8]

Cognitive therapy and the concepts of Murray Bowen

In presenting what he called "the Bowen theory," Bowen wrote that its cornerstone was the concept of *differentiation of self:*

> The concept defines people according to the degree of *fusion,* or *differentiation,* between emotional and intellectual functioning. This characteristic is so universal it can be used as a way of categorizing all people on a single continuum. At the low extreme are those whose emotions and intellect are so fused that their lives are dominated by the automatic emotional system. Whatever intellect they have is dominated by the emotional system. These are the people who are less flexible, less adaptable, and more emotionally dependent on those about them. They are easily stressed into dysfunction, and it is difficult for them to recover from dysfunction. They inherit a high percentage of all human problems. At the other extreme are those who are more differentiated. It is impossible for there to be more than relative separation between emotional and intellectual functioning, but those whose intellectual functioning can retain relative autonomy in periods of stress are more flexible, more adaptable, and more independent of the emotionality about them. They cope better with life stresses, their life courses are more orderly and successful, and they are remarkably free of human problems. In between the two extremes is an infinite number of mixes between emotional and intellectual functioning. [Bowen, 1976, pp. 65–66]

Bowen went on to claim that this concept eliminated the concept of *normal,* which psychiatry had never successfully defined. The concept of differentiation had no direct connection with the presence or absence of symptoms. He asserted that people with the most fusion had the most human problems and those with the most differentiation had the fewest difficulties. He explained that at the fusion end of the spectrum the intellect was so flooded by emotionality that it became a mere appendage of the feeling system; a person's life was determined by emotions, by what "feels right," rather than by beliefs or opinions.

Bowen's contention that the basic cause of human problems is the domination of intellect by emotion is of interest to the cognitist. On one level he seems to be agreeing that problems arise out of faulty cognitive functioning. We, in turn, can agree that it is difficult or impossible for a person to "think straight" when flooded by intense emotion in a particular circumstance. In this writer's experience, however, improvement of a client's original presenting problem was seldom accomplished by dissolving the fusion between emotions and intellect because that was rarely an ongoing, entrenched characteristic of the client. Whenever such fusing was noted, it was usually a temporary response to a specific stressful situation. This raises the question of how universal or significant a role in cognitive dysfunction is actually played by fusion.

Philosophically, the Bowen theory does not mesh with cognitive theory. Bowen implies that in periods of stress, people should strive to keep their intellectual functioning independent of their emotions. This clearly suggests that emotion is the primary force against which the intellect must be protected. Cognitive theory, on the other hand, regards thought as primary and as the shaper of emotions: there can be no emotion without a preceding thought. The disparity between Bowen and the cognitists becomes plain: Bowen believes that the chief cause of maladaptive cognition is the domination of intellect by emotion; earlier in this chapter, we listed many other personality and experiential factors which can contribute to perceptual distortion, so the most we can say is that the degree of fusion between emotional and intellectual functioning is just one of many possible influences.

Cognitive therapy and the concepts of Erik Erikson

Erikson's famous conceptualization of the Eight Stages of Man (1950) was considered a bold step forward by the ego psychology wing of the Freudian movement. It was contained in his book, *Childhood and Society.* In that work, according to Elkind, Erikson made three major contributions to the study of the human ego:

> He posited (1) that, side by side with the stages of psychosexual development described by Freud (the oral, anal, phallic, genital, Oedipal and pubertal), were psychosocial stages of ego development, in which the individual had to establish new basic orientations to himself and his social world; (2) that personality development continued throughout the whole life cycle; and (3) that each stage had a positive *as well as* a negative component. [Elkind, 1970, p. 27]

Erikson, a psychoanalyst, expanded traditional Freudian doctrine with his concept of how the "normal" individual develops by successfully solving the tasks of each of a series of developmental stages and then moving on to the next. He divided the entire human life cycle into eight stages. At the end of each one, an individual feels under pressure or tension because society is making demands on him for a more mature level of behavior. He relieves the tension by meeting these demands through completing the developmental tasks for that stage.

Elkind explained why Erikson's ideas seemed so revolutionary to psychoanalysts in 1950:

> Their presentation, for one thing, frees the clinician to treat adult emotional problems as failures (in part at least) to solve genuinely adult personality crises and not, as heretofore, as mere residuals of infantile frustrations and conflicts. This view of personality growth, moreover, takes some of the onus off parents and takes account of the role which society and the person himself play in the formation of an individual personality. Finally, Erikson has offered hope for us all by demonstrating that each phase of growth has its strengths as well as its weaknesses and that failures at one stage of development can be rectified by successes at later stages. [Elkind, 1970, p. 112]

Psychoanalysts, prior to Erikson's theoretical contribution, mostly concerned themselves with the pathology of the disturbed person, not with the development of the healthy person. They did not deal with adolescent and adult behavior in its own right, but only as a consequence of what happened in childhood. They did not consider the influence on personality of any other forces except the immediate family. Sexual libido was regarded as the underlying determinant of all behavior.

The relationship of Erikson's ideas to the cognitive orientation is that he gave Freudians a rationale for a new viewpoint that embraced some cognitive principles. Erikson opened the way for analysts to do the following:

1. Attribute behavior to other causes besides the sex drive;
2. Consider the influence of environment and society;
3. Admit that events beyond the age of six could be crucial;
4. Look at adult behavior as conceivably independent of what happened in childhood; and
5. Be more optimistic: personality was not fixed after age six, and problems not solved in one stage could be solved later on.

Cognitive therapy
and the concepts of Perry London

London's ideas (1964) provide a final perspective on cognitive therapy. He made the point that all therapeutic systems fall into two general categories, *action* or *insight*.

Action therapy stresses the functioning of the client: it aims at helping him to achieve the ability to act in a certain way. It concentrates on removing symptoms, equating symptom removal with cure. Its methods are explainable, subject to evaluation, and objective. The therapist chooses what kind of behavior the client must practice in order to overcome the distress which the client himself has decided to conquer. Action therapy is not concerned with the meaning of life or the way a person should live or the origins of his distressing behavior, but chiefly with the alleviation of the specific distress caused by a specific problem.

Insight therapy (psychoanalysis and its variations) is not concerned with function but with meaning, the premise being that when the client understands the sources of his upset, the unconscious motives of his behavior, he will then be able to alter that behavior. The action therapist takes responsibility for changing the client's behavior by teaching him how to act differently. The insight therapist takes no responsibility for the client's behavior, often does not allow him to discuss daily problems of living, and focuses on interpreting to the client his inner dynamics.

Formulating these ideas in 1964, London believed that both categories had serious limitations, and that the treatment of choice was a comprehensive therapy which aimed to elicit both insight and action. He asserted that therapists cannot avoid being either behavior manipulators or interpreters of meaning. Therefore, they should consciously do both on the most scientific basis possible, which included getting to know as much as possible about the nature of man. Some clients had problems which were exclusively behavioristic (phobia of elevators) and could be handled strictly on an action basis. Some clients had problems which involved no behavior at all but inner distress caused by confusion over life goals and values, and these could be handled strictly on an insight basis. For most clients, however, self-understanding plus change of behavior was needed.

In London's view, insight alone had proved to have very little power to change behavior; once feelings were understood, the client needed to be taught to live differently in order to feel different. Insight therapists, however, tended to veer away from discussions about how the client should act outside the therapist's office. In this sense, the insight therapist was leaving to the client the decision as to the kind of behavior he would practice.

Cognitive therapy in its contemporary form was just coming on the scene when London wrote the book from which the material in this section is summarized. He made no mention of any form of cognitive therapy in it. The point we wish to make here is that cognitive therapy now provides the "comprehensive" approach called for by London, which can offer both self-understanding and techniques for behavior change. In 1964, dealing only with psychoanalytic and conditioning approaches, he implied that all insight therapies focused on unconscious dynamics and that action methods were mechanical and disinterested in the client's inner life. Today the situation is far different. Cognitive therapy, as an insight method, aims to make the client conscious of the realities of his daily life, not of his unconscious. Cognitive therapy, as an action method, individualizes each client, explores his thoughts and emotions, and focuses on the behavior changes he himself desires. Meanwhile, as we noted previously, the behavior modification movement itself is becoming more cognitive as cognitive practitioners concomitantly seek more knowledge of behavioral techniques.

London also contended that therapists cannot avoid being moralists because what they do with clients is based on their conception of the kind of person they think the client should ultimately become. In this connection, cognitive practitioners probably hope that their clients will become people who:

1. See reality accurately;
2. Have the ability to act on their accurate perceptions;
3. *Feel* better, in addition to *thinking* and *acting* more realistically;
4. Develop "social interest" and choose goals on the "useful side of life" (Adler); and
5. Become everything they are capable of being.

The immediate agenda

Further work is necessary to increase the efficacy of cognitive therapy and to facilitate the maintenance of client gains, a problem that is beginning to draw the attention of researchers. Various writers have suggested utilizing spouses to improve client compliance with homework assignments, telephone reminders, phone call booster sessions, printed materials (bibliotherapy) for reviewing treatment techniques, and client "buddy systems."

Cognitists must remain alert at all times to minimize their own perceptual distortions. They can contribute to this aim by listening and learning from clients, participating in the life of their communities, taking continuing education courses and attending conferences, and exchanging experiences with supervisors and colleagues in a free and frank manner.

In addition to previously mentioned sources of distortion acting on the practitioner, such as stereotyped thinking, lack of information, and the setting, we should note the possibility of sexual bias in our perception of male and female roles and raise our consciousness in this area.

Meanwhile, the humanism of cognitive therapy continues to reside in the way it approaches each client with attention to all his connections in the human world he occupies.

References

ADLER, KURT A. 1979. "An Adlerian view of the development and the treatment of schizophrenia." *Journal of Individual Psychology* 35, no. 2 (November).

ANSBACHER, HEINZ L. 1970. "Alfred Adler: A historical perspective." *American Journal of Psychiatry* 127, no. 6 (December).

ANSBACHER, HEINZ L., and ROWENA ANSBACHER. 1956. *The individual psychology of Alfred Adler.* New York: Basic Books.

BECK, AARON T. 1976. *Cognitive therapy and the emotional disorders.* New York: International Universities Press.

BECKER, JOSEPH, and MARC A. SCHUCKIT. 1978. "The comparative efficacy of cognitive therapy and pharmacotherapy in the treatment of depressions." *Cognitive Therapy and Research* 2, no. 2 (June).

BELL, JOHN ELDERKIN. 1961. *Family Group Therapy* Washington: United States Government Printing Office. Public Health Monograph no. 64.

BENNETT, IVY B. 1975. "A plea for personality theory." *Social Work* 20, no. 1 (January).

BLIZINSKY, MARTIN J., and WILLIAM J. REID. 1980. "Problem focus and change in a brief-treatment model." *Social Work* 25, no. 2 (March).

BLOOM, MARTIN, and STEPHEN R. BLOCK. 1977. "Evaluating one's own effectiveness and efficiency." *Social Work* 22, no. 2 (March).

BOCKAR, JOYCE A. 1976. *Primer for the nonmedical psychotherapist.* New York: Spectrum Publications.

Bowen, Murray. 1976. "Theory in the practice of psychotherapy." In *Family therapy: theory and practice,* ed. Philip J. Guerin, Jr. New York: Gardner Press.

Carlson, Bonnie E. 1977. "Battered women and their assailants." *Social Work* 22, no. 6 (November).

Cammer, Leonard. 1969. *Up from depression.* New York: Simon and Schuster.

Carter, D. Bruce; Charlotte J. Patterson; and Susan J. Quasebarth. 1979. "Development of children's use of plans for self-control." *Cognitive Therapy and Research* 3, no. 4 (December).

Colby, Kenneth Mark; William S. Faught; and Roger C. Parkison. 1979. "Cognitive therapy of paranoid conditions: Heuristic suggestions based on a computer simulation model." *Cognitive Therapy and Research* 3, no. 1 (March).

Combs, Terri D. 1980. "A cognitive therapy for depression: Theory, techniques, and issues." *Social Casework* 61, no. 6 (June).

De Lo, James S., and William A. Green. 1977. "A cognitive transactional approach to communication." *Social Casework* 58, no. 5 (May).

Dewane, Claudia M. 1978. "Humor in Therapy." *Social Work* 23, no. 6 (November).

Dewey, Edith A. 1971. "Family atmosphere." In *Techniques for behavior change,* ed. Arthur G. Nikelly, pp. 41–45. Springfield, Ill.: Charles C Thomas.

Diagnostic and Statistical Manual of Mental Disorders. 1980. 3d ed. Washington, D.C.: American Psychiatric Association.

Directors of the Robbins Institute. 1955. "An integrated psychotherapeutic program." *Psychotherapy* 1, no. 1 (Fall).

Elkind, David. 1970. "Erik Erikson's eight ages of man." *New York Times Magazine,* April 5.

Ellis, Albert. 1958. "Rational psychotherapy." *Journal of General Psychology* 59.

———. 1962. *Reason and emotion in psychotherapy.* New York: Lyle Stuart.

———. 1973. *Humanistic psychotherapy: The rational-emotive approach.* New York: Julian Press.

ELLIS, ALBERT, and ROBERT A. HARPER. 1961. *A guide to rational living.* Englewood Cliffs, N.J.: Prentice-Hall.

EPSTEIN, NORMAN. 1970. "Brief group therapy in a child guidance clinic." *Social Work* 15, no. 3 (July).

———. 1976. "Techniques of brief therapy with children and parents." *Social Casework* 57, no. 5 (May).

ERIKSON, ERIK H. 1950. *Childhood and society.* New York: Norton.

FISCHER, JOEL. 1976. *The effectiveness of social casework.* Springfield, Ill.: Charles C Thomas.

———. 1978. *Effective casework practice: An eclectic approach.* New York: McGraw-Hill.

FISHER, PHYLLIS K. 1973. "Traditional and behavior therapy—competition or collaboration?" *Social Casework* 54, no. 9 (November).

FREED, ANNE O. 1977. "Social casework: More than a modality." *Social Casework* 58, no. 4 (April).

FREUD, SIGMUND. 1962. *Civilization and its discontents.* New York: Norton.

FURST, JOSEPH B. 1954. *The neurotic: His inner and outer worlds.* New York: Citadel Press.

FRANKL, VIKTOR E. 1967. *Psychotherapy and existentialism.* New York: Simon & Schuster.

GLASSER, WILLIAM. 1965. *Reality therapy: A new approach to psychiatry.* New York: Harper & Row.

GLASSMAN, MARJORIE. 1980. "Misdiagnosis of senile dementia: Denial of care to the elderly." *Social Work* 25, no. 4 (July).

GLOGOWER, FREDERIC D., WILLIAM J. FREMOUW; and JAMES C. MCCROSKEY. 1978. "A component analysis of cognitive restructuring." *Cognitive Therapy and Research* 2, no. 3 (September).

GOLDSTEIN, EDA G. 1980. "Knowledge base of clinical social work." *Social Work* 25, no. 3 (May).

GOLDSTEIN, HOWARD. 1981. *Social learning and change: A cognitive approach to human services.* Columbia, S.C.: University of South Carolina Press.

HALEY, JAY. 1978a. "Ideas which handicap therapists." In *Beyond the double bind,* ed. Milton M. Berger. New York: Brunner/Mazel.

———. 1978b. *Problem-solving therapy.* New York: Harper & Row.

HOLLIS, FLORENCE. 1980. "On revisiting social work." *Social Casework* 61, no. 1 (January).

HORA, THOMAS. 1962. "Existential psychotherapy." In *Current psychiatric therapies,* vol. 2. New York: Grune & Stratton.

HUSSIAN, RICHARD A., and P. SCOTT LAWRENCE. 1978. "The reduction of test, state, and trait anxiety by test-specific and generalized stress inoculation training." *Cognitive Therapy and Research* 2, no. 1 (March).

JACOBS, GORDON L. 1971. "The behavioral approach." *Poca Press* (a publication of Psychiatric Outpatient Centers of America) 7, no. 2 (Fall).

JAYARATNE, SRINIKA. 1978. "A study of clinical eclectism." *Social Service Review* 52, no. 4 (December).

KABANOV, A.N. 1955. *Anatomy and physiology of a human being.* Leningrad, U.S.S.R.: State Text-Book Publishing House.

KANNER, LEO. N.d. "Early infantile autism revisited." In *The psychiatric forum,* ed. Gene Usdin, pp. 27–32. New York: Brunner/Mazel.

KEMBLE, ROBERT P. 1959. "IBM records save staff time." *Mental Hospitals* (November).

KETTNER, PETER M. 1975. "A framework for comparing practice models." *Social Service Review* 49, no. 4 (December).

KIRESUK, THOMAS J., and ROBERT E. SHERMAN. 1968. "Goal attainment scaling: A general method for evaluating comprehensive community mental health programs." *Community Mental Health Journal* 4, no. 6 (December).

KRAUSS, HERBERT H. 1967. "Anxiety: The dread of a future event." *Journal of Individual Psychology* 23, no. 1 (May).

KRILL, DONALD F. 1979. "Existential social work." In *Social work treatment,* ed. Francis J. Turner, 2d ed. New York: Free Press.

LANTZ, JAMES E. 1978. "Cognitive theory and social casework." *Social Work* 23, no. 5 (September).

LAZARUS, ARNOLD A. 1976. *Multimodal behavior therapy.* New York: Springer.

———. 1977. "Has behavior therapy outlived its usefulness?" *American Psychologist* 32, no. 7 (July).

LOCKE, EDWIN A. 1979. "Behavior modification is not cognitive—and other myths: A reply to Ledwidge." *Cognitive Therapy and Research* 3, no. 2 (June).

LOEWENSTEIN, SOPHIE FREUD. 1979. "Inner and outer space in social casework." *Social Casework* 60, no. 1 (January).

LONDON, PERRY. 1964. *The modes and morals of psychotherapy.* New York: Holt, Rinehart and Winston.

MAHONEY, MICHAEL J. 1977. "Cognitive therapy and research: A question of questions." *Cognitive Therapy and Research* 1, no. 1 (March).

MARKOWITZ, IRVING. 1975. Remarks at a continuing education workshop on "Child and Family Therapy: Truth and Nonsense," sponsored by Psychiatric Outpatient Centers of America (POCA), Sarasota, Florida, April 26.

MASLOW, ABRAHAM H. 1970. *Motivation and personality,* 2d ed. New York: Harper & Row.

MAULTSBY, MAXIE C., JR. 1975. *Help yourself to happiness.* New York: Institute for Rational Living.

———. 1975. "Rational behavior therapy for acting-out adolescents." *Social Casework* 56, no. 1 (January).

MAY, ROLLO. 1960. "Existential bases of psychotherapy." *American Journal of Orthopsychiatry* 30, no. 4 (October).

MILLER, WALTER L. 1980. "Casework and the medical metaphor." *Social Work* 25, no. 4 (July).

NIKELLY, ARTHUR G. 1971. *Techniques for behavior change.* Springfield, Ill.: Charles C Thomas.

NIKELLY, ARTHUR G., and DON VERGER. 1971. "Early recollections." In *Techniques for behavior change,* ed. Arthur G. Nikelly. Springfield, Ill.: Charles C Thomas.

NORD, WALTER. 1977. "A Marxist critique of humanistic psychology." *Journal of Humanistic Psychology* 17, no. 1 (Winter).

O'DONEL-BROWNE, CANDY. 1979. "Bonds between battered

women and violent men." *POCA Press* (a publication of Psychiatric Outpatient Centers of America) 12, no. 2 (February).

ORTEN, JAMES D., and DIANE P. WEIS. 1974. "Strategies and techniques for therapeutic change." *Social Service Review* 48, no. 3 (September).

OXLEY, GENEVIEVE B. 1966. "The caseworker's expectations and client motivation." *Social Casework* 47, no. 7 (July).

PAUST, ANNE. 1980. Personal communication to the author, August 1.

POWELL, BILL. 1979. Remarks at "A Training Session for Youth Service Personnel," sponsored by United Way of Essex and West Hudson, Newark, New Jersey, December 5.

RADO, SANDOR. 1956. *Psychoanalysis of behavior.* New York: Grune & Stratton.

RANK, OTTO. 1936. *Will therapy.* New York: Alfred A. Knopf.

REID, KENNETH E. 1977. "Nonrational dynamics of the client-worker interaction." *Social Casework* 58, no. 10 (December).

REID, WILLIAM J., and ANN W. SHYNE. 1969. *Brief and extended casework.* New York: Columbia University Press.

ROSENHAN, D. L. 1973. "On being sane in insane places." *Science* 179 (January 19).

RUSH, AUGUSTUS J.; AARON T. BECK; MARIA KOVACS; and STEVEN HOLLON. "Comparative efficacy of cognitive therapy and pharmacotherapy in the treatment of depressed outpatients." *Cognitive Therapy and Research* 1, no. 1 (March).

SALEEBEY, DENNIS. 1975. "A proposal to merge humanist and behaviorist perspectives." *Social Casework* 56, no. 8 (October).

SALTER, ANDREW. 1964. "The theory and practice of conditioned reflex therapy." In *The conditioning therapies,* ed. Joseph Wolpe, Andrew Salter, and L.J. Reyna. New York: Holt, Rinehart and Winston.

SALZMAN, LEON. 1960a. "Paranoid state—Theory and therapy." *Archives of General Psychiatry* 2, no. 6 (June).

———. 1960b. "Masochism and psychopathy as adaptive behavior." *Journal of Individual Psychology* 16, no. 2 (November).

———. 1973. *The obsessive personality,* 2d. ed. New York: Jason Aronson.

Sarasota (Fla.) *Herald-Tribune.* "Thoughts About Religion" (editorial), March 2, 1980.

SARBIN, THEODORE R. 1964. "Anxiety: Reification of a metaphor." *Archives of General Psychiatry* 10, no. 6 (June).

SHOHAM, HARRY B. 1978. "Psychiatric social work with the aged: A new look." In *Toward human dignity: Social work in practice,* ed. John W. Hanks, pp. 178–188. Washington, D.C.: National Association of Social Workers.

SILVER, STEVEN N. 1976. "Outpatient treatment for sexual offenders." *Social Work* 21, no. 2 (March).

SIPORIN, MAX. 1972. "Situational assessment and intervention." *Social Casework* 53, no. 2 (February).

———. 1978. "Practice theory and vested interests." *Social Service Review* 52, no. 3 (September).

SMALLEY, RUTH. 1967. *Theory for social work practice.* New York: Columbia University Press.

SNYDER, VERONICA. 1975. "Cognitive approaches in the treatment of alcoholism." *Social Casework* 56, no. 8 (October).

STAR, BARBARA. 1978. "Treating the battered woman." In *Toward human dignity: Social work in practice,* ed. John W. Hanks, pp. 217–225. Washington, D.C.: National Association of Social Workers.

STENSKY, BESSIE K. 1975. "Aging—and the essence of things." *POCA Press* (a publication of Psychiatric Outpatient Centers of America) 9, no. 3 (August).

STUART, RICHARD B. 1979. "Behavior modification: A technology of social change." In *Social work treatment,* ed. Francis J. Turner, 2d ed. New York: Free Press.

THOMAS, EDWIN J.; ROLAND ETCHEVERRY; and ROBERT KELLER. 1975. "Repertoires of behavioral and nonbehavioral treatment methods used in social work." *Social Service Review* 49, no. 1 (March).

THORNE, FREDERICK C. 1963. "An existential theory of anxiety." *Journal of Clinical Psychology* 19, no. 1 (January).

TURNER, FRANCIS J. 1978. *Psychosocial therapy.* New York: Free Press.

ULLMAN, MONTAGUE, 1955. "The dream process." *Psychotherapy* 1, no. 1 (Fall).

VAN KAAM, ADRIAN. 1966. *The art of existential counseling.* Wilkes-Barre, Pa.: Dimension Books.

WEAKLAND, JOHN. 1976. "Communication theory and clinical change." In *Family therapy: Theory and practice,* ed. Philip J. Guerin, Jr. New York: Gardner Press, 1976.

WERNER, HAROLD D. 1965. *A rational approach to social casework.* New York: Association Press.

————. 1970. *New understandings of human behavior.* New York: Association Press.

————. 1973. "See Naples and live: Report on a Florida clinic." *POCA Press* (a publication of Psychiatric Outpatient Centers of America) 8, no. 2 (June).

————. 1979. "Cognitive therapy." In *Social work treatment,* ed. Francis J. Turner, 2d ed., chap. 9, pp. 243–272. New York: Free Press.

WHITE, COLBY L. 1970. "Untangling knots in casework with the experiential approach." *Social Casework* 51, no. 10 (December).

WHITTAKER, JAMES K. 1976. "Causes of childhood disorders: New findings." *Social Work* 21, no. 2 (March).

WORTIS, JOSEPH. 1953. "Comments and conclusions." In *Basic problems in psychiatry,* ed. Joseph Wortis. New York: Grune & Stratton.

YELAJA, SHANKAR A. 1979. "Functional theory for social work practice." In *Social work treatment,* ed. Francis J. Turner, 2d ed. New York: Free Press.

ZACKS, HANNA. 1980. "Self-actualization: A midlife problem." *Social Casework* 61, no. 4 (April).

ZUK, GERALD H. 1972. *Family therapy: A triadic-based approach.* New York: Human Sciences Press.

Index